It Simply *Must*
Be Said

It Simply *Must* Be Said

A View of
American Public Education
from the
Trenches of Teaching

by

Hank Warren

iUniverse, Inc.
New York   Bloomington

It Simply Must Be Said
A View of American Public Education
from the Trenches of Teaching

iUniverse books may be ordered through booksellers or by contacting:

*iUniverse
1663 Liberty Drive
Bloomington, IN 47403
www.iuniverse.com
1-800-Authors (1-800-288-4677)*

*Because of the dynamic nature of the Internet, any Web addresses or
links contained in this book may have changed since publication and may
no longer be valid. The views expressed in this work are solely those of
the author and do not necessarily reflect the views of the publisher, and
the publisher hereby disclaims any responsibility for them.*

*ISBN: 978-1-4401-3400-5 (pbk)
ISBN: 978-1-4401-3399-2 (ebk)*

Printed in the United States of America

iUniverse rev. date: 12/17/2009

For my wonderful wife
with love and deepest gratitude
and to our son who makes life
such an adventure

Table of Contents

Acknowledgments

Heartfelt thanks to those dedicated teachers who made such a difference in my life and to the thousands upon thousands who do the same for their students every day.

Sincerest appreciation to the veteran colleagues who took the time to share their expertise and help me learn the necessary skills to become an accomplished teacher.

Deepest gratitude to my "editor" KJ for all of the time, energy and courage it took to dissect this manuscript and tell me what I needed to hear. As a non-educator, I hope your conviction that this book will speak to individuals from all walks of life proves prescient. Needless to say, it's incredibly, amazingly, astoundingly fortuitous, on the other hand, how *inherently* and poignantly extraordinary is the encapsulation of permeation.

Many thanks to my in-school IT "expert" for her incredible patience in teaching me computer skills and helping me to realize that the "book" is indeed better than the "scroll."

Much appreciation to my oracle of special education proficiency. Regarding my continual inquiries, the answer is "Yes," and you're reading it right now.

Thank you to my former colleague and dear friend ML for her editorial help and enthusiastic support.

Also, to all who previewed this book. Your insights, suggestions, expertise and encouragement were indispensable.

And most definitely to MN who, despite having a business to run, takes the time to do the computer tasks that I could never dream of doing myself. So much of this wouldn't have happened without you.

Last but not least, to the wonderful friends in my "lunch crew" who help to keep me sane. If it weren't for the laughter, where would we be?

The Reality of Teaching[1]

Then *Jesus* took his disciples up the mountain and, gathering them around him, he taught them, saying:

Blessed are the poor in spirit, for theirs is the kingdom of heaven
Blessed are they that mourn
Blessed are the meek
Blessed are those who hunger and thirst for righteousness
Blessed are the merciful
Blessed are the pure in heart
Blessed are those who have been persecuted
Rejoice and be glad, for your reward in heaven is great

Then Simon Peter said, "Are we supposed to know this?"

And Andrew said, "Do we have to write this down?"

And James said, "Will this be on the test?"

And Philip said, "Will there be a study guide?"

And Bartholomew said, "What came after poor?"

And John said, "The other disciples didn't have to learn this!"

And Mark said, "How come you're still using an overhead projector when Mr. Baptist has a Smartboard?"

And Matthew went to the bathroom.

One of the Pharisees who was present asked to see Jesus' lesson plan and inquired of Jesus: "Where are your anticipatory set and your objectives in the cognitive domain?"

And Jesus wept.

1. Would You Care To Speculate On The Assumptions Heard Thus Far?

On November 12, 2001, just two months and one day after the 9/11 attack on the World Trade Center in New York City, American Airlines flight 587 went down over the borough of Queens. Apparently, the plane started falling apart in midair and pieces ended up over a wide area. Coming so close on the heels of 9/11, the frenzy surrounding this tragedy was extraordinary! Speculation of another terrorist strike splashed across the airwaves. The uproar of semi-information, misinformation and outright babble from both reporters and pundits was prolific. Nobody knew a thing, yet the need to continually fill air-time took precedence over any concern for factual content.

Although this event occurred around 9:00 a.m. eastern time, evidently nothing could be released by American Airlines until their CEO could fly from the west coast to New York to hold the official press conference which finally took place around 5:00 p.m. It quickly became obvious that in the course of eight hours very little of substance had been confirmed. After a brief statement to that effect, the CEO began to field questions from the hundreds of reporters cramming the room. It was truly remarkable how many variations of "I don't know" this gentleman was able to espouse. Eventually, however, came the *coup de grâce*. A female reporter asked, "Would you care to speculate on the assumptions heard thus far?"

It wasn't until later in the evening, when Jon Stewart began to dissect the day's insanity on "The Daily Show," that the absurdity of this statement began to sink in. The reporter was basically asking, "Would you care to make something up about what has already been made up?" In the ensuing days I began to realize how precisely this notion applied to the entire realm of American education. At the time, being well into my 27th year as a teacher, I had long been contemplating the puzzling nature of this unique enterprise we call "teaching." Because the classroom experience is so insular, the opportunity for misunderstanding and misconception abounds. There is perhaps no other profession so clearly unique as that of a teacher, and the enormity of this truth did not become clear to me until I finally stood in front of a classroom. The simple fact is, there are few experiences that can be so isolated while, at the same time, so extraordinarily public.

Consequently, the ground is infinitely fertile for the formation of every conceivable opinion from every possible perspective, with the exception of the most important one——that of the Teacher. It is the one key viewpoint that only comes with the attainment of the position. Because we have all been students at some point, each of us has an opinion on education from that singular perspective. And, since everyone's experience in school is distinctly personal, there are as many different opinions as there are citizens who have attended school. Therefore, as we become parents, business people, politicians, bosses, workers, and general participants in every walk of life, these experiences shape our perceptions on education. However, because the reality of teaching itself is so unique, none of these perceptions apply to actively "teaching." They are *only* the product of having been in the passive position of "student." As a result, everyone has an opinion about how it should be done, while having absolutely no idea of what it is like to actually do it. In other words, everyone is "speculating on the assumption" that they possess complete understanding.

Perhaps you may recall the huge splash that the movie "Pleasantville" made during the 1990s. By all accounts, the film's combination of black and white with color imagery was a major technological breakthrough. The plot concerns a squabbling brother and sister who mysteriously find themselves transported through their television set into a "Leave it to Beaver" world in which they are forced to live. Aside from the ever-timely message of needing curiosity and creativity in life, I was most struck by the depiction of the school children sitting at their desks with perfect posture, rapturously absorbed in the classroom lesson.

This image became even more meaningful as I began to contemplate the attitudes towards public school education that pervade our society. Regardless of how any individual behaved or misbehaved, contributed or detracted, achieved or squandered during their high school years, somewhere around the age of thirty this image of sitting quietly at desks, as if they had been sucked through the TV into "Miss Lander's" class, takes over. On a regular basis there are TV commercials for any number of products portraying the classroom setting as one filled with fresh-faced, eager, cooperative, enthusiastically engaged students. Even if only by wishing it were so, we all seem to want to picture ourselves in that environment. In fact, it is precisely because pop culture plays such a huge role in the public's perception of teaching, that I will be referencing pertinent films, television shows, etc., throughout this book. In addition, I have included a number of my favorite parodies and anecdotes that I've collected through the years. If you happen to be familiar with them, I hope you will enjoy the "modifications" I've infused.

Ultimately, the teacher is in charge of his or her classroom. This is what we call teaching. On the other hand, the teacher has absolutely no control over the abundance of outside forces that so powerfully influence all that occurs in the classroom. Whether it is the extraordinary consequences of the "No Child Left Behind" legislation, right down to if a child has had breakfast; all these elements have a tremendous effect on learning, but are factors over which a teacher holds little sway. Against all odds, the teacher is expected to run an efficient, educationally sound classroom while having virtually no input into the policies that govern the process. Take, for instance, this simple example: An administrative directive goes out that there is to be "no food in the classrooms." It has been proven time and again that students who are physically comfortable are apt to learn better. Hungry students don't. While certainly being mindful of healthy nutrition and children with food allergies, if a teacher is okay with having food in class, shouldn't they be allowed that professional discretion?

I was recently reading an article about the former South African President and Nobel Laureate, Nelson Mandela.[2] He attributed much of his success to attaining a level of comfort with contradiction and expressed a concern about the inclination of Americans to see things strictly in black and white. It was striking how clearly he understood that the world is infinitely nuanced and every problem has many causes. However, in our public discourse there is a tendency to try to identify the *one thing* that is the cause of all our problems, and public school is a perennial favorite. While all the finger pointing goes on, the truth is, America's public schools are actually doing *more* for a more diverse student demographic than ever before in our history. We serve an increasingly varied population: ethnic, socioeconomic, and disabled. But, in our current fast-paced society that expects instantaneous results (quarterly measurements—not long term five to ten year plans), schools simply can't measure up.

Compare the overall school population in the 1950s and 60s to today. Each school tended to have a characteristically similar student makeup and, even though grouping was heterogeneous, it was understood that, while there would be some slow kids and a few really smart kids, the vast majority would be "average." Now we have the severely handicapped, the emotionally/socially disturbed, the mentally disabled, and the special needs. In short, we service students with every conceivable diagnosis, *as well as* the slow, average and smart ones, all grouped together in the same classroom. In addition, each one is expected to be highly successful, regardless of ability, interest, effort, desire, parental involvement/control/concern, home life, or background; whether or not they speak English, are living in a mansion, a car, or a cardboard box; have two parents, one parent, or no parents; are living with one parent while the other is in jail; have foster parents, are being abused by parents—the list is endless. While in the 50s and 60s it was commonly accepted that some kids would be auto mechanics, a select few would be doctors, and the vast majority would be in the middle, now the expectation is: They are all going to Harvard!

There is an absolutely wonderful sequence in the 1975 film "Monty Python and the Holy Grail," that should be required viewing for anyone interested in gaining even the slightest understanding of the world of teaching. The scene in question occurs directly before the wedding at Swamp Castle when the prince is hiding in his room because he doesn't want to marry the princess with the "huge tracts of land." Concerned that the prince may try to escape, the king attempts to instruct two guards to watch the prince until he (the king) returns. However, no matter how many ways the king tries to rephrase the order, one guard just stands there hiccupping while the other keeps misinterpreting the directions in every manner possible. The saintly patience of the king as he repeatedly explains the instruction to the ever-increasingly confused guard is absolutely priceless! Yet, similar to the previous parody where Bartholomew asks "What came after poor?," this is exactly what teachers confront on a daily basis.

I saw a bumper sticker the other day which stated "Everything is Connected." Considering the vast number of interconnected topics related to education, discussing every issue in detail would require volumes. In order to avoid a treatise of encyclopedic proportions, I have tried to adhere to these main topics:

- Separating the facts from the myths about teaching.

- Analysis of the chasm between "educating" (teaching) and "education" (the entrenched bureaucracy).

- Examination of crucial teacher, student and parenting issues.

- Analysis of the impact of legislation and case law decisions concerning children with disabilities on the school/learning environment.

- Presentation of five core recommendations to improve American Public Education.

My ultimate goal is to initiate thoughtful dialogue which hopefully will result in truly meaningful improvements to the educational process. The teachers who previewed this book prior to publication, found it served as a catalyst for sharing additional experiences and ideas. I hope these kinds of discussions abound. Equally encouraging was the enthusiastic response from those outside the field of education. This makes me hopeful that, should both educators and the general public ever unite in common purpose, meaningful change may well see fruition.

As this book was nearing completion, it became amusingly apparent that there were at least two dozen places where I had written something to the effect of "This is the honest truth," or "Believe it or not," or "I'm honestly not kidding." In order to avoid this unnecessary repetitiveness, I can emphatically state from the outset (cue "Dragnet" theme): The stories you are about to hear are true, only the names have been changed to protect the instigators.

2. Learning to Swim by Drowning

If you happen to start teaching at the high school level straight out of college, the fact that there is only a four to five year difference in age between you and the students you are teaching can be rather challenging. It is *so* easy to fall into the trap of thinking you're going to be really "hip" and able to relate to them on a personal level, only to suffer the immediate shock of teaching reality: Sustained resistance to nearly everything. First you have to come to grips with the fact that you are not one of the kids. In their eyes, regardless of your age, you are simply one of "them" (the teachers). Because you have yet to develop any classroom management, behavioral, or control skills, the kids are constantly challenging your every directive. This is where so many new teachers fail—they can't get past this initial "shock and awe." Colleges, in vastly variegated efforts to teach the skills you are going to need to be successful, put potential teachers through endless classes of educational philosophy and applied theory. Therefore, when these novices finally get in front of a class, it's largely on-the-job training.

I clearly remember how dismayed and downright angry I was with my first high school classes. I couldn't understand why the students were giving me such a hard time. We listened to the same music and watched the same TV shows for heaven's sake! The fact that most of the other teachers on staff were older only added to my feeling of disconnectedness. I looked at them as if they were *my* high school teachers—basically out of touch old farts. Why couldn't my students see what a cool guy I was, especially when I was so much closer to them in age? Then came the real killer. I began to see the really nice relationships the kids had with these other teachers. What on earth was this about? Why were they giving me nothing but crap while treating these old crows the way I wanted to be treated? Truthfully, a blind man could have seen it in a minute, but this was long before first year teachers had "mentors" or anything of the sort. The hard reality? I simply had to grow up, realize that I was the teacher, and start acting like one. Needless to say, it was the hardest year of my life.

Now in my 34th year of teaching, it's impossible to recount the number of new teachers I have seen fail; especially those who fall into the same trap that I did during my first year: focusing on being "buddies" with the kids. First and foremost, children need teachers, not pals. Developing close rapport and becoming a role model/mentor to students is an outgrowth of establishing appropriate adult authority as the instructor. In addition, it took years for me to finally accept the fact that, no matter how extraordinary your efforts and/or instructional ability, some kids are going to love you, some kids are going to dislike you, and the vast in-between will basically remain indifferent.

Recently, a former student appeared in my room to substitute for my cellmate (a colleague who shares my room) who happened to be out sick that day. It was nice to have a few minutes to reminisce before the helter-skelter insanity of the day began. Even though this girl was now 27, she had yet to hold down a permanent teaching job. In fact, she had been going to college continually since graduating from high school. She held degrees in elementary education, special education, and school psychology and was currently working on a degree in educational law. She said she thought she would really like to teach special education. However, because you are dealing with the most severe learning and behavioral issues in the school, this is unquestionably one of the greatest challenges in teaching. In addition to looking like she was 15, this girl was so sweet and soft-spoken, her demeanor almost bordered on ditzy. She told me about her previous three days substituting in a math class and described the amount of trouble some of the children gave her. Then she started proudly listing how many of them she sent to the office, completely oblivious to what a bad idea that is. First of all, the students learn you can't control them, and secondly, the administration doesn't want to be dealing with any kids, never mind a steady stream.

I had numerous occasions throughout the day to watch this girl in action, or rather "inaction" as the case turned out to be. The children were so poorly behaved that I had to intervene a couple of times to keep full chaos from breaking out. All the while I couldn't help but wonder: What on earth is this girl thinking? How is she ever going to survive in a classroom? All those degrees and all that money invested in something for which she is apparently not the least bit suited.

This brings me back to teacher training. There is one distinct truth that I have come to realize through all these years: Just like the Ministry, teaching is a calling. It genuinely has to be in your blood. You can immediately identify the young teachers who are going to be successful because they have that indefinable aura about them; the spark in the personality and the effortless connection to the kids. Aside from these select few, however, I'm really concerned about what motivates the majority of young people to think they want to teach. Are they falling victim to the fictitious myths that permeate society about teaching; for example, six hour days and summers off? Do they watch those ridiculous commercials on TV, like the one for an investment fund where the client says, "What if I want to teach when I retire?" He's talking as if it's some kind of a hobby, similar to taking up sailing or shuffleboard. And I love the fact that the commercial shows a class of high school students sitting quietly—all enthusiastically raising their hands to participate. *Obviously* paid actors on a set. Assuming he has a college degree, at least this TV commercial retiree will have the advantage of being able to follow the alternative certification route which, due to the incredible teacher shortage, can be as little as a six week summer program in many states. This way, when he gets to the reality of the job, he won't have invested very much when he drops out to pursue something easier and less stressful. Bullfighting perhaps?

The most essential pieces of advice that I can offer to any new teacher are: 1) establish strong relationships with veteran staff and regularly seek their guidance and, 2) make friends with the school secretaries and custodians. In my experience, most secretaries are very helpful and friendly, but, should you encounter unpleasantness, redouble your efforts. Establishing good relations can be as simple as a regular "hello" and an occasional chat. Learn something about them, show interest in their lives, and be sure to regularly thank them for all they do. As you will soon discover, the principal's head secretary basically runs the school. It's wise to nurture camaraderie. Similarly, you'll be amazed at all of the little "extras" that come from a good relationship with the custodians. Something as simple as never finding your paper towel dispenser empty is a pleasure. Having done custodial work during graduate school, I fully understand the lack of respect they endure. Recognition of their efforts and validation of them as human beings will go a long way.

Earlier this year, my wife, an exemplary high school teacher, witnessed a classic example of new teacher "disconnect" at her school. A thirty-something man, who had completed a brief alternative certification program, was hired to teach math. Towards the end of the first week of school, with a look of total bewilderment on his face, he said to my wife: "These kids are completely unmotivated! They don't want to do a thing!" So my wife gently pointed out that this is our job as teachers; the daily challenge to get students motivated to want to do something, *anything*, that will vaguely resemble active participation in the educational process. By the middle of the next week, he was gone.

In contrast, college students have spent tens of thousands of dollars on four to five years of schooling. Regardless of completing up to twelve weeks of student teaching, they are still vastly unprepared for what is about to hit them. In my own school I've watched scores of new teachers finish one or two years before leaving for more lucrative, less stressful jobs in the business world. In terms of brevity, I thought I'd witnessed the record: A teacher who lasted one day! That was until a friend in another school system told me about the one who bailed out after half a day. It seems fourth period came around and someone alerted the office that there was no teacher in his room. Apparently, the guy just up and walked away—never notified a soul.

Here's my suggestion: Prior to admission to any teacher training program, be it college or alternative certification, anyone who is thinking about teaching must complete at least one week *actively* volunteering in a public school classroom. This is not sitting in the back of the room and observing, but actually working with kids. After surviving the week, if you still want to teach, go for it!

Equally important, colleges must make experience in a public school setting an integral component of any four year teacher education program. Interfacing with real students in a genuine classroom must occur during *each* semester, starting freshman year and continuing throughout. The current system of student teaching only in the last semester before graduation provides little connectivity between the college classroom and practical application in the real world. Revamping the college curriculum to more accurately reflect the tools needed for actual teaching would also help. In the meantime, I will continue to recommend that students get a college degree in something practical for the business world and, if they still think they hear the calling, go the alternative certification route during a summer. Then, if it doesn't work out, there will be no need for any further course work to pursue a business career. A college degree in education allows for no such direct transference.

I recently happened upon a radio interview with a film crew that was shooting a movie locally. The young female director was lamenting the inadequacies of her preparation for the realities of movie-making after four years of majoring in film at college. In fact, she said, the most essential components of working with unions, production crews, financing, and personnel issues were basically absent from her training. I found it fascinating that her observations were almost identical to those stated by beginning teachers concerning their college training. Especially interesting was her conclusion that being provided with opportunities to work on film crews throughout her college studies would have been invaluable.

About a year ago, one of my son's friends, who had dropped out of college and was currently working sixty hours a week as a manager in an auto parts store, told me that he thought he might try teaching because the hours were so easy. I suggested he use some of his vacation time to volunteer in a public school. On last check . . . . . he's still at the store.

3. Reality Bites

In discussing the countless classroom realities for which teacher training programs offer no preparation, I am reminded of Don; a short, ruddy, red-headed sixth grader who had the ability to single-handedly turn a room upside down. Mind you, this was nothing malicious by any extent of the imagination; it was simply Don being Don—a mini-tornado in the making. He personified a wonderful quip that applies so perfectly to so many children in school:

We spend the first two years of a child's life trying to teach them to walk and talk, and the next sixteen trying to get them to sit down and shut up!

During my very first year of teaching, I learned the effect that one child can have on a classroom of thirty. I was working at a private parochial school and one of my classes always seemed to be in a state of upheaval. Suddenly, one day in early October, the room was a picture of orderliness. About ten minutes into class, I remarked to the children how wonderful they were being. In unison they said, "That's because Jim isn't here!" Amazingly, the very kids who were constantly fooling around when Jim was there were sitting like angels! It was one of those instantaneous on-the-job lessons that tend to define the first few years of every teacher's career. Whereas Don was merely a whirlwind of energy, Jim was absolutely incorrigible. Despite the earnest efforts of every teacher and the principal, most of whom were nuns, little progress was made towards controlling his behavior. By the start of second semester in January, Jim was gone. And thus you have the essential difference between public and private schools. Private schools can weed out the disruptive, nonacademic students, living with uninvolved parents in unstable home situations. Public schools must take them all!

Anyway, Don scurried into my room one day buzzing with energy; simply aglow with this huge grin on his face. "Mr. Warren," he bellowed, "you won't believe this, but somebody let a big crap down in the hallway!" Immediately considering the source of this information, I gestured dismissively to Don to have a seat. "No," he said, still grinning like a Cheshire cat, "It's really true!" Skeptically, I surveyed the faces of a few of the other kids who very tentatively nodded in agreement. "If you don't believe me," Don continued, "come take a look!"

It is essential to understand that whoever designed the school building in which this was taking place, apparently thought it was going to be used as IBM corporate headquarters or an Embassy Suites Hotel. The building surrounded a huge, skylight-topped atrium which encompassed three split-level floors that were accessed by a convoluted combination of open stairs and ramps. Most astoundingly, the library opened directly onto this area, subjecting it to an unimaginable noise level as 650 students passed from class to class and/or made use of their lockers. In short, this school's construction served as the perfect visual for a regularly occurring phenomenon in education: Ideas and initiatives that look great on paper but, in reality, are fraught with problems. To add to the excitement, the hallway outside my classroom had an open railing that overlooked another hallway about ten feet lower. The kids quickly discovered that, if you hung from the railing while placing your toes on the top lip of the locker bank below, you could drop to the lower floor unscathed.

In any event, as soon as I indicated the slightest hint of acquiescing to Don's challenge, the entire class barreled to the railing. Wouldn't you know it, there's the custodian down below mopping up what looked like a trail of droppings after the horses pass in a parade. As I made some utterance of disbelief, Don, completely vindicated, shouted, "See! See! I told you so!"

And this is the way it goes sometimes in school. Whereas Don wanted to believe that some kid had "dropped-trou" right there in the hallway, it turns out that a student with a large dog had collected the excrement in a bag and distributed it in the hallway. The next day I joked with Don that, based on the previous day's events, should he come in and announce that there was a T-Rex in the hallway, I'd be compelled to go have a look. Needless to say, Don ran with that for weeks.

4. Teacher Shortage

The Steve Martin movie "Bowfinger" contains a wonderful scene where Martin's character holds up the pathetic amount of cash he has on hand and says, "We're going to get the finest film crew this money can buy!" The movie immediately segues to a scene of illegal Mexicans scurrying into the back of his pickup truck while dodging bullets being fired by border guards. The relevance here is that this is exactly where we are heading in education if we don't do something substantial and meaningful to offset the already extraordinary and ever-growing teacher shortage. We'll be at the point where any warm body in front of the room will have to suffice.

If you work hard and supplement your college program with summer courses, you just might be able to finish a bachelor's degree in education in four years. However, many states are now requiring that new teachers obtain a double certification; both in their major subject area and in special education. So, now you need a *minimum* of five years of college to be eligible to go to work for a starting salary of $35,000-$40,000 per year (many areas of the country are lower—a handful are higher). In addition, numerous states are now placing beginning teachers in probationary periods of one to three years. This involves working with mentor teachers, building portfolios, being evaluated by state auditors and even having to pass written exams to receive a Professional Teaching Certificate. When I started teaching, these certificates were permanent. Now they are only good for five years, during which time every teacher—fifth year to thirty-fifth year—needs to amass a certain number of hours of continuing education (workshops, conferences, technology training, etc.) in order to get re-certified for another five years. Once you obtain re-certification, you start the five year process all over again. Many states also expect teachers to earn a master's degree (at their own expense) within ten years. This is, of course, on top of every other challenge a teacher must face to be successful in the classroom. Is it any wonder we have a teacher shortage?

While my son was growing up, especially during high school, our house was the hangout (another book's worth of stories there!). As a result, we got to know his friends very well and have been able to stay in the loop throughout college and beyond. One of these young men started his first job at $60,000 with incentives and opportunities for salary enhancement too numerous to mention. Our son, now three years out of college (bachelor's degree only) is on track to earn what I am making after thirty-four years in teaching with a bachelor's, master's and sixth-year certificate. He works very hard but is also compensated accordingly, especially for every extra hour he puts in. How does this compare to the "opportunities" in teaching where, no matter how many hours you put in, the pay is the same?

Let's take a look at some average salaries in the geographic area in which I work, which happens to be in a state considered to have some of the highest teacher salaries in the country. It's also one of the most expensive states in the country in which to live. A new teacher, fresh out of college with a bachelor's degree and possibly $25,000 to $100,000 (or more) in loans to pay off, starts at $39,350. Do those 12 hour days, weekends and holidays—basically surrender your life to the job—and in the second year your pay will go all the way to $42,000. In year three: $44,750. And thus it continues; basically $2,700 salary increases each year until you get that master's degree (at a cost of $15,000-$20,000 out of your own pocket), at which point you get a *onetime* $2000 dollar bump in your base salary, over which the yearly $2,700 increments continue.

The woefully inadequate earning potential of this salary schedule is perhaps the greatest disincentive for young teachers to continue in education. It makes no difference if you are the best or the worst, work the hardest or the least, there it is: your value, worth, and earning potential, all laid out in front of you for the next twenty years. No bonuses, promotions, incentives, rewards, Christmas gifts. . . . . Nada! Here's one that just jumped out at me: Next year, a teacher with 9 (NINE!!!) years experience *and* a full master's degree will earn $59, 750! That's not even what my son's friend earned his first year with a bachelor's degree. And one is only left to imagine: What is *he* going to be making in 9 years? $150,000? More? Now, here's the *real* kicker; something that is impossible to fully comprehend until you get there. Once a teacher makes it to the top of the scale, the yearly salary increases don't even cover the cost of living! In fact, when you add-in spiraling health care costs and co-pays, the salary for top-of-the-scale veteran teachers is actually decreasing each year.

So, what's to be done? The sad but real truth in education is that the only path to any form of substantial salary increase is to go into administration. This basically entails completing a course of study requiring approximately 30 credits beyond the master's degree. In my school system, the starting salary for a first year assistant principal is $96,000 per year. That's $56,000 more than a first year teacher, and the best part is *you don't have to teach anymore!* Plus, you get a nice office, a secretary, and a *telephone*! Mind you, at least as a building administrator (principal, assistant principal) you still have *some* degree of contact with students.

Which brings us to the most fascinating irony of all: As an administrator, the further you get from any contact with students whatsoever, *the more money you make!* So, the curriculum coordinator, director of special education, assistant superintendent and superintendent usually get housed in a town office building completely separate from any school buildings that have kids in them. And, as an added bonus for having achieved a position requiring no daily contact with real students, you get to make all of the decisions regarding those students: how and what they are to be taught, how they are to be disciplined, how many in a class, how many classes, how many teachers, aides, custodians—*EVERYTHING!* And, because you never have to actually work with the kids, you have no practical understanding of the impact of your decisions; except what gets reported to you by building administrators who, as we have already pointed out, don't have to teach either!

I am fascinated to see that the issue of equal pay for equal work is back in the national discussion. It seems study after study has shown that women in the workplace earn approximately 70% of what men earn for doing the same job. I can emphatically state that, in teaching, equal pay between the genders is *not* an issue. Everyone, male or female, earns the 70%.

Here's what needs to be done if America is serious about recruiting and retaining good teachers:

1. *Immediately,* **double salaries!** No strings attached. No further requirements, demands, or expectations. Just pay these new salaries for *exactly* what teachers are already doing. It's still a bargain.

2. Get every teacher a full time clerical assistant to take attendance, copy papers and deal with routine e-mails, notes, etc., from both the front office and parents. They could also do bus, lunch, recess, study hall and detention duties, as well as handle routine office tasks and general paperwork. This would free teachers to do what they are supposed to be doing with all of that education and training: planning good lessons, working with students, keeping current in their subject matter/instructional pedagogy, and vibrantly

and enthusiastically *teaching!* A properly trained assistant could also handle the latest administrative darling—creating and maintaining Web pages. This involves posting homework assignments, worksheets, lesson plans and class notes on a daily basis. In addition, many school systems are now installing software which requires teachers to record all individual student grades (test scores, research papers, presentations, etc.) on a daily basis for easy online parental/student access. And when on earth are we supposed to find time to do this? The administration's answer is, because the program is easily accessible from any computer, teachers can "conveniently" do this from home. With student loads of 80-120, just try to fathom the time consumption.

3. *Significantly reduce class sizes.* Being certified for grades K-12, I have had the opportunity to teach at all levels and in a variety of circumstances in my 34 years. Believe it or not, I have taught classes as small as two students, up to as large as 50! I can emphatically state that the optimal class size is 10-12 pupils.

4. Get every teacher a phone. The administration claims that they want teachers to make frequent contact with parents but, in my building, over 75 staff members have access to a total of four phones—only two of which are in private, quiet locations.

If anything, I know that item four is certainly reasonable. The fact that some school systems already offer this amenity is most promising. And I'm not saying that it needs to be a land line. A cell phone might actually be better, taking into account all of the after school, evening and weekend work teachers are expected to do. Meanwhile, let's look at some of the more popular schemes currently under consideration for nominally enhancing teacher salaries.

Merit Pay

Because it is virtually impossible to objectively quantify or even define exemplary teaching, any attempt to base salary on something so hard to measure is an exercise in futility. This truth has been substantiated in every experiment with merit pay nationwide. Virtually every case ends-up as a reward system for garnering favoritism with the administration; the lapdogs and yes-men reap the benefits. The only possible measurement with any hint of objectivity is the use of standardized test scores. But, seeing as standardized tests are supposed to measure cumulative knowledge, who gets the credit? The current teacher? Last year's teacher? Perhaps there should be a sliding scale; current teacher gets the most, while teachers from previous years receive a lesser percentage the further back we go. Or, maybe it should be the other way around; earlier teachers get the most because they taught the basics—how to read, for example. But then, what about the art, music and physical education teachers? There are innumerable studies showing that the study of music is inextricably linked to academic success. There is also an abundance of new research hailing the importance of exercise to physical, emotional and mental well-being. Shouldn't the school social worker or psychologist get a piece of the pie for helping with emotional and mental well-being?

Finally, the school nurse. She keeps the kids' medications balanced and provides the necessary treatment for the sudden stomach pains and nausea associated with math-itis, science-itis, history-itis and the like. She deals with the "forgot my homework" histrionics and distributes all of those magic frozen sponges in the little plastic bags that work for everything from a bump to a severed arm. In case you aren't familiar, these sponges are employed as an easily reusable icepack. Honestly,

I've had classes with six or more children sitting with the magic sponges at the same time. "So, Johnny, Jim and Mary, what are your sponges for?" "Oh, my finger hurts." "I bumped my locker." "My cat died." Perhaps the nurse should receive extra pay based on the number of life threatening, CDC illnesses she cures with the frozen sponges.

The short of it is, attempting to base merit pay on some unverifiable measure of teacher performance is simply tilting at windmills; for no other reason than the fact that teaching is only part of the equation. The *learners* have to also be willing to work and achieve. What kind of a measurement scale do we use to factor "student desire to learn" into teacher evaluation? Or, is this also the exclusive responsibility of the teacher? If so, only the teachers of motivated students will get recognized. Those of us who work with the most difficult learning and behavioral problems (the greatest challenge of all) will never see a penny.

I was reading about a program in Colorado[3] that is attempting to reward good teaching through a series of incentives with exact dollar amounts attached:

1. You get an extra $1,000 for working in a high risk school. Not being a math major, I pulled out the calculator and, based on a 180 day school year, you get an extra $5.56 *per day* to risk being what: assaulted? knifed? shot? I'm guessing it took a full administrative team weeks to come up with that one! And I don't doubt for a minute that they got scores of teachers to sign up. Lord help us, but we teachers can be so easily manipulated. I guess if you pay us poorly enough, we'll jump at anything!

2. You can get an additional $1,000 if the students in your school exceed expectations on the state exams. I'm a little unclear here: All of the kids? 50%? Two? And who sets the expectations they are supposed to

exceed? If it's "spell your name correctly," you are probably out cashing your check. Anything more becomes iffy. And how many exams are we talking about? The academic achievement test in my state consists of multiple sections on numerous topics that take some twenty hours of testing time to complete. Do they have to do better on all of it? Half? Sample question A?

3. The third incentive pays $350 and should be a cinch to earn unless you don't have a good relationship with your evaluator. To fulfill this incentive you simply have to meet the professional academic objectives you helped set at the beginning of the year. Make up something you can do in your sleep and you're in the money. But if your administrator puts the screws to you, this one's gone with the wind. Come to think of it, doesn't this essentially boil down to good old-fashioned "apple-polishing?" Talk about a pioneering work-place transformation.

4. Incentive number four really makes me start to wonder how innovative this program is. You get $1,000 if you get a good evaluation from your principal. Hmmm, I don't think we need to waste any more ink on what's involved here (see incentive three). However, what really has me alarmed is, with incentives three and four paying a total of $1,350 for merely checking your dignity at the principal's door, how does that compare with putting yourself in the possible equivalent of downtown Fallujah for a piddling $1,000, as is the case with incentive one? I really would like to know how that's working out.

5. Last but not least, incentive five: A $700 reward if your school is judged to be a "distinguished school." I

don't know what's involved here, but it certainly seems like you're banking on the perfect alignment of the planets or something of a similar celestial magnitude. Of course, it might simply boil down to who's judging and how much they are willing to take for a bribe. If everyone chips in $50, each of you just might come out $650 ahead. Then there's always the possibility that your building administration is doing to their bosses something similar to what you're doing to them for incentives three and four. Also, depending on what one receives for being principal of a "distinguished school," the casting couch may be in full swing! Once again, I hate to beat a dead horse, but if I can get $700 by just praying, wishing, and hoping that my school gets judged "distinguished," what again is my motivation for selecting incentive one?

Anyway, if by some miracle you manage to cash in on all five "incentives," you get a total of $4,050 (it almost seems like the $50 'fix' for incentive five is built in). Seriously, I know people in the business world who get anywhere from $3,000-$5,000 just as a Christmas bonus, with only a bachelor's degree; no master's that they had to pay for themselves. As if to add insult to injury, the wife of one of my colleagues works as a general office secretary in a small area law firm. She received an $8,000 bonus this past Christmas; right in the midst of this huge economic meltdown!

Even more alarming, merit pay appears to be the cornerstone of President Obama's new education plan. I don't know who's advising him, but I wonder if there are any *active* teachers involved. As the kids would say, "Mr. Pres., you need to get *schooled!*" Better yet, invite me over. I'd be honored to give you some "grassroots" input.

Mentor/Master Teacher

Numerous programs assign beginning teachers to a mentor or master teacher. The basic concept is to have novice teachers meet one on one, or in small groups, with an accomplished veteran teacher on a regular basis for structured lesson planning and evaluation. In general, experienced teachers can advance professionally three ways: 1) continue to teach while becoming a mentor to other teachers, 2) discontinue teaching to become a full-time master teacher responsible for overseeing 12-15 teachers, or 3) take the traditional route into administration. One can only assume that option one pays the least, while option three continues to be the most lucrative.

During my years in education, I have observed a singular hard truth: Once *any* individual is removed from the classroom to "advance" into administration, it usually takes less than a year to completely sever any connection with the reality of teaching. I have seen this happen to the most capable of teachers. No matter how exemplary their classroom performance, the transition into administration cuts all ties.

Therefore, the only one of the three possibilities outlined above that does not basically add more administration, is mentoring. The opportunity to work under the direct guidance of an inspiring, innovative, *practicing* teacher is absolutely invaluable! As a new teacher, you can experiment with ideas, actively participate in their implementation, evaluate effectiveness, and adapt, change, and discard as needed; in an atmosphere of creative inventiveness. The simple act of becoming a mentor teacher elevates all involved: mentor, teacher, and students. To be a mentor requires a fundamental love of the art of teaching. As I look back on my years as a pupil and teacher, it becomes glaringly apparent that the truly inspirational teachers created a unique realm in their classrooms that was theirs alone. The thought of leaving this for the front office would have been sacrilege!

An outstanding teacher who uplifts both students and colleagues is the educational ideal. In our hearts we know this to be true, if for no other reason than our own personal experiences with teachers of this magnitude. But sadly, in the hierarchy of American public education, this is the least respected status. We revere and applaud advancement through the administrative echelon when, in fact, the exact opposite should be true. The ones who are in the trenches, doing the actual teaching, should be given the highest recognition, respect, and salary.

Recommendation #1: Teach!

Thus we arrive at a core recommendation: *All who wish to call themselves "educators"* <u>*must*</u> *be actively teaching in some capacity.* Except for secretaries and maintenance workers, everyone, from superintendent to the first year novice, must be in charge of a classroom of students. In this manner, the essential purpose of our profession will be realized and practiced by all involved. Even if the superintendent were only teaching one class per day, it would be a massive step in the proper direction. Imagine the clarity and efficiency if all were immersed in the common mission. No more decisions by individuals who have long since forgotten the reality of the classroom. No more bloating of the administrative hierarchy to provide room for the ever-burgeoning numbers of those pursuing "advancement." The monetary rewards would go to those involved in innovative teaching and mentoring. *Practicing* master teachers, honing their craft in concert with others, would be the highest advancement attainable.

Guide to Qualitative Evaluation[4]

Performance Degrees

Performance Factors	Far Exceeds Requirements	Exceeds Requirements	Meets Requirements	Needs Improvement	Does Not Meet Minimum Requirements
Achievement	Leaps tall buildings with a single bound	Must take running start to leap over tall buildings	Can only leap over a short building or a medium building with no spires	Crashes into buildings when attempting to jump them	Cannot identify building
Timeliness	Is faster than a speeding bullet	Is as fast as a speeding bullet	Not quite as fast as a speeding bullet	Has difficulty finding bullets	Wounds self with bullets when shooting gun
Initiative	Is stronger than a locomotive	Is stronger than a bull elephant	Is stronger than a bull	Shoots the bull	Smells like a bull
Adaptability	Walks on water consistently	Walks on water in emergencies	Washes with water	Drinks water	Passes water in emergencies
Communication	Talks with God	Talks with the angels	Talks to himself	Argues with himself	Loses argument to himself

5. Teacher Longevity

For the longest time, the attainment of ten years in teaching was the benchmark for achieving accomplished veteran status. However, with the extraordinary demands that are now placed on teachers, this general time-frame has compacted to two years for mastering the basics of classroom management and five to seven years to become a fully proficient teacher. Those with this fortitude learn the true fundamentals of excellence in teaching, which include: effective interaction with students and delivery of instruction, classroom control and discipline, dealing with administrative and parental demands, the ability to separate the important from the mundane, finding time for ongoing self-education, and striking a balance between the overwhelming requirements of accomplished teaching and actually having a personal life.

Ultimately, it is the ability to combine all of these elements into a caring, nurturing classroom environment that makes good teaching truly indefinable. Think about the great teachers you can remember in your life and then try to quantify what made them so. One quickly realizes that, because its nature is so inherently affective, quality teaching is virtually unmeasurable. Sadly, in the current hell-bent rush to teacher accountability, the entire hierarchy of administrators, boards of education, local, state, and national governments are attempting to quantify the un-quantifiable. Having engaged in exhaustive discussion with individuals both inside and outside of education concerning this issue, the ultimate challenge is this: Make a list of irrefutably *objective* criteria for teacher evaluation. See if you can produce even one specification. It is incredible to report that, after spending months on this endeavor, the current result is nil. I find it mind-boggling to realize how long we have been evaluating teachers using entirely unverifiable subjective measures.

This brings me to an issue that I'm sure is at the forefront of everyone's mind: The marginal *career* teachers we have all encountered at one time or another as students. Years of analysis and discussion on this topic have led me to one broad observation: If you are over forty years old, your chances of having endured an incompetent *veteran* teacher is much greater than for those who are in their 20's and 30's. The simple reason? The demands of the job have become so overwhelming that only the most dedicated survive. Any pretense of "coasting through" rapidly began to disappear with the issuance of the federal government's "Nation at Risk" report in 1983. In the wake of this study, the burgeoning school reform movement, coupled with mushrooming governmental mandates, created a profusion of demands previously unheard of in teaching. Combine this with dramatic changes in standards of parenting and an increasingly litigious public mentality, slackers disappeared like the Dodo. On the other hand, these same elements are significant contributing factors to the frequent turnover of first and second year teachers, which greatly increases the possibility that those in their 20's and younger have encountered incompetence as students of inexperienced and/or uncommitted novices. This is why we must pursue every possible means to ensure teacher longevity as well as the expedient acclimation of dedicated beginning teachers, so that all students have the opportunity to work under highly competent instructors.

Considering the necessary years of applied effort that is required in order to gain proficiency in teaching, the proliferation of new programs designed to lure potential candidates requires some examination. Given the current absence of any real efforts to drastically improve working conditions and salaries for committed teachers, these programs may serve as the last bastion for providing a modicum of basic classroom coverage.

At least thirty-nine U.S. states offer some form of teacher incentive program. Most involve scholarships, tuition waivers, stipends, loan forgiveness, and/or lower interest rates on loans for students pursuing degrees in education. Some programs offer salary enhancements, signing bonuses, and even mortgage assistance to starting teachers who are switching careers via accelerated certification programs or are teaching in "shortage" areas like math and science. When tuition waiver programs were first instituted during the 1990's, they required three to five year teaching commitments. But, because the tuition payments were made while the students were in college, there was no penalty if the obligations weren't fulfilled. Fortunately, most of these programs now forgive a percentage of the loan balance as each year of the teaching commitment is completed. Regardless, the multitude of outright scholarships or low interest loans that are based solely on maintaining a prescribed grade point average while studying for a degree in education, have no such requirements. If the student decides not to teach after graduation, no punitive action ensues.

In a slightly different vein, programs like Teach for America focus on a national service concept of sending recent college graduates for two year commitments to the poorest inner city and rural school districts. In return, participants are eligible for tuition stipends, college loan reimbursements, and/or transitional funding, in addition to standard starting teacher salaries. I have a former student who is well into her first year of a two year commitment in a similar type of program called New York City Teaching Fellows. Lori is teaching fifth grade in the Bronx for a full entry-level New York City teacher's salary ($46,000 per year) and is earning her master's degree at New York City College for a total cost of $3,000.

Apparently, a number of excellent colleges and universities participate in this program including Pace and Fordham. The acceptance requirements are very comprehensive and include passing the Liberal Arts and Sciences Test, completing an intensified NY State Teachers Certification program and, just as any regular applicant, interviewing and being hired for the job at the school at which you will teach. According to Lori, the NYCTF program is designed for people with a college degree in something other than teaching. In fact, a number of the participants are changing careers in their 40's and 50's; supposedly some very successful business people who are simply unhappy in their current jobs (after a few weeks of teaching, I can't help but wonder how their old jobs will begin to look).

Because these types of programs are necessary only as a result of *not* making teaching the viable, well-paid profession that it should be, I have questions on which Lori has been giving me regular updates. Having previously taught at a Catholic K-8 school for two years, Lori knew exactly what she was getting into and openly admits that she would be "freaked" if she did not have this experience under her belt. She knows how much needs to be learned and was extremely conscientious during the certification program which, thankfully, included in-depth classroom management training, lesson plan development, and teaching strategies.

But what about all of those who have never taught? Do they have any idea what they are getting into? Is there an escape clause for the ones, like the math teacher at my wife's high school, who want to bail-out after the shock of reality hits them? If we know that it takes five to seven years to become a truly proficient teacher, is it best to place teachers with little or no experience in the neediest schools? Stories proliferate concerning the lack of preparedness for the settings into which these new teachers are thrust and the paucity of promised support they receive. I personally know of two individuals who dropped-out of the NYCTF program because they were totally overwhelmed by class sizes and discipline issues, not to mention the vast differences in student learning ability, including non-English speaking children, placed in the same classroom. Sadly, Lori's early reports confirm the class make-up, lack of mentoring, and, most disturbingly, the number of participants who withdrew in the first month or two (I can only imagine the scramble to get substitute teachers to come in on a permanent basis).

And what about the overall attrition rates in these types of programs? Of those who actually complete the two years, how many continue teaching in these schools? Teach for America claims 44% are working as K-12 teachers and 9% as administrators. However, after four years, the number who choose to stay in these challenging districts can be 15% or lower.[5] Consequently, how many of America's most needy children are being subjected to the continual upheaval of an 85% (or greater) turnover rate of basically novice teachers. In Lori's case, her previous teaching experience and "born to teach" personality are paying immense dividends. But her latest update states that, although she loves the kids, she finds the support from NYCTF to be insufficient and she often feels overwhelmed. And she's a third year teacher! What must it be like for those in their first year?

It is perhaps providential that most teachers start when they are still single, so that during those first few years of learning the art of teaching they can afford to spend the necessary 12 hour days, weekends and summers honing the craft. As the years go by, one learns to consolidate the ongoing demands to fewer hours after school and at home. But it is never eliminated—not by a long shot! After 15 years of experience (which is an undeniable benchmark for achieving veteran status), I was finally able to limit the need to stay after school until 7 or 8 p.m. to one or two times per month. A few years back, I was working at the school copy machine around 8 p.m. and a second year teacher walked in whom, due to of the size of the school, I did not encounter often. "So, how are you enjoying the 12 hour days?" I inquired, to which she answered, "Once I get past this current stage, I know it will get a lot easier." Before I had time to respond with something like "Please let me know when *that* is," she came to the realization that she was standing there with a 25 year veteran, doing the exact same thing as she was, at the same hour of the night. We now work in different buildings but, on the occasions when we meet at a system wide function, we still share a chuckle over that one.

A colleague in a nearby city school system had the opportunity to experience a unique program designed to provide veteran teachers with the opportunity for an alternative one-year assignment after every three to four years of regular classroom teaching. The purpose was to counteract the ongoing yearly grind of teaching while offering professional growth and renewal: working as curriculum specialists in reading, math, science, etc., or as department coordinators, or, depending on certification, in mid-level administrative positions—the possibilities were numerous. Ultimately the program was suspended; one reason being the reluctance of many participants to return to the classroom after their taste of freedom from the rigors of teaching. Isn't that just priceless?

Throughout the years, I have kept regular notes on the issues that teachers consider major contributing factors to "burnout." The most frequently cited are:

- Time and energy expended on superfluous and constantly changing administrative/legislative programs, initiatives, mandates, and demands.

- Class sizes, student load, and hectic pace of the day.

- Lack of parental support, oversight, and general "parenting" skills.

- Lack of support and backing from the administration.

- Ongoing student issues: work habits, effort, behavior, interest, etc.

- Time/effort expended on special education/special needs students.

- Exhaustive personal time demands for paperwork and lesson planning.

- Time expended on duties (monitoring students at lunch, recess, study hall, etc.) and menial clerical tasks.

- Insufficient equipment, classroom supplies, and teaching materials and the resulting need to expend personal funds for necessities.

- General lack of recognition, respect, and appreciation.

- Salary/working conditions/schedule.

In addition, high school teachers are more frequently noting the difficulty of mentoring kids that live in increasingly fragmented home environments. I have always found it interesting that salary seems to be the one item that teachers inextricably understand is going to be woefully inadequate from the start. Everything else seems to be discovered with experience. However, during in-depth discussion, the thought of vastly increased salaries tends to make the other issues far more palatable.

The fact of the matter is, the more dedicated you are to becoming an outstanding teacher, the harder it is to learn to balance the demands of the job with maintaining a personal life. Many of you may recall the accolades that surrounded the 2007 movie "Freedom Writers" starring Hilary Swank. It tells the story of acclaimed teacher Erin Gruwell and her extraordinary work with minority students in a Los Angeles high school during the 1990s. One exquisitely represented element was how "Ms. G" consumed her life with the job, even to the point where she and her husband divorce. Of course she was doing great and inspirational things with the kids, but at what cost to her personally? How long can one sustain such a thing? In reality, it was only four years before Erin went off to teach community college.

This brings me to the veteran teachers in the movie and the excellent portrayal of how tenuous and vulnerable they felt. Because there is so little valued recognition bestowed on experienced teachers, they tend to grasp at whatever sense of territoriality they can garner. Although the movie portrayed the veterans as sternly inflexible, the truth is, they had learned how to survive long-term in that particular school atmosphere. Granted, they weren't doing much for this particular group of minority students but, from their standpoint, along comes the idealistic kid who turns everything upside down and then leaves. So who's teaching those children now?

Once again, what Erin accomplished was wonderful, and the Freedom Writers Foundation she created is attempting to implement her program in other inner city schools. In the final analysis, however, the success of her program was 95% Erin Gruwell. Implementing it elsewhere will require finding similar dedicated personnel. While there is no question in my mind that there will be ample candidates, the question remains: How many can continue this all-consuming effort long term? Leaving to run a foundation is certainly noble but, similar to those who move to administration, who is left to do the actual teaching?

Another movie, "The Ron Clark Story," clearly substantiates my concerns. While Ron was living in a squalid apartment, his life consumed by his teaching job at a New York City public school, he became quite ill with pneumonia. The fact that Ron continued to push himself regardless of his sickness, concerned me greatly. I was also in my twenties when I got pneumonia, and for the exact same reason as Ron; working 24/7 doing incredibly wonderful things for the kids

(Hey! where's my movie?). I know from experience that it took a full two to three weeks of bed rest to regain any semblance of basic function, and approximately three to four months before I felt completely recovered. Once again, the question is: How long can one sustain such a frantic, all-consuming pace? Similar to Erin Gruwell, it only took a few years before Ron was off to bigger and better things. In his case, it was starting his own school.

I particularly remember the scene where Ron received his own special parking place at the North Carolina school at which he was teaching prior to leaving for New York City. My wife and I turned to each other bemusedly. From experience, she and I both know the "reality" of teaching dictates that no one teacher can receive sustained recognition over everyone else for an extended period of time. If Ron had stuck around long enough, the administration would have engaged in every possible tactic to thwart his enthusiasm: larger class sizes, more students with learning and behavioral issues, less desirable teaching space, transfer to another grade level or building, to name a few.

Several years back, after one of my more notable accomplishments with the children, a group of parents wanted to hold a school-wide assembly to plant a tree in my honor. Because the only time I had ever seen a tree planted was in memoriam, I knew there was absolutely no way a tree was going to be planted in honor of one teacher and not all of the others. The principal managed to squirm her way out of it by saying we couldn't do anything permanent due to a pending addition being added to the school. The parents suggested that, knowing exactly where the addition was to be erected, couldn't the tree be planted somewhere completely removed from that area? Apparently, the principal successfully argued that the addition would entail laying waste to the entire neighborhood. So instead, I received a small garden fixture during a very subdued gathering in the school courtyard.

Eventually, the administration completely dismantled the program I had created.

I recently read a statement by John McCain about patriotism. He said, "Patriotism is countless acts of love, kindness and courage that have no witness or heraldry, and are especially commendable because they are unrecorded." It struck me immediately that simply adding "Teaching" to this statement provides the perfect definition for the consummate selflessness that is the essence of our calling. Just the other day my wife's principal said to her: "Why do *I* need to commend you for doing that? You know you did it and, hopefully, so do your pupils." That statement offered an incomparable summary of the teaching conundrum. It truly is the countless daily acts of kindness and selflessness that have no heraldry and, for the most part, go completely unrecorded; except for the possible hope that an occasional student might notice.

Fortunately, as you persevere from a novice to a more experienced teacher, you get to the point in your classroom where there is far more cooperation than not; but *every* period of *every* day there is at least one incident requiring resolution. In addition, each and every period you have to set the tone from the outset—it is never automatic or routine. As the following incident will clearly illustrate, dealing with this continual resistance can be exhausting.

It was the late 1970s, and, being in the pre-cable/satellite dish era, the selection of television channels was limited to whatever you could receive off an antenna, which in our case consisted of "rabbit ears" on top of the TV set. At best, we were able to get fuzzy reception on two of the three major networks and one local start-up station. I distinctly remember coming home in such a state of mental and physical fatigue that my wife and I would plop down in front of the only show available: "Quincy, M.E." The plot centered on a forensic medical examiner named Quincy, who would find himself at odds with his bosses and other police personnel during each and every episode. Suffice it to say, the acting on this show consisted of Quincy, in a state of continual agitation, shouting every line with exactly the same grating inflection. This being pre-Oprah/Ellen DeGeneres, "Quincy" was on every day. Although we laughed at the embarrassing lameness of the whole thing, due to the exhausted state in which we found ourselves each day, there we sat. Think of it, healthy young people in their mid-twenties, ensnared in this frightening ritual.

It didn't take long before we discovered that my wife's brother, a special education teacher, was doing exactly the same thing! However, his participation in this viewing activity was quickly curtailed after a student pulled a knife on him and he decided to bail-out of teaching for greener pastures. As an estimator for a moving company he now earns more than my wife and I combined. Although his work involves the usual stresses of a job in sales, he continually says his worst day at his current job can't compare to anything he experienced in teaching.

So, when tackling the issue of longevity, it would be quite understandable for you to wonder why my wife and I stayed in a profession which necessitated watching shows like "Quincy" to unwind after a long day. Essentially, it is because we, and so many teachers like us, are believers. We believe that we can make a positive difference in the lives of our pupils; sowing the seeds of the future. Like Don Quixote, we ride on with hope and, no matter how "impossible," continue the Quest.

6. Teacher on Teacher

"Elementary school teachers have it easy!" "Those high school teachers don't do a thing!" From my first day of teaching, I heard comments like these spew-forth from the mouths of the very people who had the audacity to bemoan the fact that the general public makes these very same comments about teachers as a whole. While I was astounded at this colleague on colleague denigration, I was simultaneously intrigued that nobody made these comments about middle school teachers. There appeared to be an intrinsic understanding that teaching kids of this age, those "walking hormones," was a nightmare. Middle School teachers, on the other hand, were able to raise complaining about elementary teachers and especially high school teachers to an art form. It was simply no contest! Something similar to sending the New York Yankees out to play a bunch of "T" ballers. Then again, all teachers of core subjects (math, science, history, etc.) universally agreed that special area teachers (art, music, physical education) had it made in the shade.

What astonished me the most was my reaction. Listening to this venom, I came away from each encounter with the feeling that everyone had a point. Right then and there I began what has become a career-long analysis of this "gut" reaction. While the comments have never ceased, my efforts to understand this bewildering phenomenon have been ongoing. *Why* would teachers do to themselves the very thing that is done by everyone else to teachers in general? It struck me as being akin to adults eating their young. I have come to believe that this issue is key to any pursuant understanding of the enigma we call teaching.

Throughout this book I use the term "career" to describe my years in teaching. In the Random House dictionary, the first word in the definition of career is "*progress*"—progress through some phase of life. Herein lies what is perhaps the greatest incongruity in teaching:

Regardless of whether you are a beginning teacher starting your first day on the job or a thirty year veteran, your "official" job assignment, level of responsibility, and expectation of accomplishment are identical!

The fact that the only difference between the novice and veteran teacher is salary brings to light a key element underlying the frustration inherent in teaching. Whereas a traditional professional career path is linear in advancement, with steadily increasing levels of responsibility and prestige, teaching is cyclical. In essence, teaching becomes a one year career, repeated over and over for the duration. I believe this basic discrepancy is the cornerstone to which all related concerns can be linked. This is why, despite the many flaws that need to be resolved, I find myself enthusiastic about veteran teachers having the opportunity to pursue a true linear career path by becoming mentor and/or *practicing* master teachers.

While contemplating this cyclical career stagnation, I was drawn to a major frustration expressed by the controversial new Washington, D.C. School Chancellor, Michelle Rhee, during a recent interview in Time Magazine.[6] Apparently, she proposed offering D.C. teachers up to $130,000 per year in merit pay incentives (almost double the average salary) in exchange for giving up their tenure (a protection requiring due process against arbitrary firing). Much to Ms. Rhee's consternation, the teachers were adamant in their opposition to this measure. As every veteran teacher thoroughly understands, because the administration regards the value of all teachers as equal, and one can hire three beginning teachers for the same $130,000 salary, any teacher who relinquished his or her tenure would unwittingly find themselves in a one-year position. With the protection of tenure removed, the administration could surely concoct any number of reasons to fire that individual by the close of the school year, while more than likely using those same fabrications to deny the proposed merit pay incentives in the process.

Every year, as the school calendar winds-down, teachers are required to participate in an evaluation process. Often this involves a self-evaluation linked to some preset goals wherein the teacher reflects on his or her accomplishments throughout the year. It is at this time that I, and many of my colleagues, ponder the 99% of time, effort, and energy expended on students, behind closed classroom doors, that goes completely unnoticed; not only by administrators and parents, but oftentimes by the vast majority of the pupils as well. Herein lies another glaring incongruity of teaching: We function in this extraordinary "fishbowl," where everyone is watching and dissecting all that we do, when, in reality, almost everything that we do is completely hidden behind the four walls of our classrooms.

Despite the current groundswell towards collaboration between teachers, the truth is, even though two classroom doors may be directly adjacent to one another, what goes on behind those doors can be as different as night and day. Consequently, even teachers of the same subject, content area, and curriculum often have no idea what is happening in neighboring colleagues' classrooms because there is no time allotted in the daily schedule for visitations of this type. Therefore, we are left with nothing but totally superficial perceptions about what everyone else is doing. Now, if our own colleagues are wallowing in false perceptions, what does that say for the administration, parents, and public at large? Teachers may be doing great things every day, but the vast majority of it goes completely unrecognized. Thus, the frustration mill grinds even finer.

Since administrators no longer teach, their disconnection from the classroom experience further feeds this downward spiral. As a result, teachers who are "schmoozing" the administration get elevated in stature. I am certainly aware that this issue imbues all professions but, because teaching produces such a paucity of tangible evidence to substantiate any claim of superiority, cultivating the perception of significant accomplishment to those in charge balloons in magnitude. The mere hint that some may be elevating themselves at your expense is all that a teacher needs to justify a sense of intense unease.

Let me be clear. I fully understand from friends in the business world that cutthroat, back-stabbing subterfuge is basically considered standard operating procedure. While in the corporate structure this behavior may result in career advancement, what does a teacher get? An easier duty assignment? Perhaps one fewer disruptive child in their class? With no meaningful advancement available, these are the scraps over which we are left to squabble.

I remember the brief tenure of an assistant principal who suddenly started showing up in my room every day for brief visits. Alarmed, I immediately went to our union representative to ask if I should be concerned about this selective treatment. It turned out this woman was doing the same thing in every classroom, every day. Aside from wishing she had announced this in advance, the uniqueness of the activity filled me with curiosity and provided an opportunity to open some positive dialogue. Lo and behold, it just so happened that this approach was actually taught in one of the classes she had taken for her administrative certificate: "Management by Walking Around" (MBWA, as she liked to call it). I gained an immediate respect for the institution where she received her training because, during the vast majority of my career, I had only worked for administrators with exclusive expertise in MBHIYOAD (Management by Hiding In Your Office All

Day). Of course, with the advent of computer technology, another key administrative course has apparently been added to supplement MBHIYOAD; that being MBWE (Management by Writing E-mails).

As I'm sure you can deduce, MBHIYOAD coupled with MBWE has created the current environment in the building where I work. After four years under the present principal, it's astonishing to report that she has been in my room a total of two times. Once was to get a kid for a disciplinary issue that had occurred in another teacher's class, and the other was for a department meeting. I can easily go through an entire week without seeing her once. The result of working in a building with such an extraordinary administrative disconnection is that a complete lack of trust begins to ferment. Since our building is divided along a clear line separating the "haves" (administration buddies) from the have-nots, I don't think anything further is necessary to describe the rampant distrust that permeates our staff.

While we are on the subject of e-mail, I must reiterate that teachers are under tremendous time constraints. There is only so much time before the next bell rings and the onslaught continues. I find it interesting how school is the only place, besides fire stations, boxing matches and horse races, where jumping to bells is part of the job assignment (Of course, there's always Pavlov's dogs, which is much too disturbing to contemplate). The need to continually watch the clock is perhaps the one aspect of teaching that is inconceivable to anyone outside of education. The school day progresses in strict adherence to measured segments marked by ringing bells. Add to this the fact that we don't sit at a computer all day long, and you'll understand why teachers are at odds with school administrators who do have the time to sit at their desks writing e-mails.

In light of this, I find it amazing how long it has taken for administrators to become diligent about how and what they write in e-mails. Perhaps the turnaround can be traced to the U.S. Supreme Court decision stating that e-mails in the workplace are *not* protected under privacy statutes. Even so, the reversal has been amazingly slow. As a result, I have collected several years' worth of the most incredibly embarrassing, absurd, and potentially incriminating administrative statements imaginable. Whether or not the initial cause can be attributed to the casual nature in which e-mail technology was first put to use, it seems as though administrators had no inkling they were putting these things in writing or that a simple click of the "print" icon would save them in hard copy forever. Verbal statements have a built-in "plausible deniability." The administrator can simply say, "Oh, you must have misunderstood." Written statements have no such retractability. Truthfully, if I didn't have the following example in writing, there is no way I would ever have believed it!

At the beginning of every school year, each department (subject area) sends home a syllabus that explains the course content and the requirements/expectations for student achievement. Because my department has used the same basic handout for the past dozen years, we were flabbergasted to receive a lengthy e-mail from the principal concerning the "grading" section in this year's document. In our subject, we not only evaluate demonstrated "skills and understanding," we also assess student "preparedness" which includes the level of responsibility shown by completing homework and bringing all required materials to each class. Unbelievably, the principal stated, "If you remove the word "responsibility," I am comfortable with what you want to send home." Considering the current infatuation over increased expectations on schools, I find it truly inconceivable that a principal would deem it inappropriate to assess student responsibility. Not only that, but to remove any possibility that we misinterpreted her instructions, it's *in writing!!!*

So, when considering the effect of MBHIYOAD and MBWE on the issue of teacher insularity, if the administrative perception of the teacher is based almost exclusively on hearsay, parents simply serve to put gasoline on the fire. In over thirty years, I can count on ten fingers the number of times parents have brought a *major* concern directly to me as their child's teacher. To the contrary, the occasions when parents have gone directly to the administration are plentiful. Please understand, these instances are not in any way an attempt to resolve a concern. They are for the singular purpose of spewing parental venom. If I had a nickel for every time an administrator has told me how much I have their support in these situations, I'd probably have a good $3.35 by now. They claim that they hate dealing with this stuff, yet do nothing to end it. It would be a simple matter of just telling the parents that they *must* speak to the teacher first. But, because they don't, the result is:

The 15% policy

When *any* incident occurs in school, by the time the child gets home no more than 50% of what they are telling the parent is actually true. First of all, he or she has completely eliminated their own culpability from whatever tale they are telling. Secondly, one must compute the spin, half-truths, and complete fabrications the child's friends may have added to the mix during lunch, in-between classes, or on the bus ride home.

Regardless, upon hearing this yarn the parent will immediately infuse their own preconceived notions. They will factor-in whatever they have already "heard" about this teacher, then add their own childhood memories of a similar situation, and perhaps call some other parents to gather a few more inaccuracies. Therefore, by the time the parent finally calls the principal to foam and fume, at the absolute best, 25% of what the principal is hearing has any authenticity. Then it's the principal's turn to affix all of his or her perceptions of the teacher, the kid, and the parent, and combine that with whatever politically correct "spin" they feel needs to be applied. Consequently, by the time the teacher hears the story, any resemblance to what *actually* occurred is at most a 15% probability.

So, here's the poor teacher, agape and aghast, attempting to explain what really happened. And the kicker is, the vast majority of these incidents take you by complete surprise. Most teachers instinctively know when something of significance has occurred and a good teacher will have the sense to proactively resolve the situation—"nip it in the bud" as it were. Usually a phone call home is all that's required. Regrettably, procedures like this 15% policy create a general pall of unease that can have a devastating effect on staff morale. However, even a mere 15% is preferable to my principal's latest approach, which I can only dub the 0% policy. Teachers are now being called to the office concerning issues raised by complaining parents who are *allowed to remain anonymous!* How can a teacher possibly address a matter in which all specifics, including the names of the students allegedly involved, are withheld? And talk about staff morale. Now *every* teacher is wondering what sort of fabrications anonymous parents are making about them!

My former principal, Karen, had a very simple policy for dealing with complaining parents. Her first question would be, "Have you talked with your child's teacher about this?" When, of course, the answer was "No," the parent would be instructed that he or she *must* speak with the teacher first. Then Karen would say, "If you are still dissatisfied with the outcome, you, the teacher, and I will have a meeting in my office." In five years of working for Karen, I had three one-on-one conferences with disgruntled parents and never had any in her office.

Every time I tell this story, the inevitable response is "Karen must have had a wonderfully supportive relationship with her superintendent!" In fact, nothing could be further from the truth. But, because her policies were so fair and consistent, she had extraordinary support in the community. You see, making a parent meet with the teacher means the issue will actually be resolved; hopefully to the satisfaction of the parent, but definitely to the benefit of the child. Trust and contentment abound when such policies are employed.

The "my door is open for you to come in and say anything you want" policy of most other administrators for whom I have worked solves nothing. The problem never gets resolved and the parent just continues to gripe. The administrator is left with an inaccurate perception of the teacher, and the teacher is left with a hopeless sense of being trapped in a process that always leaves him or her floundering. Ultimately, the biggest loser in this whole process is the child, because any teacher with a lick of sense simply backs off. With so many other students in the class to concentrate on, this is just one less problem to deal with. As a result, the kid begins to think he's doing better because he's no longer being challenged, while the parent revels in the erroneous thought that they "really fixed *that* teacher."

The sense of uncertainty created by the policies and issues discussed in this chapter cultivates an absence of trust and a general air of skepticism and unease. In the unique, isolated atmosphere of public education, the product is festering suspicion and insecurity which far too often find an outlet in teacher-on-teacher denigration. Because there is no way to absolutely know what another teacher is doing (aside from shadowing that teacher all day long), it is very easy to get drawn into the perception game. Mere speculation simply feeds on itself, round and round in a vicious cycle. The only thing you do know with absolute certainty is how difficult, challenging and oftentimes dismaying you find your own situation. So, when a group of teachers of the same age level and subject commiserate over common issues, the resulting assumption simply has to be that all of those *other* teachers have it easier!

I have been most fortunate throughout my career to have a broad certification. This has allowed me the unique opportunity to teach at all levels, kindergarten through 12th grade. Therefore, I can personally attest that every grade has its unique challenges and any suggestion that a teacher or group of teachers, no matter what age bracket or subject area they work in, has it "easier" than you do, is absolute nonsense! My answer to teachers who denigrate other teachers is the same as I say to anyone chastising teaching in general: If you have not taught that grade or subject, you have no basis for your critique. If you think they have it so good, get certified in their discipline and find out. You'll be in for a shock! This is exactly what happened to me when I discovered— contrary to commonly held perceptions—how extraordinarily difficult it is to teach kindergarten. Don't believe me? Go give it a try!

7. Celebrity Musings

I was recently reading a Time Magazine interview with Steve Carell, of "40 Year Old Virgin" and "The Office" fame.[7] The question was asked, "If you didn't pursue acting, what would you be doing?" Steve's answer was, "I would teach history and coach a couple of sports. I think that would make me very, very happy. That's always been my backup plan" (p6). To this veteran teacher, that answer simply flew off the page! It perfectly summarizes the common mindset about teaching that permeates our society: *If all else fails, I can always teach!*

Perhaps more than anything else, this misconception is the precise reason teachers get so little respect. This "fall back on teaching" mentality may have been marginally accurate during some idyllic past, but in the 21st century, nothing could be further from the truth. The demands and expectations of the job absolutely require the most dedicated individuals. Just for the fun of it, however, let's play out Steve's "backup plan" a bit. Aside from the fact that he probably makes more in a day than the average teacher makes in a year, if he has invested wisely he just might be able to make the transition and still live somewhat in the manner to which he's become accustomed.

If Steve showed up as the new history teacher at any given high school, his celebrity status would automatically make him a student favorite. They would flock to his class in droves to see this hilariously funny star. But, for poor Steve the pressure would be enormous! Unlike filming a movie where you get numerous "takes," this would be live. And, unlike a stand-up show which is over in two hours, this performance would last a minimum of five periods. Furthermore, unlike any other gig, you don't fly to another destination when it's over. Nope, you come back tomorrow and do the whole thing again for another five periods! And, you can't compare it to a multiple-night stand at the same venue where the audience is comprised of mostly new people each night. In school, your entire audience consists of the same pupils day after day.

Just say, by some miracle, Steve is able to pull this off for a week or so. Eventually, the nagging issue of what he is really supposed to be doing would finally creep to the forefront: Teaching History! Giving him the benefit of the doubt, there is no question he could weave some of his outstanding comedic skill into the delivery of the history curriculum. Even so, bearing in mind the unrelenting schedule of five periods a day, day upon day, it would take two or three weeks, possibly a month, before Steve Carell the movie/television star would become just plain ol' Mr. Carell the history teacher. Again, perhaps he would have the gift to transition into successful delivery of instruction, but at the end of this grace period all of the other demands of teaching would come raining down. In addition, if there was anything the least bit phony or put-on in Mr. Carell's demeanor, this lack of genuineness would certainly have a detrimental effect on his rapport with students—a most essential part of successful teaching.

While I certainly don't doubt the sincerity of Steve's musings, there are numerous other media personalities who regularly "chime in" on a subject about which they know nothing. A refreshing exception occurred a few years back in an article in Newsweek by Anna Quindlen. After spending a day at a New Jersey elementary school, she was describing the daunting task faced by teachers and the urgent need to drastically increase teacher salaries. The most extraordinary thing was that, unlike the vast majority of pundits who offer opinion after opinion while never setting foot inside a real school building, Anna actually attempted to *teach!* After just three classes she says, "I staggered out the door and wanted to lie down for the rest of the day" (p100).

On the other hand, Joe Klein of Time Magazine regularly "chimes in" on the need for longer school days and school years, the benefits of merit pay, and the need to abolish teacher tenure. Yet, unlike Anna, I haven't seen any indication of a similar in-school classroom experience. One of Joe's recurring themes is to write disparagingly about teachers' unions; perpetuating the myth that they only serve the status quo and protect lousy teachers. Surprisingly, I've also heard HBO's Bill Mahr and some other unexpected luminaries spouting this same line. In my experience, nothing could be further from the truth; especially considering the demands that are currently placed on teachers. However, if we continue to fixate on this one issue as the root cause of the problems facing our schools, there is simply no hope that we will ever engage in meaningful discussion and an intelligent resolution of the myriad issues facing education.

The National Education Association, of which I am a member, is dedicated to improving teacher effectiveness and delivery of instruction. In addition to sponsoring regular workshops, their publications at the state and national levels focus on teacher training. Unfortunately, due to ongoing negotiations and legislative battles at every level, a substantial portion of the union effort is focused on teacher working conditions and salary. Because these issues never get resolved, one could easily conclude that the union is stagnantly perpetuating a rigid, narrow agenda. While not perfect by any means, without the union teachers might find themselves back in one-room schoolhouses working for room and board. Although this is a bit of an exaggeration, because schools are largely funded by local property taxes, how far do you think people might go to cut their yearly tax bill in half? Look at what happened in California after the passage of Proposition 13. They went from one of the best funded education systems in the country to one of the very worst. The outcome of Proposition 2½ in Massachusetts was the immediate layoff of

9,270 teachers, the closing of 200 schools, and the elimination of many music, art, and reading programs across the state.

While education tends to be a fairly regular topic of television news stories, I particularly remember one investigation where the commentator was ruefully lamenting the fact that he was being blocked from coming into the school building. He wanted to get the "true" picture from the inside: observe classes, see teachers in action, and talk to students to get their perspective. The only problem was that he wanted to bring in the whole production crew with cameras, microphones, sound technicians, etc. The artificiality created by all the hoopla would completely negate any legitimate understanding of the natural school setting. If you want to get an honest perspective of the school environment, come in anonymously—not as the flashy television reporter—just as "average guy."

Now there's an idea! Due to my admiration for his insightful reporting, allow me to offer this challenge to our friend Joe Klein. Want to find out what is really going on in school? Let's you and I switch jobs for a week. Hopefully I have demonstrated some writing ability, so you come in and do what I do. Not as the esteemed magazine/TV commentator. Just show up with no fanfare, write "Mr. Klein" on the blackboard, and go at it. I'll do your schedule for a week and you do mine. Mind you, there's no bailing out at lunch on the first day. You *must* do the whole week! Most importantly, because you probably earn in one month what I earn in a whole year, switching salaries is definitely part of the deal!

Come to think of it, this may be just the solution for anyone who wishes to speak ill of the teaching profession. Come in and do a week. If you manage to make it through, then at least you'll have a basis for your comments. As a matter of fact, if we really want to elevate teaching to the status it deserves, let's make this a "national service" commitment. If every adult in America had to do one week in front of a class, their esteem for teachers would skyrocket! (Plus, this process might unearth potential teachers who had not yet realized their "calling.") In the interim: *If you haven't done the time, you aren't allowed to "chime."*

I have always enjoyed the work of the actor Bruce Willis, going back to his "Moonlighting" days. However, I recently became a full-fledged groupie upon hearing that he regularly advocates the immediate doubling of teacher's salaries. I have no idea if he plans to contribute any of his millions to the effort, but his empathy is heartwarming.

I find it uncanny that coinciding with the time frame in which I'm writing this, there's an interview with John Madden in Time Magazine where the question is asked, "If there wasn't football, what would your life be like instead?"[8] Amazingly, he says, "I'm sure that had I not been a coach, I would have been some form of teacher." Then he adds, "I'd like to work with kids in special education" (p6). All I can say to the "great drawer of circles and arrows" is: What's stopping you? Go ahead, give up your millions and head right into that special education classroom! They'd be delighted to have the extra body! And since you seem to be a very outspoken, independent and skilled commentator, I'd love to have a chat after you experience what it's like to work within the confines of special education laws that restrict what you can and can't do, and what you can and can't say. Teacher expertise must conform to the guidelines, required services, protections, and rights of the children. Your opinions and beliefs are not a consideration. In fact, if you say something that is marginally insensitive or wrongly interpreted by a child, you could find yourself sitting in a lawyer's office. Still sound like fun?

8. The Business of Education

Possibly one of the greatest dichotomies one will ever encounter is the cavernous dissociation between the teacher in the classroom and the "business" of education which includes administrators, boards of education, parental advisory boards, local, state, and national legislative branches/education departments, education advocacy/lobbying groups, institutions of higher education, and teacher training institutes. Whenever one encounters a panel or policy discussion, from the local level to the national, ordinary teachers are bound to be absent. Perhaps there may be a building principal, but that too is not the norm. The participants tend to be exclusively superintendents, college professors, elected or appointed officials, legislators, governors, college administrators, and/or additional "experts" in the field. The one group of individuals that is rarely invited to discuss issues, provide input, offer expertise, answer questions, or participate in setting policy, are the ones who do the actual educating: Teachers!

Once the establishment has identified and immersed themselves in the current talking point or *issue du jour*, the individuals who will be responsible for the implementation become inconsequential. Having teachers involved would only complicate the situation by inserting the actualities of the real world of education. Teachers understand that the multifaceted, complex world of genuine contact with students cannot be reduced to a single catch phrase. This blurring of reality becomes even more obvious every time an administrator talks about "seeing the big picture." It really has nothing to do with the size of the picture or the clarity of vision; it's simply that administrators and teachers are looking at completely different canvases. Living in their separated realm, administrators tend to gravitate towards the vision of a tidy, bucolic John Constable landscape, while teachers function within a disjointed, fragmented Pablo Picasso-esque creation.

Understanding the complexity of this chasm between the realities of "educating" (teaching) and "education" (the entrenched bureaucracy) is paramount to resolving the overwhelming problems currently facing public education. Whereas these two entities should be one and the same, the gap is ever-widening. Attempting to shed clarity on this extraordinary situation is indeed a daunting task.

In 1971, the year I entered college, James Herndon published his brilliant exposé on the state of American education: "How to Survive in Your Native Land." This book became the cornerstone of thoughtful discussion throughout my college studies. When I began teaching in 1975, it instantly became clear that the classroom experiences Herndon had encountered in the 1960s were completely unchanged a decade later. In fact, in the 38 years since its publication, there have only been three major changes to the conditions chronicled in his book: 1) we no longer use movie projectors to show films, 2) bowling alleys now use automatic scoring, and 3) special education/special needs students have been assimilated into regular public school classrooms. Despite scores of landmark educational mandates and initiatives, classroom structure remains astoundingly unchanged. Certainly the addition of computer technology has had an incredible impact, but outsized numbers of kids still sit at desks, in rows, in classrooms that are too small, while the teacher, against all of the same odds described by Herndon, tries to teach.

At the same time that life *inside* the classroom has only changed minutely, everything occurring *outside* the classroom door has changed immeasurably. Without exception, every educational initiative, revamping, and overhaul has had little positive effect on conditions in the classroom, but has caused for extraordinary additional demands on teacher time, endless streams of paperwork, and the never-ending expansion of the administrative bureaucracy. And the sum total of it all? Only the "appearance" of change. As long as the public is manipulated into *believing* there has been meaningful change: Mission Accomplished!

Individuals of a certain age may remember the hand-wringing consternation that surrounded the release of the 1983 National Commission on Excellence in Education report entitled: "A Nation at Risk: The Imperative for Educational Reform." This document stated that American education had declined precipitously over the previous twenty-five years and recommended higher graduation standards, more demanding curricula, better teacher training and more reliance on standardized testing. At that time, the standard classroom consisted of 25 students, seated at desks, in rows, under the direction of a single teacher. Almost 20 years later, when the "No Child Left Behind" legislation was enacted, the standard classroom consisted of 25 students, seated at desks, in rows, under the direction of a single teacher—a situation that continues to the present day. Interestingly, "No Child" contains the same performance demands on schools, teacher training/accountability, and reliance on standardized testing as "A Nation at Risk."

Most disquieting was my recent perusal of President Obama'a March 2009 speech announcing his major educational reform initiatives. I have so many notes written in the margins that it looks like I was correcting a student research paper. While I am heartened by the call for more parental accountability and the need to reward accomplished educators who serve as mentors to new teachers, many of the proposals are essentially a reworking of the same talking points of the last twenty-six years. When expressing my concerns to a colleague, it was surreal to hear him say, "Don't worry, after all the fanfare and multi-million dollar expenditure, nothing will be any different." It is mortifying to contemplate the likeliness of this outcome.

So, what has changed since the original "Nation at Risk" imperative? Aside from a burgeoning administrative bureaucracy, the 1983 report spawned a spectacular new growth industry: "*Educational Reform.*" This movement has become an institution unto itself, with extensive studies, reports, assessments, recommendations, lobbying efforts, curriculum developments, and a vast network of in-school workshops, lectures, and teacher training initiatives. While growth in the educational reform movement from 1983 to 1999 was substantial, the turn of the millennium served as a catapult for launching commissions, associations, partnerships, and educational alliances dedicated to promoting "educational excellence 2000," "school reform for the new millennium," and "skills for 21st century learning." The explosion in publications, websites, companies and institutions dedicated to educational reform is simply mind-boggling! A quick Internet search of "school reform" or "21st century learning" will clearly substantiate this verity. The business being generated must be in the hundreds of millions of dollars.

This brings me to my favorite James Herndon (1971) insight about the two essential characteristics of institutions (p109-110):

> The first characteristic of all institutions is that, no matter what the inevitable purpose for which it was invented, the institution must devote all of its energy to doing the exact opposite. Thus, a Savings Bank must encourage the people to borrow money at Interest, and a School must inspire its students towards stupidity.

> The second characteristic is that an institution must continue to exist. Every action must

be undertaken with respect to eternity. This second characteristic is the reason for the first. For unless a Savings Bank can persuade the people not to Save, the Savings Bank will go broke. But the Savings Bank must continue to exist, since otherwise the people would have No Place To Save. Just so, the School must encourage its students not to learn. For if the students learned quickly, most of them could soon leave the school, having Learned. But, if the students left the school it would cease to exist as an institution and then the students would have No Place In Which To Learn.

"An Institution Is A Place To Do Things Where Those Things Will Not Be Done"

Could the entire school reform movement be defined any more perfectly than by these two characteristics? Can you imagine what would happen to this vast industry if we ever actually *achieved* meaningful school reform? It would cease to exist! Therefore, the movement must persevere in vigorously promoting a school improvement agenda that will *never* reach fruition, because, if the institution of School Reform ceased to exist, where would the educational bureaucracy turn for the continual "reform" initiatives that are the foundation of 21st century learning?

In the final analysis, it's not the teachers or the union that are responsible for the lack of meaningful school reform––it's the entrenched bureaucracy. It seems that the instant administrators began to talk about "thinking outside the box," we started doing everything but. That's because preserving the status quo serves the bureaucracy perfectly. Why would those in charge want to institute policies that would drastically impact their job assignments? They aren't going to send themselves back to the classroom any more than sitting politicians are going to enact term limits. It would be an act of pure insanity! As long as the bureaucracy is responsible for instituting school reform policies, you can bet that *meaningful* reform will continue to be illusory.

I just attended a faculty meeting during which the principal was exhorting all of the changes put in place during the past year. It essentially boiled down to a list of insignificant window dressing, in a long line of the same, dating back to my earliest days in teaching. In terms of any relevant impact on what goes on in the classroom, all of this infatuation with change has had virtually no positive effect on "real" education, i.e., the teacher/student dynamic. There is a phrase that teachers have long used to express the futility of this ongoing obsession with change: "Reinventing the Wheel." Ultimately, after the fanfare and grandstanding have subsided, we end up exactly where we started. In this regard, I perceive that this book will probably speak most vibrantly to veteran teachers with ten or more years of experience. The novice teacher, having yet to endure sufficient instances of "recycled" change, may not fully appreciate the poignancy of the truths presented here. (Just give it some time.)

There is another much more intriguing phrase which I never fully understood until I applied it to education: "Rearranging Deck Chairs on the Titanic." Aside from the extraordinary paperwork and time expenditure, all of the aforementioned administrative and governmental initiatives are totally irrelevant to the essential process of teacher/student interaction. However, unlike "reinventing the wheel" where the result brings you back to where you started, the crushing weight of paperwork and time expenditure involved in "deck chairs" is drastically different. Left to their own devices, the bureaucracy would simply ride the ship to the ocean floor. It is the teachers, with their unlimited resourcefulness in the face of seemingly insurmountable odds, who keep education afloat.

In short, we care passionately about teaching—the process of working directly with students. To witness a burgeoning administrative hierarchy continue to distract and exhaust the practitioners of the art of teaching is simply heartbreaking. No matter how earnestly we try to face each new academic year with a sense of satisfaction over previous accomplishments and an excitement for what lies ahead, it becomes increasingly necessary to simply learn "How to Survive In Your Native Land."

9. How Shit Happens[9]

In the beginning was the plan. . . .

*A*nd then came the assumptions

*A*nd the assumptions were without form

*A*nd the plan was completely without substance

*A*nd the darkness was upon the face of the Teachers

*A*nd they spoke amongst themselves, saying:

"It is a crock of shit and it stinks"

*A*nd the Teachers went unto their Department Coordinators, saying:

"It is a pail of dung and none may abide the odor thereof"

And the Department Coordinators went unto the Assistant Principal, saying:

"It is a container of excrement and it is very strong such that none may abide by it"

And the Assistant Principal went unto the Principal, saying:

"It is a vessel of fertilizer and none may abide its strength"

And the Principal went unto the Assistant Superintendent, saying:

"It contains that which aids growth and it is very strong"

And the Assistant Superintendent went unto the Superintendent, saying:

"It promotes growth and is very powerful"

And the Superintendent went unto the Board of Education, saying:

"This new plan will actively promote the growth and efficiency of this organization and these areas in particular"

And the Board of Education looked upon the plan and saw that it was good and the plan became policy.

This is how shit happens

10. The Others

My first two years of teaching, I worked in a parochial school system under the supervision of nuns. True to every stereotype, these women were no-nonsense, structured educators and disciplinarians. I was then hired for my first public school position by Karen, the finest administrator for whom I have had the honor to work. To offer a perspective, it took less than a year after Karen retired for a grassroots effort by parents, teachers and the general citizenry to result in the school being named after her. This was in spite of every possible resistance by the superintendent and board of education. If you are wondering how these people could be so out-of-sync with the general public, similar to outstanding individual teachers, an outstanding administrator makes all the others pale in comparison. For superiors it turns into a continual issue about why everyone isn't like Karen and why the other schools aren't as good as hers. In fact, in a vain attempt to make things harder for her, the superintendent kept dumping so-called "difficult" teachers into Karen's school (me?). However, contrary to his hoped for effect, under Karen's outstanding leadership these teachers would flourish! Interestingly, the two parents who led the effort for the school name change were both eventually elected to the board of education and subsequently appointed chair and vice chair. Not unexpectedly, a bit of housecleaning resulted in a new superintendent and assistant superintendent.

Immediately following Karen's retirement, however, because the existing superintendent and board of education were looking for a principal who would be exactly Karen's opposite, they hired Fred. And they achieved their goal brilliantly! Everything that Karen was, Fred wasn't, and the shock was enough to cause me to seriously consider leaving teaching. I even went so far as to sign-up with a career counseling/management service. Aside from working in construction with my dad when I was a kid, I had no idea what I wanted to do other than teach; except that I absolutely *knew* I didn't want to work in construction.

Career Counseling and Teacher Skills

The career counseling service wound up being *very* expensive because I foolishly paid the entire $3,500 fee up-front in order to take advantage of a 10% discount. This was completely on impulse, as the result of an hour long meeting with the CEO who gave a fantastically inspirational promo about his "finest in the region" service. He *guaranteed* that, no matter what it took, they would place me in the job of my dreams. I vividly recall questioning him multiple times about why so much of what he was promising wasn't in any of the written materials or the contract I ultimately signed. It is so easy to exploit the fragile psyches of those who engage services such as these, and he did it masterfully. People who are out of work or unhappy in their jobs are very easily manipulated.

In actuality, this service gave you some aptitude and personality tests to help you define what kind of a job you should be pursuing, and then sent you to the Thomas Registry to peruse job descriptions. Ultimately, you were directed to "shadow" anyone *you* knew who had a job in the business world. No, this service didn't provide these opportunities; you had to pursue them on your own. As one might expect, the strain this put on some of my personal relationships was, in a few cases, friendship ending. Truthfully, how incredibly awkward it was to put the pressure of a request like this on friends and acquaintances.

On the positive side, this experience helped me to clearly define the extraordinary skills required for good teaching. These include, but are not limited to:

- Outstanding organizational and people skills.

- Extraordinary self-motivation, self-initiative, and follow-through.

- The ability to juggle multiple tasks simultaneously.

- Remarkable creativity and adaptability.

- The ability to resolve issues and solve problems independently.

- Very little need for supervision.

- The ability to think on your feet and make good decisions instantaneously.

- The ability to work under incredible pressure and time constraints.

- The ability to thoroughly research any given topic.

- Continual immersion in ongoing technology education and skill development.

- Possessing an in-depth understanding of human psychology.

Through the years, it is truly astounding how many times, both inside and outside the school setting, I have witnessed teachers instantaneously observe, analyze, take charge, and resolve the most baffling of situations. This is especially instinctive for veteran teachers. Even so, as I tried to shop myself around, it became exasperatingly clear that people in the business world have absolutely no understanding of the skills involved in teaching. They are ensconced in the mindset that teachers are amply paid for short, easy days, coupled with lots of vacations and summers off. The utter fallacy of this assumption is borne out by the massive number of teachers who, if they don't teach during the summer, work as cashiers, floor clerks, house painters, etc. It took twenty-five years before I reached the point financially that I didn't have to teach during the summer.

The truth is, if business leaders had any inkling of the extraordinary skills held by successful teachers, they would have recruiting booths set up in the parking lots of every school in the country. Just imagine the teacher shortage then! Similar to the way high gas prices have finally made people demand more fuel efficient cars, America would have to start paying teachers what they are worth.

Teacher Survival Skills

Despite the cost, my foray into the business world yielded nothing and I ended up enduring the four year tenure of Fred. But all was not completely futile, because Fred inadvertently taught me some invaluable survival skills which have served me well throughout my career. Unfortunately, leaders of Karen's ability are not the norm. However, administrators on Fred's side of the spectrum have graced numerous leadership positions in the buildings in which I have worked.

Take, for example, Fred's idea of an inspirational statement. At his very first meeting with the entire staff, Fred stood in front of the room with a bucket of water. While demonstrating, he said, "If you want a perspective on the impact teachers make, put your fist into a bucket of water and then remove it. Notice how there is no evidence that your fist was ever there." As you can imagine, all of us sat there dumbfounded! No one had a clue as to what he was trying to say, but nobody said a word. Who wants to appear obtuse in front of the new principal, especially after this big extravaganza with the bucket of water? All the same, it sure succeeded in giving us plenty to talk about afterwards. Nobody could really believe that this new principal's message would be that, as teachers, we have no impact whatsoever! A few months later, after we all knew him *a lot* better, Fred made the same statement again, minus the bucket. A veteran teacher had the courage to raise her hand and ask him exactly what he meant; because it sure appeared that he was saying teachers make no difference. Fred clarified that the point was "Don't take yourselves too seriously!"

Fans of the movie "Office Space" will certainly appreciate the fact that, when working under certain levels of incompetence, sophomoric inclinations are oftentimes the only available avenue to maintaining one's sanity. Consequently, the first survival skill that Fred taught us was *Out of sight, out of mind.* Anyone who has worked for such an individual knows incompetence breeds chaos, and Fred was continually in the throes of battle. If you happened to be anywhere in sight, he would grab you to "cover this" or "help with that." Many times it might even interfere with a class you needed to teach. Although it was fabulously entertaining to observe this man in action, if you got caught in his field of vision you would invariably get snared in his ever-widening net of disruption. So I learned to stay in my room as much as possible. I only went to the office when absolutely necessary and, since I was fortunate enough to have a single stall lavatory right next to my room, I was able to keep travel in the hallways to a minimum. In addition, because my room was in a more remote corner of the building, it became a "safe haven" of sorts, where many of my colleagues would come to escape detection. This location may also account for the reason why I can only remember one time that Fred deliberately came to my room to involve me in something.

The second survival skill went hand-in-hand with the first: *If an issue/instruction/declaration, etc., was really important, Fred would come and tell you personally.* Having previously worked exclusively for outstanding administrators, this second survival skill took much longer to learn. Under competent leadership, nothing is decreed that isn't expected to be followed. Conversely, incompetence results in directives that are regularly adjusted, amended, or completely reversed. Actually following instructions in a chaotic atmosphere like this only causes one to expend needless time and effort when, in the end, you will either have to do the exact opposite or, more than likely, nothing at all. Soon one learns to ignore all blanket directives and wait for one specifically addressed to you. Because this type of administrator is always operating in chaos, a lack of response on your part may very well be completely overlooked.

The third and most important survival skill was learned as the result of a particularly extraordinary incident with Fred. I had been teaching summer school since being hired at this building and, this being the first summer under Fred's supervision, he was struggling to understand what would occur. As far as he was concerned, there was an expected summer building maintenance schedule that was to be followed without fail. This consisted of every teacher clearing all materials off the walls, desks, and countertops to facilitate general cleaning, painting, and repairs during the summer. To aid in this task, ample boxes were provided for storage. This being my sixth summer, I had an established arrangement with the head custodian whereby I would clear my room at the conclusion of my course and they would clean it during August. This particular year, the last day of school was on a Thursday and I was starting my summer program three days later on Monday. Therefore, I spent the last couple of days of school setting materials throughout my room so that everything would be ready for the next week. Mind you, Fred had been repeatedly apprised that I was teaching this five week summer program and that the issue of cleaning my room was already arranged with the maintenance staff.

On the second to the last day of school (Wednesday), Fred came into my room, looked around and said, "What's all of this stuff?" Startled, I said, "These are the materials for my summer course that starts on Monday." Now, wouldn't it have been logical for Fred to say something like "Oh, yeah, that's right" and then, in a vain attempt to cover the fact that he had forgotten, add some highly essential administrative directive like "Just be sure it's all packed up at the end of the five weeks." Yes, that would seem reasonable. . . . However, quite unbelievably, Fred said,

"All of this stuff needs to be put into boxes!"

Completely taken off guard, I simply reiterated, "All of this is for my summer course that I start teaching on Monday." Fred stood there bewildered for a moment and said, "But Tom (the custodian) needs to clean the room." "Yes," I said, "but Tom and I have it all arranged that he will clean the room during August when I'm done." "Oh," said Fred, at which point I assumed that we're all set. Then, out of the blue, as if absolutely none of the previous conversation had occurred, Fred said,

"All of this stuff needs to be put into boxes!"

Astounded, I responded with the only thing I could assume would be logical: "Of course, Fred, I'll be sure it is all put away at the end of my summer program." Curiously, Fred continued to eyeball all of the teaching materials on the tables and countertops and, just as I'm assuming he is about to turn and leave, he said,

"All of this stuff needs to be put into boxes!"

"Fred!" I exclaimed, "I need these materials to teach my summer course that starts on Monday!" "But," said Fred, "Tom needs to clean the room."

As I stood there stunned, in total shock and disbelief, a commotion in the hallway caused Fred to turn and start heading towards the door. As my hopes began to soar that this distraction might be enough to get him to leave, Fred stopped at the door and turned back towards me. As he surveyed the materials on the tables and countertops as if for the first time, he said,

"All of this stuff needs to be put into boxes!"

As he went off, leaving me in a state of sheer, deer-in-the-headlights bewilderment, I proceeded to spend an hour and a half putting all of the materials into the boxes in a manner that would ensure the most expedient retrieval when I came back four days later. As a direct result of our discussion, sure as clockwork, Fred was back the next day to be sure everything was as he directed. Of course, come Monday, one would assume that I needed to arrive an extra hour and a half early to take all of the materials out of the boxes to prepare them for teaching. The only problem was that my first class began very shortly after the custodians opened the building. Thus my entire day was a mass of unnecessary disarray as I desperately attempted to set the tone for each class as I pulled materials out of boxes in a perceived state of unpreparedness.

I learned an invaluable lesson from this experience that has served me time and again over the years. When Fred first came into the room and said, "All of this stuff needs to be put into boxes," I should have immediately replied, "You bet, Fred, right away!" And that would have been the end of it. Fred would have gone off completely satisfied that his directive was being followed—not to be heard from again. What if he had come back, you say? In the 25 years that I have been playing the "absolutely, right away" card, never once has anyone come back to check. How is this possible? Because, once you establish yourself with every new administrator as a cooperative "team player," the stage is set. One of my colleagues has dubbed this third and most important survival skill: ***Nod 'n Do*** *- Anytime you know a discussion with an administrator is going to result in a no-win situation, simply nod in agreement and then go do what you were planning.*

In a perfect world it might seem reasonable for administrators to defer to the expertise of accomplished veteran teachers. However, the reality is, the first time you attempt to discuss any administrative directive, no matter how absurd, you plant the seed of discontent in the back of their minds. My wife continually questions the veracity of "Nod 'n Do" even though I have been successfully employing it for years. Why? Because being a reasonable, forthright, "play by the rules" kind of person, she is always attempting to address and resolve every issue. As a result, she has the administration around her all the time, poor kid.

Recently, I overheard an acquaintance lamenting that he constantly finds himself arguing with his boss. While a number of people within earshot were nodding in sympathetic understanding, he added, "The only problem is I'm self-employed!" I find this especially meaningful because, when I talk about administration, I speak from 14 years of experience as Founder, CEO and CFO of a community-based educational program. Student participation averaged 90-110 each year. The fact that parents paid tuition to have their children participate in this program year after year, and entire families chose to join us for educational trips all over the country, speaks volumes about its scope and viability.

This brings me to Rob, a fabulous veteran teacher who also ran his own part-time home repair/carpentry business outside of school. Rob opted for early retirement after enduring Fred for just two years and has been successfully operating his business on a full time basis ever since. Similar to my wife's approach, Rob would regularly attempt to discuss issues with Fred. Having worked under Karen for numerous years, he simply found it impossible to transition to any other manner of deportment. However, by regularly attempting reason in the face of total disarray, he became front and center on Fred's radar screen.

As I mentioned earlier, all teachers are expected to set yearly goals which provide the basis for their end-of-the-year evaluation. Somehow I had managed to get Fred to sign off on some incredibly skeletal statements. Rob, on the other hand, was struggling to come up with ideas. Knowing my goals had already been approved, he asked if he could see them. Basically, the mere thought that these things had been approved, caused us to laugh 'till we stopped. But, when one works in an atmosphere of complete upheaval, anything is possible. So, taking a chance that the iron might strike twice, Rob rewrote my goals to fit his subject area and handed them in; to which Fred bellowed, "What the heck kind of goals are these? I'd never dream of accepting something like this!" It was everything Rob could do to not rat me out! Believe me, I would have understood.

Leadership Skills

Show your employees loyalty, and they will be loyal.
Show them it is about the job, and
they will make it about the job.
Make it into a game, and they will play the game.

The Wire, Season One

I'm continually asked by colleagues to describe what made Karen such a phenomenal administrator. In a nutshell, she held herself and her staff to the highest professional standards. She treated you like a professional and, in return, expected you to be one. At the opening day faculty meeting, for example, she would hold up the faculty handbook and say, "This is the faculty handbook. As professionals you are expected to know its contents." That was it. No further discussion or elaboration. She didn't point out any highlights, changes, or specific portions. And she positively never read a word of it to us! She was the only administrator I have ever worked for who didn't read to us like we were children; a practice that is especially rampant in the current "PowerPoint" era. The slide goes up and it gets read to you! Ironically, every PowerPoint presentation is preceded by ample discussion, movement and adjustment to be sure everyone can see the screen. What's the purpose if it's going to be read to you anyway?

Karen expected you to function independently. In direct contrast to the current micro-managing administrative mentality, there was never any hovering. You were responsible for any and all information set out in memos or discussed at faculty meetings. The school functioned smoothly because there was never a superfluous directive; every instruction was the result of thoughtful analysis and discussion. She was up-front and honest. Consequently, the trust that developed between Karen and her staff was unshakable. She was a true teacher advocate and, as long as you carried out your responsibilities as a professional, you had her complete support.

Unlike other administrators for whom I have worked, she never sent out blanket memos concerning the fulfillment of responsibilities. If you were late to a duty, she would come to see you individually. You can't imagine how quickly the word about something like that gets around. I distinctly remember my second day working for her. The faculty handbook plainly stated the time that teachers were expected to arrive at school. As I was walking in the front door, Karen said, "Good morning Mr. Warren, school starts at 8:20." As I looked at my watch, she responded, "Not 8:21, . . 8:20." Lesson learned? Upholding the highest professional standards encompasses all aspects of the job.

Perhaps you may recall the massive uproar that occurred during the early 1990s, when the idea of hiring "non-educator" administrators first made the rounds. In virtual lock step, the teachers' unions and almost every teacher I knew voiced adamant disapproval. How could someone without a background in education, having never taught, be in charge of an educational institution? But, based on my then almost twenty years with numerous administrators, I was intrigued by the notion. Curiously, as I spoke with colleagues and they began to examine their own administrative histories, the inadequacies of the current system became evident.

The requirement for administrators to be ex-teachers simply baffles me. There is not one dedicated veteran teacher I know who, aside from dreaming about the pay, would ever consider leaving the classroom for a position that removes them from direct immersion in the education of students. During moments of unguarded candor, a number of administrators have confided to me that, aside from the massive salary increases, a major incentive to go into administration was to be removed from the daily grind of teaching. Because it rarely takes more than a year before most school administrators completely forget what the reality of teaching is like, all that remains is whatever degree of administrative skill they possess. Simply put, the desire to escape the classroom and make more money does not necessarily translate into good administrative practice. I would much rather have an excellent administrator without a background in education, who possesses all of the necessary leadership skills, than one who does not, but may have once been a teacher. However, if we must be restricted to only using former teachers as administrators, continuing to teach should definitely be part of the job description. Having all "educators" directly immersed in the instruction of children would be ideal. But, if administrative positions are to continue being exclusively managerial (a veritable certainty), let's get the most skilled and effective by casting the widest net possible.

So, what are the attributes of an outstanding administrator from a teacher's perspective? The following list is gleaned from years of discussion and analysis:

- Possesses honesty, integrity, and self-respect.

- Treats staff like professionals with dignity, respect, and support.

- Builds trust by serving as a teacher advocate. Shields staff from unnecessary distractions and superfluous mandates.

- Encourages self-reliance and independent function; no micro-managing.

- Operates with fairness and consistency, acting without prejudice or favoritism.

- Never betrays a confidence or speaks unfavorably about one teacher to another.

- Follows through on issues in a timely manner.

- Communicates clearly.

- Solicits meaningful input from staff. Listens and acts on the needs of the teachers, not a separate personal agenda or resume building.

- Shows open-mindedness to new ideas. Encourages risk-taking without fear of retribution.

- Acts with a stable, reasoned, and thoughtful approach to issues and crises, devoid of erratic behavior or emotional outbursts. Always seeks to lessen stress and difficulty for teachers; doesn't insert his or herself in a manner which exacerbates situations.

- Is knowledgeable on a wide range of topics and issues; seeks personal growth.

- Possesses and encourages perspective; it's a job, not our lives.

I was watching a political rally on TV last year where the speaker was exhorting "small town values" to the thunderous cheers of the enraptured crowd. Afterwards, an interviewer asked people in attendance if they could name some of these values. As I watched person after person stumble and fumble for answers, I questioned how similar the response might be if individuals at a gathering of school administrators were asked to clearly articulate their purpose. I wonder how much of the above list would be included in their answers. For instance, while programs are being cut and a number of teachers are being overwhelmed with outsized classes and student loads, my current principal expends extraordinary energy on continual "school spirit" activities. I like to joke that she must have been passed over for social secretary of her college sorority. Now, before you peg me as a grumpy old curmudgeon who can't get with the current youth culture of "fun" at work, I'm only suggesting that perhaps the goal of providing optimal educational opportunity for students should come first.

Consider this example: Because students and parents complained that study halls were essentially a waste of time, they were removed from last year's school schedule. In the meantime, despite our collective protestations, some of the principal's favorite cronies convinced her that the lack of study halls eliminated valuable time to work individually with the kids. Therefore, study halls were reinstated during the current school year under the guise of "on team time"—a euphemism for extra time with "core" subject teachers (math, science, reading, etc.). However, due to the expansion of the foreign language program, the only way to find time in the schedule for study halls was to cut the art, health and computer programs in half! Somehow the administration was able to sell this absurdity to the public by emphasizing that the students would have more time with core teachers. Just in case you're thinking that this sounds even marginally reasonable, prepare yourself for a shock. At the start of the current school year, the art, health, and computer teachers discovered that they were *assigned to monitor study halls!*

Truthfully, you need a chain saw to cut the irony! The very teachers whose programs were cut are now covering study halls during the exact same periods that they were previously teaching. Incredibly, core teachers have been assigned to group teacher planning sessions during these periods instead of working with children individually as the public was led to believe. Those of us who are a little more familiar with the complexities of the scheduling process feared this outcome from the start. Our point is, once it became clear that the schedule made it impossible for this "on team time" concept to be implemented, study halls should have been abandoned and the program "cuts" reinstated. One can only conclude that, either the administration is completely obtuse, or they just don't care about providing students with a well-rounded education. If these are the kinds of actions taken by administrators with a background in education, I'm all for trying something else.

This brings me to the current assistant principal at our high school. He taught fourth grade for three years, then spent two years as the computer specialist in a grade 3-5 elementary school and one year as the grade 6-8 technology specialist. During his three year computer/technology stint, he earned his administrative degree and was subsequently promoted directly to high school assistant principal! Apparently, they counted his year at the 6-8 school as his administrative internship. What, if anything, in the background of this 28 year old would qualify him to be assistant principal at a 1200 student high school? The only conceivable explanation was that he understood how to create the high school class schedule; indeed a daunting task, but one that is done during the summer and could easily be subcontracted to any competent IT specialist. To pay someone with absolutely no administrative experience a $106,000 salary as high school assistant principal because he is good with computers, is a travesty. Recently, two of my high school colleagues were in the hallway when one of our more "upstanding" citizens went tearing by. As they were about to intercede, this assistant principal came running after him. As my friends watched in amazement, one of them speculated: "What is he going to do if he actually catches the kid?"

As incredible as it sounds, in 34 years of teaching I have never sent a student to the office for a disciplinary issue. When I was working for Karen, the behavioral standards were so clearly defined and enforced that the parameters were unmistakable. Conversely, under an administrator like Fred, sending pupils to the office could result in punitive actions ranging from the marginal to the totally inconsequential. Therefore, I began to apply Karen's criterion within the confines of my room—a practice I have continued ever since. It's amazing how children will respond to fair and evenly enforced standards. This, of course, needs to be coupled with the necessary parental contacts but, even in the cases where home support is absent, clear classroom expectations still tend to be effective. In addition, the essential process of earning the respect of the students is severely undermined when you send behavioral issues to the office. They learn that you can't handle it yourself and, once the office takes over, you lose all control over the matter. The outcome may be completely contrary to what you desired and/or deemed appropriate.

Either unintentionally or deliberately, my building administration recently developed an elaborate "Disciplinary Referral Form" that basically serves as a disincentive for teachers to send students to the office. Just last month, a colleague spent 45 minutes completing the form only to find herself called down to the office for a meeting with the assistant principal anyway. After a recent ruckus in the hallway outside my room, a teacher in the adjacent room said she would deal with sending the kids involved to the office because she had seen most of the incident. Knowing that, like me, she usually handled discipline herself, I wasn't the least bit surprised when later, in a state of utter exasperation, she exclaimed what a convoluted, time consuming process it had been. Her conclusion: "I'll never send anyone to the office again!" (I wonder why I have this odd feeling that the administration is down there "high-fiving" each other!?)

"Children of the '60s" will enjoy this one. In the early 1990s, the PTO (Parent/Teacher Organization) brought a beautiful carved wooden bench for the front foyer of the building. This became the spot where students who were sent to the office sat while waiting to see the principal. Thus we dubbed it: "The Group W Bench."[10]

Hank's Rule

There is one inexplicable disciplinary procedure that I have seen used repeatedly by administrators through the years: Coming down hard on a "good kid" to set an example for others, while repeat offenders get off lightly. I remember an incident when I was teaching high school that involved a student who switched into one of my classes early in the year. This girl followed the appropriate office protocol and completed all of the necessary paperwork required to drop one class and add mine. Understandably, she assumed it was "all set" and began attending my class. Apparently nobody told her that she needed to keep attending the previous class until the office sent out the official word, which took four days. If you think it is nonsensical for a child to continue to sit in a class that they are dropping while falling further behind in the class they are adding, then you need to get "schooled" in the unique logic of educational administration. This is best summarized in what has come to be known as "Hank's rule of administrative practice:"

Whatever is the logical, correct and educationally sound thing to do, devote all of your energy to doing the exact opposite.

Take this poor girl for instance. She was so adamant in her assertions that the process was completed that I allowed her to start attending my class. Meanwhile, the previous teacher was sending notification slips to the office that the girl was skipping class. Now, wouldn't it be logical to think that once the office realized this was merely a procedural misunderstanding, all would be forgotten? Not a chance! The assistant principal decided to follow the "letter of the law" and, because the girl had skipped class four times, she was *suspended from school for three days!* You couldn't ask for a more perfect example of the above "rule." As a result of skipping class in one subject, your punishment is to get sent home to skip *all* of your classes for three days.

I was introduced to these aberrations in administrative logic way back when I was student teaching. Part of my training involved going to a grade 7-8 Junior High School on Wednesday afternoons. On my very first day the fire alarm went off. In a matter of minutes it became apparent that this was not a prearranged drill. With the building evacuated and all of the students out in front of the building whooping and cheering, a fleet of fire trucks arrives; sirens wailing, bells clanging, and an entire attachment of firefighters all decked-out in full gear: coats, pants, boots, helmets, goggles, etc. It was a show worthy of a firefighter's jamboree. As I looked on in amazement, my cooperating teacher explained that this "entertainment" was due to the kids pulling false alarms and that it was a regular Wednesday afternoon occurrence.

Supposedly, the administration had exhausted every avenue for putting a stop to this. Even though I was only a student teacher, it quickly became obvious to me that if the children exited to the rear of the building instead of the front, they wouldn't be able to see the fire trucks arrive. With their viewing capabilities curtailed, the incentive to pull the alarm would be eliminated. My cooperating teacher, along with a number of other teachers, thought this was pure genius and they all went to share it with the principal. The result? For the remaining ten weeks of my student teaching assignment, we all stood out in *front* of the school every Wednesday afternoon and watched the show.

I see a similar scenario played out year after year at high school graduations. A few years back, I was in the early planning stages for a large outdoor event which required me to investigate a variety of possible venues. While touring the grounds of one particular facility, the owner posed a question that should be at the forefront of any plans involving an outdoor function: "What are you going to do when it rains?" In my naiveté, I immediately responded, "You mean, *if* it rains." "No," he said, "*When* it rains."

If you have yet to experience an outdoor graduation adversely affected by inclement weather, count yourself blessed. Perhaps if you live in an arid area like Arizona or New Mexico, the issue is moot. However, in my state, graduation upon graduation is impacted every year, but nothing is done to address the situation. There are vendors virtually everywhere who can provide rental tents for any size event. I have personally attended a function in a tent the size of a football field with supports that were larger than telephone poles! For an occasion that occurs once in a child's lifetime, to which family members often travel great distances, wouldn't appropriate precautions be advisable? If expense is an issue, I can't imagine anybody balking at a small per-person fee to be able to sit in dry comfort. Yet it seems the only possibility entertained by administrators and boards of education is to "hope" it doesn't rain. Wouldn't logic dictate trying something else? Adamant adherence to "Hank's Rule" is honestly not an oath of office.

Please understand, similar to my previous statement concerning marginal teachers, I do realize that, out of the approximately 250,000 elementary and secondary school administrators serving in America's public schools, there are undoubtedly thousands with excellent leadership skills. If you are fortunate enough to work for one of these individuals, rejoice! I am also aware that, no matter how lacking in managerial prowess, every administrator has positive attributes.

Through the years, I have joked with students regarding any number of minor issues with statements like, "That is surely a violation of Board of Education statute 131, section C, paragraph 3." It has been a great way to humorously diffuse various situations, rather than resorting to standard admonitions such as, "Knock it off," "Cut it out," "I'm going to break your kneecaps," etc. But last year, when I was reading our newly completed "Student/Parent Code of Conduct Handbook," my jaw dropped to the floor! There it was in black and white: A policy numbered 5221.3.2.4 on pupil misconduct in school. Despite the fact that there were multiple pages of similar listings (policy #5183.2.4 concerns student conduct on busses), in a state of disbelief I went to the district website only to find over 200 pages of numbered policies on everything from student dress (#5273.4.2) to HIV infection (#5421.1.3). Now when I say to the kids that they are in violation of Board of Education policy number 5361, section 4, paragraph 3 (failure to follow the directive of a staff member), it can elicit some levity and be true.

Of course, because few of the kids (or parents for that matter) actually read any of these documents, it always results in an extra bit of fun when I open the handbook and produce the evidence. For full effect, I've even taken classes onto the website to show them the entire monolith. Aside from the 203 pages of policies on students, there are nine other sections of district policies for a total of 522 pages! I now have enough policy numbers to cite a different one every day for the rest of my career! And this is for a school system comprised of a total of six schools! What must a major city have? Five thousand pages?

Honesty

I worked 12 years for a principal named Gail who epitomized the concerns that Harry G. Frankfurt lays out in his wonderful 2005 book: "On Bullshit." "The essence of bullshit," he states, "is a lack of connection to any concern with truth; that a statement is grounded neither in a belief that it is true nor, as a lie must be, in a belief that it is not true" (p.33). "Whereas a liar must reject the authority of truth, the bullshitter pays no attention to it at all. By virtue of this, bullshit is a greater enemy of the truth than lies are" (p 61).

After coping with this precise disregard for honesty on a daily basis for twelve years, I clearly understood the extraordinary viability of this assertion. Gail went beyond a complete lack of credibility into a dangerously murky territory, totally devoid of any guise of factuality. If you are wondering how a person like this could stay in their position for so long, you only needed to experience the utter lack of respect, if not downright disdain, with which the superintendent treated her. To say she was a lapdog doesn't begin to describe it. Needless to say, during these twelve years, I refined the three survival skills I learned from Fred to an art form.

As I was reviewing Dr. Frankfurt's book, I was amazed at the number of times I had written word definitions in the margins. To approach a subject such as this in such a learned and scholarly way, adds immensely to the value of the discussion. I thoroughly enjoyed statements such as, "the phenomenon itself is so vast and amorphous that no crisp and perspicuous analysis of its concept can avoid being procrustean" (p 3). Although the teacher in me desperately wants to "help" you analyze this (i.e., do it for you), I'm going to encourage you to make use of a dictionary just like I did.

If you tell the truth, you don't have to remember anything[11]

A colleague, with whom I have worked since she started teaching, recently became an assistant principal. Because she knew of my admiration and respect for Karen, she asked me for possible insights into what might be the key to her enjoying some modicum of similar success. I told her it all boils down to honesty. The first time you tell a lie, knowledge of it will be building-wide before the day is over. However, as the administrator, you will have no realization whatsoever that this has happened because absolutely nobody is going to come down to call you on it. Therefore, it becomes very easy to fall into the trap of thinking you got away with it.

If administrators had any understanding of this simple truth, every school environment would be like the one that existed between Karen and her staff—trust would reign supreme. But the extraordinary fissure that develops with the first lie is very hard to mend. Sadly, because there is no knowledge on the part of the administrator that he or she has been "outed," standard practice usually becomes a continuation, if not escalation, of dishonest practices. Ultimately, the question is: As an administrator, do you want to be honest and forthright and earn the respect and loyalty of your staff? Quite simply, if you treat teachers with dignity and respect, their reciprocation will be manifold. Regard teachers as professionals and there is no limit as to what their loyalty will achieve.

Blanket Dictums

Another major issue about which many administrators appear to have no understanding is the total ineffectiveness of blanket memos or e-mails concerning violations of protocol. In fact, the final outcome can be completely contrary to the bosses' intention. Individuals who are guilty of the infraction feel they have eluded detection, while the ones who are following instructions feel they are not being recognized. Because there are no direct consequences, not only is the problem not solved, it can actually escalate.

Take, for example, the issue of recording student attendance in my building. Every morning during homeroom, the teacher is expected to tabulate absences and e-mail the names to the office before students pass to their first period class. The guidance secretary then types up a complete list and e-mails it to the entire staff. In order that everyone will know which classrooms have not been tabulated, she indicates the names of the teachers who have not submitted attendance at the top of the list. Virtually every day, it is the same individuals who neglect to submit their attendance. So, when they see their name on the list they will send a building-wide e-mail listing the absentees from their homeroom with an accompanying "Sorry" or "I got a little tied up this morning"—something of that nature. Astoundingly, they seem oblivious that they are guilty of this infraction almost every day!

Karen would have solved this problem by immediately going to the individual perpetrators and reminding them, in no uncertain terms, of their responsibilities as professionals. What do my administrators do? They send out a blanket e-mail to the entire staff reminding everyone of the need to get attendance in on time. The result? Absolutely nothing changes. For me it boils down to simple self-respect. I would be mortified to see my name on that list day after day. Similarly, as an administrator, I would feel humiliated if my directives were being completely ignored.

Because the guidance secretary is responsible for contacting parents concerning all unexcused absences, she sent the following e-mail to the entire staff:

To: Staff
Subject: Attendance
I think if I explain the process, we can resolve this mess!

- Parents are supposed to call-in their child's absence by 8:00. **Doesn't always happen**.

- Teachers are supposed to submit their attendance to the guidance office every morning. **Doesn't always happen**

- Teachers are supposed to submit ANY notes/emails/ communication of any kind to the office concerning anticipated absences or tardies. **Frequently doesn't happen**.

- The guidance office is required to call every child's home if they are on the absence list and have not been called-in by the parent. Depending on the number of students, this can require a substantial amount of time. Many of these calls are completely unnecessary simply because the information has not been communicated to the office.

Today I made 10 unnecessary calls, only to find out that these kids are on vacation and teachers had this information in advance.

Please help!

And, can you guess what happened? That's right, absolutely nothing! The administration is obviously unaware what a negative impact this has on their credibility. If they went directly to these individuals and told them to start fulfilling their responsibilities, word would get around immediately and the administration's esteem in the eyes of the staff would skyrocket! But no, they sit in their offices and write blanket e-mails addressing issues that only involve a few errant individuals.

In a strikingly similar manner, blanket e-mails *praising* everyone for doing a great job are equally ineffective. Not everyone is doing a great job and we all know it! Therefore, those who are doing a great job feel trivialized and may quite possibly throw up their hands in futility. Similarly, those who are doing the minimum (or less) certainly won't be inspired to do more, especially if they are being led to believe that what they are currently producing is considered a "great job." If, as an administrator, you truly wish to praise an individual for outstanding work, make the effort to hand-write a note on nice stationery. If it's a group, do one for each participant. Believe me, that means something.

Teacher Input

About 15 years ago, I attended a workshop introducing an innovative administrative process entitled: The Inverted Pyramid. Essentially, this concept involved reversing the "top down" system of administrating to a "bottom up" approach. In brief, the teachers would become the most important part of the chain of command with the administration answering to their needs and recommendations. While all of us laughed at the notion that this would ever be enacted in anything vaguely resembling the format being presented (administrators relinquishing power to mere teachers?), this concept did spawn a fabulous new catch phrase: "Teacher Empowerment." Once again, on paper this was a tremendously worthwhile idea: Solicit the input and expertise of the very individuals who are most directly affected by administrative directives prior to their formulation and implementation. To make a long story short, the practical application of this teacher input initiative involved a vast increase in meetings where teachers provided the administration with valuable information and ideas and the administration went out and did whatever they wanted to do in the first place. I distinctly remember a conversation with an administrator addressing this exact issue. Without blinking an eyelid he said, "Well, you *did* have input, didn't you?"

This process became most disruptive when the administration began pulling us out of class for half-day and full-day meetings and workshops. This means that, for every one of these release days, classes need to be covered by substitutes. You must understand, with the incredible paucity of substitute teachers, more often than not, the substitute has no training at all in the subject they are covering. So, essentially, the educational process comes to a halt while the kids do busy-work. What perfect irony! We are hampering student learning under the guise of improving student learning; all so the administration can profess that their initiatives "come from the teachers." On the plus side, this entire process emphatically confirmed that reverse "Nod 'n Do" (administrators to teachers) is alive and well. Thus, any possible hint of guilt that I may have been feeling over my own "Nod 'n Do" behavior was tossed joyously to the four winds.

One question that I have heard repeatedly from parents through the years is "Why are you doing it this way?" This is usually in regard to issues over which I, as the teacher, have absolutely no control: class size, making do with inadequate materials, class schedule—things that are simply dictated from higher up. Two years ago, I was talking with a parent about the increase in my student load and class sizes, to which she posed that same question. She honestly spoke as if I had chosen to make my life more difficult and purposefully impede student progress. I made it quite clear that I had absolutely no say in the matter with the added emphasis of: "I'm just a peon."

Lo and behold, two nights later, this same woman got up at a board of education meeting to express her concerns about these very issues, and chose to include the comment "Hank Warren said he's just a peon." Mind you, this was an open public session with the entire administrative staff, parents, general public, and reporters in attendance. I was later told that the general reaction was one of levity, but it still did not spare me the trip to my principal's office to explain this little faux pas. So much of what we do as teachers requires parsing our words like a politician.

The most egregious example of "pretend teacher input" I've been forced to endure concerned the shift of a school in which I was teaching from a grade 4/5 to a grade 5/6 format. For three full years we met on a monthly basis to discuss this transition process. Very early on it became quite evident that the administration had decided from the outset that the "new" grade 5/6 school would be a full-blown Middle School Model (students pass from class to class) rather than the Elementary School Model we were currently using (students spend most of the day with the same classroom teacher). In spite of the fact that all of the teachers unanimously agreed we wanted to retain the elementary school model, they made us endure over 25 meetings concerning this grade level shift. They insisted, even up through April of year three, that they weren't going to impose a full middle school model; continuing to profess that there would be some form of a hybrid between the two. And the final outcome of all this teacher input? When the superintendent announced that we were going to a full Middle School Model, she was able to say to the public that this decision was the product of three years of meetings with the teachers!

I must include one final story on this topic. This one involves curriculum writing—a perennial administrative favorite. My wife and her entire department were granted multiple "release" days from teaching in order to completely rewrite the high school curriculum in their subject area. After five full days of intense, earnest effort, they submitted their completed document. Because it so accurately reflected what they were actually teaching, my wife and her colleagues considered it a done deal. The administration called it a first draft. After approximately one month, they reconvened to review the superintendent's recommendations. Astonishingly, she had completely rewritten the entire thing, first page to last! Dumbfounded, the teachers spent another two days revamping the document to incorporate as many of the superintendent's dictates as possible, while still retaining the original "meaningful" structure. This, of course, was deemed a second draft.

Approximately two weeks later, the superintendent called them together in her office. As I'm sure you can guess, the document was reverted to the exact form she had returned it to them the first time. Apparently she wanted the curriculum to appear as a model of current educational jargon, not as a document reflecting what was really being taught in the school system. In addition, she made it emphatically clear the process was over. Of course, when the document was officially presented to the board of education, all of the teachers who were involved in "writing" it were prominently displayed on the title page. So, in the end we have a curriculum that has virtually nothing to do with what is really being taught and everyone—board of education, town officials, and general public—thinking that the teachers were completely responsible for its creation. And talk about disruption to the educational process. How about subjecting all of those students to substitute "busywork" for a full seven days?

Now that she's been mentioned, I simply must elaborate on the extraordinarily harsh management style of this particular superintendent. She ruled with such an iron fist that our nickname for her was Darthie Vader. We were all aware of the exact moment she arrived at an event or entered a room because the first to spot her would alert the others by humming Darth Vader's theme (The Imperial March) from Star Wars.

Of many additional examples I could give, there is one that probably illustrates her methods even better than the curriculum story. One of the music teachers in our system also directed an outstanding vocal ensemble at an area youth music school. Incredibly, this group was invited to perform at one of the holiday parties given at the White House (yes, *that* White House). Because about half of the kids in this group were students in our school system, the teacher submitted the appropriate form to apply for two Professional Service Days. It seemed reasonable to her that performing at the pleasure of the President of the United States would be considered a "professional service." Being a reasonably sane person, the assistant superintendent approved the days. Then, most incredibly, Darthie learned of this, overrode the assistant's approval, and forced the teacher to use Personal Days instead.

By contract, teachers in our system are allowed two days each school year to use for "personal business which cannot be conducted outside of the school day." Now, because this teacher had already used her personal days to attend an out of state wedding earlier in the year, she didn't have any more personal time available. So what did Darthie do? She docked this teacher two full days pay! (yes, you can take a moment to get your jaw off the floor). Imagine, here's this choral director performing in the East Room of the White House with students from our school system, and it's costing her two days pay.

Because the granting of professional days is at the total discretion of the superintendent, the teacher had absolutely no recourse, with the possible exception of making a public issue of it and risk getting fired. Now, if you say they would *never* fire you over that, in a technical sense you'd be right. However, there are insidious ways to effect the same result, and I've seen it done a number of times. They simply give you a teaching assignment that, while within the parameters of the teachers' contract and your certification, is so miserable that you either quit or stick it out under such extreme duress that your life becomes a living hell.

I won't go into how a creature like Darthie could have been employed for 13 years, except to say that a like-minded board of education with a "thumb on the teacher" mentality, allowed it to be so. As of this writing it has only been a short while since she left, yet you can't find a single soul in the entire school system that misses her. Not only that; but the expressions of relief still continue.

Principal's Advisory Council

Gail, my principal of 12 years, provided an invaluable opportunity to watch the process of "pretend input" play out among students. With great public fanfare, she instituted the Principal's Advisory Council, which consisted of any and all children who wished to discuss school improvement issues. Unbeknownst to the kids, we already had a faculty School Improvement Committee which was basically a committee in name only. They were about to find out why.

Even though it required them to arrive at school 45 minutes early, about 50 children attended the first meeting. Who would be surprised that the initial topic of intense interest was none other than cafeteria food? You could have convened this meeting in 1949, and the primary topic would have been exactly the same. See how much has changed in school in 60 years? Anyway, the students produced a long list of things that they felt could be improved—from eliminating bread sticks to reducing the fly population. My two personal favorites were complaints that the kitchen staff had unpleasant attitudes and that they needed to wear hair nets! Evidently, the kids have never been told that there is a test given to all kitchen staff applicants to be sure they possess the prescribed level of miserableness. In all seriousness, it's fascinating how students don't consider their sterling cafeteria behavior to be the slightest factor in contributing to the demeanor of the kitchen staff.

In case you've forgotten, there is a massive gap between "kid time" and what the students love to hear me call "old fart" time. Whereas adults have a certain perspective on the relationship between various time segments, in "kid time" a week, a month, or three months can become quite blurred, especially for eleven and twelve year olds. Therefore, the vast majority of the children who attended that first meeting expected most of those changes would be implemented by lunch time *that day* or certainly by the end of the week.

In fact, absolutely nothing happened. After a few principal cancellations, by the next time the council met, only twenty children were in attendance; all adamantly complaining that nothing had changed in the cafeteria. Knowing Gail, she must have given them enough of her "signature product" to require a dump truck to haul it away.

Undeterred, the kids launched into the topic of homework. They produced another long list of grievances and, once again, nothing changed. In contrast to teachers, who are forced to participate in these pretend input activities, the students were there purely because of an earnest desire to produce meaningful change. Consequently, after a few more cancellations, the final meeting consisted of only four children and the whole initiative died a quiet death. While the principal's motivation was exclusively the public hype, she apparently didn't understand that, unlike teachers who don't complain publicly due to a desire to retain employment, students have no such compunction. They let it be known loudly that "this whole thing was nothing but a joke." Fortunately for Gail, kids have short attention spans and it didn't take long before they were consumed by some new aspect of their lives. Nonetheless, I will never forget the huge number of children who told me that they probably wouldn't believe anything the principal said ever again. What a painfully sad lesson for an earnest group of young people to learn. And we wonder why students get turned off.

I feel it is essential to reiterate that, as Nelson Mandela observes in Chapter 1, there are no absolutes. No administrator is all bad, nor is the outstanding one without flaws. If you look back on the previous list of leadership qualities, even Karen didn't embody 100% of them, but she sure came close. And, aside from Fred, no administrator is completely devoid of any of these characteristics and Gail was no different. For example, she recognized that I have excellent writing skills (whoops!). In addition, despite her tendency to immediately cave-in to almost any parental complaint, on the sporadic occasions when she encountered a student/parent that she felt comfortable muscling, there were cases she handled quite well.

You may recall my mentioning the railing outside my room that overlooks a hallway about ten feet below. When I previously taught at this school, kids would regularly hang off the railing and drop to the floor below. When the school was reopened after an extensive renovation (which unfortunately did not include rectifying this open space), the first student to jump over the railing was immediately suspended by Gail. Needless to say, the news of this definitive action shot-around the student body in an instant and "railing jumping" was halted in its tracks.

With the retirement of Gail and a new principal in place, the kids decided to test the railing activity again. When the first culprit was caught, nothing remotely resembling Gail's action took place. In fact, the child didn't even get a detention; just a good "talking-to." *That* piece of news also spread around the school like wildfire. As a result, not only was there a vast increase in railing jumping but, if you remember my mentioning those convoluted ramps in the middle of the building; the kids added "ramp leaping" to the repertoire. In addition, because the roof of this building is constructed in tiers, the students discovered a spot where they could boost each other onto a lower section of the roof and thereby gain access to the remainder of the building. The first time the PE teacher caught children on the roof, he made the effort to fill out the necessary paperwork only to discover that the punishment was *one* detention. Is it any wonder that I hear from the school secretary how disrespectfully many of the students treat the principal and assistant principal?

This is the entire point: No one is willing to say "No." Parents and administrators won't say "No" to the kids. Administrators, boards of education, government, and courts won't say "No" to the parents. Yet we publicly decry the loss of respect for authority and lament the growing sense that the fabric of our society is in decay.

Resume Building Initiatives

One of my closest colleagues and I were counting the number of administrators for whom we have worked during the 32 years since we were both hired by Karen. We only included superintendents, assistant superintendents, principals, and assistant principals. In a system comprised of just six schools, there have been seven superintendents and thirteen assistant superintendents! All told, we have worked for a total of 38 different administrators (and this includes the unusually long tenures of Gail and Darthie). Although some of this number reflects our having worked in multiple buildings, an even greater portion can be attributed to the fact that the average national tenure of a school administrator in any given position is four years. . . . Four!

In comparison, teachers who get past the initial five years tend to average a full career in one school system. This is because, as previously discussed, the nature of teaching is cyclical. For fiscal reasons, school systems don't hire more expensive veterans to fill the same position for which they can hire someone fresh out of college. Therefore, very little turnover occurs as a result of teachers moving from job to job, school system to school system. Ultimately, you have a basically stable teaching force which endures a constant administrative "changing of the guard."

Karen, on the other hand, started as a teacher in the school that bears her name and then served as its principal for 27 years. Uncannily, the current principal of Karen's school, Fred's successor, has just completed 22 years! Along with Karen, Peter is absolutely the most stable, even-tempered, reasonable principal for whom I have worked. He is not a flashy innovator—full of himself and bent on self-promotion. He simply provides a stable and supportive educational atmosphere where teachers can pursue excellence. This is possible because Peter is content to spend his career as principal of an elementary school. Accordingly, he is focused on doing the best for the teachers and students in his building, rather than being consumed with career advancement.

Perhaps this is the best way to describe what made Karen so outstanding: It was always about you and never about her. Self-promotion was simply not in her vocabulary. For example, as well as I knew her, I never found out until long after she retired that for years she and her husband had been publishing a popular guide to discount outlets under pen names.

What so ails our school systems today is the constant turnover of administrators and the attendant need for continual resume building. Leaders like Karen and Peter, in the true spirit of teacher empowerment, allow building needs to flow from the teachers and then facilitate resolutions and improvements. To the contrary, "resume builders"—whether or not they cloak their efforts under the guise of having solicited teacher input—tend to arbitrarily institute. Therefore, in the ongoing parade of administrators and initiatives, there is a continual disruption to the instructional process as teachers are forced to implement ever-changing changes. Now, add-in mandates that are dictated from the state level, and a teacher can very easily be juggling initiatives from multiple sources at once.

By no means is attaining the superintendency any longer the final step. Whereas a number of superintendents still continue the practice of "retiring" to teach or administrate at the college level, many superintendents are now actively pursuing employment opportunities at the burgeoning state and federal education departments. And, trust me, superintendent generated "resume building initiatives" are much grander in scale and impact than anything a mere building administrator can dream up. For example, to enhance her resume, Darthie instituted block scheduling in grades 1-4. Whereas block scheduling is a familiar concept at the high school level, expanding it to include elementary school had extraordinary ramifications. From her standpoint, this was a fabulously successful way to augment her resume for potential advancement after retirement, while the rest of us were left to deal with the impact of this career enhancing initiative. Thankfully, after only four months on the job, our new superintendent has already indicated that he intends to dismantle this and a few of her other more disruptive decisions.

While we are on the subject, after Darthie's unusually long and difficult 13 year tenure, our new gentleman is like a breath of fresh air. Because his interview process included meetings with teachers, high school students, and the general citizenry, I had multiple opportunities to hear him present his philosophy of education and administration. Most impressive were statements such as, "He works for us" (the teachers) and "His job is to do whatever he can to help us in our efforts." Similar to Karen and Peter, it seems we may have a practitioner of true teacher empowerment. Another extraordinary comment was, "If the answer to any teacher's request, idea or initiative is 'No,' he or she deserves the dignity and respect of a sit down explanation as to the reason why."

While I listened to him speak, I was intrigued to find myself drawn into his aura of sincerity. To realize that, after 34 years, I still yearn for *real* leadership, is thrilling! I would love to emerge from my cocoon of insularity and shed the layers of defense mechanisms that have developed through years of working for marginal administrators—to castoff doubt and skepticism and believe again!

11. The Joys and Perils of Broad Certification

Hollywood has the most creative ways imaginable to _in_accurately portray teaching. Whether it's through highly misleading TV commercials, or via situation comedies like the early John Travolta vehicle "Welcome Back Kotter," or by means of dramas like the 1970s show "Room 222," I find it fascinating that, 90% of the time, teachers seem to be anywhere but in the classroom, or, if they are, anything resembling active teaching is rarely portrayed. That being said, one place where Hollywood got it exactly right was in the Arnold Schwarzenegger film "Kindergarten Cop." No, I'm not talking about that absurd business of blowing the police whistle to get the children to change activities; although I did experience a beginning teacher actually doing that with her fourth grade class a few years back. Fortunately, she stopped that embarrassment after a few days. Even so, I have always remembered what a sad indictment it was on the gross inadequacies of teacher training that the best model of exemplary teaching a novice could find to emulate would be "Arnult."

Aside from this, the movie flawlessly depicted how kindergarten children simply blurt-out whatever comes into their minds, no matter how little relationship it has to what is happening in class. I remember that one little boy in the movie who kept saying during circle time: "Boys have a penis, girls have a vagina." My wife, the high school teacher, thought this was way over the top. However, being K-12 certified, my job assignment at the time had me intimately involved with the irreplaceable joys of teaching kindergarten. As a result, I knew all too well the reality of this situation.

Say, for example, you pick up a yardstick and ask the class: "Does anyone know what this is?" There will be at least five kids frantically waving their hands. "Yes, Johnny?" Without hesitation, Johnny shouts, "I'm going to be Batman for Halloween!" Instantaneously, the entire room erupts: "I'm going to be Cinderella!" "I'm going to be a pirate!" "I'm going to be Superman!" "Superman Sucks!" "Does Not!" (as the tears burst forth). . . . After about five minutes of total bedlam you finally get the class calmed down, the tears dried, anyone who wet their pants off to the nurse for a change of clothes, and you attempt, for the zillionth time, to get the children to understand that they *must* focus on what is being discussed at the moment; in this case—the yardstick!

This is so exemplary of the fundamental rules of classroom protocol that must be taught in kindergarten: how to speak in turn, raise your hand, and share with others. Basically, all of the things Robert Fulghum spells out so delightfully in his 1989 book "All I Really Need to Know, I Learned in Kindergarten." The task is easier with children who have spent time in daycare or have been enrolled in a preschool program. They have the basic notion of how to be one of a group and interact with other children in this type of setting. Conversely, I've experienced some of the most extraordinary moments with "stay at home" mothers who had the singular ability to come into a class of 22 kindergartners and see only their child, and their child alone! I remember talking to one mother about some issue that required my gesturing towards the remainder of the class to emphasize that there were other students in the room. I'll never forget the puzzled look on her face. She honestly had absolutely no idea to what I was referring! She simply went on discussing her kid like he was the only one in the room—as if I was working with him exclusively, one on one, all day long.

I recently overheard a mother bemoaning the exhaustion she experienced at her child's eighth birthday party. She stated there were ten kids in attendance and exclaimed, "Two hours!" while the other mother nodded in total agreement and complete understanding. "Wow, was I ever glad when they all finally went home" the first mother said. I simply couldn't let the opportunity pass by to interject: "And just think about the classroom teacher who has 25 of them all day long!" Their looks said it all. . . . spoil sport! Now, imagine that the kindergarten teacher is dealing with *five year olds* who have virtually no interactive skills and have to be taught *everything!* Essentially, it takes a teacher with a superhumanly calm, controlled demeanor.

So, while you're imagining the exhaustion of trying to teach the basics of life to oversized groups of these very young children, consider the fact that kindergarten teachers are generally assigned to more "contact" time with pupils than teachers at any other level! Contact time is the number of minutes every teacher is assigned each week to be actively instructing students (as opposed to duties, prep time, etc.). I find it astounding that, in my school system, kindergarten teachers are assigned to 400 more contact minutes per week than teachers of grades 5-12. How can this be, you ask?

Here is a prime example of why teachers' unions are not perfect. Considering that all teachers are paid the same, how is it possible that one group can be teaching significantly more minutes than everyone else? In our school system it simply has to do with majority rule as delineated by the grade level configurations of the various schools. Because they were housed in a separate facility for a number of years, kindergarten teachers became a distinct entity. Teachers working at the three grade 1-4 elementary schools became another, and grade 5-12 teachers, since they use the same "passing from class to class" model, are treated as a single block. Consequently, grade 5-12 teachers form the clear majority, grade 1-4 teachers are a distant second, and kindergarten teachers constitute a miniscule minority. Therefore, in addition to the 400 minute inequity at the kindergarten level, grade 1-4 teachers are assigned to 100 more contact minutes per week than grade 5-12 teachers.

The thought process behind this criminality is explained by the union leadership this way: Attempting to lower the number of teaching minutes at the K-4 level during contract negotiations would result in too much of an impact on the grade 5-12 majority! So!!?? If fairness is the continual battle cry of the union, why on earth would this flagrant disparity be in the least bit acceptable? And, as if to pour salt on the wound, do you want to know what happened in a recent meeting with our state union representatives when the K-4 teachers started to complain? They were told, if they didn't like it, to go get a job in another school system! Now, mind you, we all pay the same amount of union dues, but this is the type of trade-off the minority must endure to be properly represented in salary negotiations. I wonder if you can figure out in which grade level block our local union representatives teach.

I must reiterate a point I made in the "Teacher on Teacher" chapter. Every level, kindergarten through 12th grade, has its own distinct challenges. It is virtually impossible to equate the frustrations of teaching five year olds how to focus on the yardstick with the demands of teaching advanced level classes at the high school. Elementary classroom teachers are basically expected to teach every subject, whereas high school teachers essentially concentrate on one academic area. But, the requirements for teaching more developed subject matter at varying levels (freshman English as opposed to senior), is a very different challenge. In addition to preparing more advanced lessons, further time is spent evaluating in-depth student work. The high school science teacher has a tremendous amount of preparatory work and equipment to setup for a laboratory class, but so does the physical education teacher regardless of grade level. What happens when he or she sets-up all of the equipment for an outdoor lesson and it suddenly rains? Clearly, any attempt to equate differing levels or subject areas is an exercise in futility.

When I first obtained a teaching license, my mother, a career-long teacher, was extolling the benefits of the fact that my broad certification would qualify me to teach any grade level from kindergarten to 12th grade. During my first ten years I wisely took advantage of this opportunity to gain teaching experience in every grade. This enabled me to finally settle on the age level to which I was most innately suited. However, the downside to a broad certification is that administrators can place you anywhere your services are needed, which resulted in the following scenario.

During the period I was doing the kindergarten stint, my job assignment had me traveling between the primary school and the high school. This was an experience in and of itself. Because it was so easy to mix speaking styles between the two levels, I would catch myself addressing the high school students like they were five year olds and vice versa. For example, having tried an "open" bathroom policy with the older kids, it didn't take long before the constant in and out began to resemble Grand Central Station. So I adopted an "Is this an emergency?" policy. Well, it seems that one day a kindergartner asked me if he could go to the bathroom and I reflexively asked, "Is this an emergency?," to which the boy tenuously shook his head no. I didn't think another thing about it until the next day when Peter invited me into his office to inquire, "Did Joey Smith ask to go to the bathroom yesterday?" Quickly interpreting my blank stare, Peter calmly explained, "When a kindergartner asks to go to the bathroom, *Let him Go!*" Apparently the kid sat right there and peed his pants! Amazingly, not one of the other children said a word. One would assume that, as the wet spot expanded, someone would squeal some note of displeasure. Nope, not a thing. I immediately realized that when I asked my signature "Is this an emergency?," the boy wasn't shaking his head because he didn't have to go, he was simply expressing that he had no idea what the hell I was saying! Ah, the perils of teaching older and younger students concurrently.

Because the differences between kindergarten and high school are so profound, this "broad" job assignment also offered the opportunity to focus on circumstances that are unique to teaching high school. Adolescents tend to have one foot in childhood while desperately seeking the "independence" of adulthood. Invariably, the juxtaposition of thought processes in their minds causes decision-making that can be clear and even-handed at one moment and wildly irrational the next. Attempting to work through this quagmire requires teachers to have a distinct understanding of the adolescent mind. I sum it up as "Saving Students from Themselves."

Being in the unusual position of simultaneously working with older and younger children gave me a deep appreciation for what high school teachers must confront on a daily basis. While younger students generally take your authority for granted and do what you ask, older students need to be convinced of the value and worth of what they are attempting to accomplish. Consequently, the process of obtaining the desired result requires the development of a specific skill set that is key to becoming a successful high school teacher. Yes, student confidence in your knowledge of subject matter is of paramount importance, however, your skills and abilities to transfer this information becomes the essence of effective instruction. Ultimately, success in teaching at any level boils down to the ability to enable another individual to understand and execute.

I particularly enjoy telling the story of participating in "team teaching" an experimental humanities course at the high school. I was overflowing with excitement at the prospect of sharing insights and information about topics that I love to eager, wide-eyed pupils who were taking this class as an "elective." This means they were there by choice, not as a requirement. So, here I am up at the blackboard expounding about the "Age of Enlightenment" and its great representative figures such as Voltaire, Rousseau, Goethe and the like. After approximately ten minutes, I suddenly realized the kids were just sitting there with blank looks on their faces. "Shouldn't you be taking notes?" I asked incredulously. "What!?" they exclaimed! "You mean we're going to be tested on this stuff?" The ensuing flurry of activity was truly a wonder to behold. Students scurrying for notebooks, pens, pencils, and paper, accompanied by all of the attendant pencil sharpening, pleas for someone to loan them some paper, and requests to go to lockers. After what seemed like an eternity, they were finally ready to get down to business. "Who's that first guy?" V..o..l. . . .

All high school teachers are intimately aware of the questioning and griping that develops when a test, project or research paper involves receiving an evaluative "grade." We call this "grade-grubbing." My initiation into the phenomenon was indeed "enlightening" (pun intended). As we were going over the first test, a girl raised her hand to inquire why a question concerning the country in which Mozart lived was marked wrong. "The correct answer is Austria," I said, "You wrote Australia." Without blinking an eyelash, the girl responded, "Austria, Australia—close enough!"

As an outstanding teacher, my wife establishes close relationships with many students which results in her being invited to their senior graduation parties. I recently observed her yearly ritual of purchasing and wrapping gifts; an outlay of personal funds that, similar to the time expended writing college recommendations, is unique to high school teachers. I have always admired her ability to maintain a "live in the moment" perspective in her relationships with students. In my case, this was an important factor in my decision to transfer out of high school teaching. I became so personally involved with the kids that the separation of graduation was tremendously difficult for me; especially when so many tend not to be heard from again.

12. No Hope of Parole

There is an absolute, indelible truth to American public education: It does not matter if you are a straight "A" valedictorian or a false alarm pulling miscreant, as a child in America you are sentenced to a minimum of 13 years of public school (kindergarten through grade 12) with no hope of parole. If you want to get a high school diploma you have to do your time. This fact is as etched in stone as if Moses brought it down from the mount, and it is the one thing that absolutely must be changed about public school.

Having taught all levels, I have watched survival skills develop in the youngest of children. They learn very quickly that, no matter what, they must endure the prescribed length of the school day for all of the days that are assigned to the school year. If they do their work quickly or slowly or not at all, nothing will change. You don't get to go home at noon if you finish that day's work early, nor are you released from school in April if you have managed to finish that year's curriculum by then. Not on your life! You are stuck there come hell or high water!

So, what can possibly be the incentive in something like this? It certainly isn't to strive for excellence as the educational hierarchy insists. The real incentive is for students to find ways to kill the required time as painlessly and effortlessly as possible. Unfortunately, circumventing productivity becomes the focus. What is the point of a child doing their best to attain maximum achievement? Are they going to advance quicker, go to harder material, develop more skills? Absolutely not! They will be given some additional worksheets to complete, told to read a book, or be forced to do some "extra credit" research;

anything to fill time while the remainder of the class tries to catch up.

Because most of the teacher's attention is absorbed by the demands of servicing the neediest children, achieving students are left largely on their own, finishing out the year just like everyone else; trudging on to the next grade level in a slow, dreary, slogging march—day by day, year by year. The end result is, by the time children are halfway through kindergarten they are learning an adaptive strategy that they will studiously perfect right up through high school graduation: How to survive by doing the absolute minimum possible. And this is an in-depth, 13 year course of study that graduates gladly bring with them to the work place.

I am well aware that being the optimistic "make the best of any situation no matter how dismal" group we teachers are, most of us look for the silver lining. Of course we try to give meaningful material to the advanced students. And all of us can point to the occasional child who's been allowed to skip a grade or jump to upper level classes. A handful may even have the opportunity to take college level courses. And, without question, there are the sporadic magnet schools or privately funded advanced placement academies. I'm not saying these aren't positive steps, but providing a minute percentage of the public school population with these opportunities is not solving the problem. We need to address the larger issue.

No Man

Thus we return to James Herndon's outstanding 1971 book "How To Survive In Your Native Land," wherein he makes another very telling analogy about how decisions are made in education entitled: "No Man" (p. 99-102). His basic premise concerns the passing of responsibility up the chain of command. Who decides the policy? Certainly not the teacher! And the principal will say it's the superintendent, who in turn will say it's the board of education, who'll say it's the town officials, who'll say it's the state legislators . . . on and on it goes until, ultimately, no one is responsible: No Man!

I was recently monitoring a classroom of children taking our state academic achievement test and couldn't help but marvel at the fact that, just like when I was a kid (40-plus years ago), they are still seated at desks, in rows, with 25 students in the class. It was as if I was watching an episode of "Little House on the Prairie," except in a more modern environment. While we herald the so-called advances in 21st century education, we perpetuate a classroom structure that is virtually identical to the one used by Nathan Hale!

All teacher contracts are the cumulative product of years of ongoing negotiations between teachers' unions and boards of education. These contracts always contain an extensive section concerning class sizes; generally giving a lower range of 18-22 pupils and an upper range of 28-32. While I have never seen 18 students in a standard classroom in all my years—the upper end occurs frequently! In the final analysis, it conservatively averages out to around 25, and it seems to have been this way since the birth of the nation. Today, students have instantaneous access to an entire world of information at the touch of a computer keypad, but we find ourselves mired in a 19th century classroom format as if our standard text was still McGuffey's Reader. When was it ordained that kids were to sit at desks, in rows, in classrooms of 25? Although there is no Biblical record, it simply must have been a Divine proclamation, because certainly No Man has ever been responsible!

A colleague of mine just attended a workshop on the new state curriculum standards for high school history. I specifically asked her to see if she could discover who actually wrote these standards: names, credentials, etc. As I have experienced numerous times before, nothing was available. The same is true for any inquiry into standardized testing: who wrote the questions, who does the grading, who determines the type of questions, quantity, importance, etc. Again, it is impossible to find out. Take the Scholastic Aptitude Test (SAT) for example. Every college bound child in America has their entire future hanging on the results of a test which is conceived, developed, and evaluated by "No Man."

The truth of this assertion was borne out by the experience of some friends. While in high school, their son, who is now Communications Director and Head Speech Writer for a United States Congressman, received a very low score on the written portion of our state's high school academic achievement test. Because this young man was a straight "A" student with excellent writing skills, his parents embarked on a long, frustrating, and ultimately fruitless effort to get some answers. It was solely by engaging the school administration that a copy of the written portion of his test was finally acquired. Curiously, it showed absolutely no markings or corrections of any kind—just the low score. All of his teachers unanimously agreed it displayed outstanding work but, no matter how hard anyone tried, an explanation of why the test was scored so low or who did the correcting was never disclosed.

Fascinated by this experience, and being challenged by a number of skeptics to substantiate the veracity of this "No Man" theory as it applied to standardized tests, I launched into what became a lengthy and exasperating effort to see if I could receive an answer to the following question:

"Is it possible to obtain the names and titles of the specific individuals responsible for constructing test questions and evaluating written portions of the (name of standardized test)"

I began with the academic achievement test for the state in which I teach. Because this test is a major component for assessing compliance with the "No Child Left Behind" legislation, the pressure to perform well is extraordinary. With so much at stake, wouldn't it seem reasonable that the names of those responsible for constructing and evaluating the test would be easily obtainable?

My initial phone call to our State Department of Education was most encouraging. I was immediately connected to the test program manager who, after requesting that I e-mail my inquiry, responded with a detailed account of the test purpose and procedures. He also provided links to the plethora of reports and assessments available at the state department website, all of which I had already accessed. Although the amount of material available is overwhelming, there is not a name in sight.

I replied with an enthusiastic thank you and reiterated that I was specifically in search of the names of the *actual individuals* who construct and correct the tests. He responded that the test is developed and scored by a private contractor called Measurement Incorporated (MI). Amazingly, he did provide the names of some teachers and administrators from my state who are involved with giving sample tests to students and providing data on the accuracy of test questions. However, it is exclusively up to MI to determine how or if the information is incorporated into finished tests. The test program manager also said that there are a handful of paid item writers from our state whose names he would need to ask his managers for permission to release. And from that moment on, all communication stopped. Subsequent e-mails and phone calls went unanswered. I can only assume that his managers must have lambasted him for releasing any names in the first place.

That avenue being clearly exhausted, I went to the Measurement Incorporated website hoping to find information about who to contact with my question. The website gives a brief overview of MI and its various functions as a test development company and then lists the names and resumes of the president and various vice presidents. Because there is no e-mail address given, I faxed a letter to both the VP of test development and the VP of scoring. After a few days I called each of them and, since they weren't available, left messages. A few days later I called again. Despite assurances from the receptionist that both VP's had received my messages and would definitely respond, I never heard a word.

Having obviously reached the termination point for finding out who writes the questions for my state's achievement tests, I turned my attention to the Scholastic Aptitude Test (SAT) and the Advanced Placement Test (APT). A through scouring of the Educational Testing Service (ETS) website revealed that, while the *Preliminary* Scholastic Aptitude Test (PSAT) and the APT are administered and operated by ETS, the SAT is under the sole jurisdiction of The College Board (are you on acronym overload yet?).

Under the "Who We Are" section of the ETS website it proudly states: "More than 1,100 of our professional staff have training and expertise in education, psychology, statistics, psychometrics, computer sciences, sociology, and the humanities. Six hundred have advanced degrees, and 250 hold doctorates." This is followed by a bulleted list on which the first item is: "We Are Test Developers." So I called them up and asked the receptionist to connect me to whoever might be able to answer my question. To my stunned amazement, she responded: "There is nobody I can transfer you to; you have to e-mail your question." In a state of total incredulity I said, "Do you mean to say that, out of the 1,100 professional staff declared on your website, there is nobody I can talk to?" Answer: "No, you must use e-mail." So I did. Despite asking my same question about tests such as the California High School Exit Examination that are clearly developed solely by ETS, I did not hear from them again.

On the other hand, I was quite pleasantly surprised when, four days later, I got an e-mail from the College Board, to whom ETS had apparently passed my inquiry. Although they didn't make even a marginal attempt to answer my question, they were profuse about how important I was and how they wanted to do everything possible to assist me. They also provided five links to different sections of their website which I had already scoured. I was delighted, however, to see a phone number which I promptly dialed in unbridled anticipation of the "do everything possible" help I was about to receive. As I cheerfully asked the receptionist if she might connect me to someone who could answer my question in regards to the SAT and APT exams, she promptly asked me what state I was calling from. Immediately upon hearing my response, she told me that this was the national office and that I must dial my regional office. Taken back, I asked, "Aren't the SAT and APT the same nationwide?" She confirmed that it's national, but the policy is that any and all business for each region must go through the appropriate regional office.

My feeling of deflation was rendered complete when I called the regional office only to once again be told that I must e-mail my question. Four days later I received a response that directed me to the portion of the College Board website that provides nineteen pages of guidelines for the release of data and a data request form, none of which pertained to my question. Thankfully, they also included a name I could e-mail with further questions, which I promptly did. After a week passed, I simply assumed that I was getting the MI treatment. Then, much to the College Board's credit, I received a response stating that, for privacy reasons, they do not disclose the names, titles or other professional information on individual test developers. The answer was not the least bit unexpected, but I do give them kudos for actually responding.

So there it is! Despite the fact that so much of the success of our students and our public schools as a whole rests solely on the results of standardized tests, those responsible are shrouded in secrecy. "No Man" is accountable!

But of course it has to be someone, many of you are thinking—the test doesn't get created by itself. However, akin to that perennial favorite concerning the tree falling in the forest, we can only *assume* it makes a noise if no one is there to hear it. Similarly, we can only *assume* that qualified individuals are creating and correcting standardized tests if it's impossible to find out who they are. For all we know, it could be Joe the Plumber! Think about this: Have you ever seen an official committee report or similar issuance that didn't proudly list all those who participated, with their official titles prominently displayed, no matter how minute their role? Not with standardized tests! You want to know who holds your child's future in their hands? Try as you might, you simply can't find out! I certainly pressed as hard as I could but, ultimately, it's "No Man."

Recommendation #2: Class Size

An integral part of the 21st century educational reform movement has been the introduction and implementation of "differentiated instruction." This instructional strategy contends that each student should be taught to his or her individual learning style and strengths. Try to envision a teacher attempting to enact this in a classroom of 25 pupils. To comply with this concept in its entirety, a teacher could conceivably be expected to instruct a class 25 different ways.

As if this weren't enough, our statewide initiative for the current school year couples differentiated instruction with the development of "common assessment" strategies. Just think about this incongruity. While we are supposed to be teaching to individual student learning styles, we are now expected to come up with strategies to evaluate all students the same way. My colleagues and I can only assume that this is an attempt to address the major concern we have had since differentiation was first introduced: If the instruction of each child is being tailored to his or her individual needs and learning traits, how can they all be expected to perform equally on the same standardized tests?

Nonetheless, the administration is currently devoting numerous after school faculty meetings and workshops to discussing differentiated instruction. This basically involves reading and analyzing books by authors who are considered to be experts on this subject. One of these 'gurus' offers the following example for using differentiated instruction to teach the water cycle (rain cycle for those of you over forty) to a fourth grade science class.[12] Children who are proficient in verbal/linguistic skills are instructed to write a report, the visual/spatial learners are expected to draw the water cycle and label the parts, and the more active bodily/kinesthetic kids are directed to "act out" the water cycle (I'll give you a moment to dry your eyes).

So what do you have as a final result? The verbal/linguistic students genuinely learn something about the water cycle by researching and writing a report, the visual/spatial children get to draw raindrops, lakes, and rivers, and the bodily/kinesthetic kids get to fool-around pretending they are raindrops. The book offers no suggestions as to what the common assessment for such an approach should be, but I suspect that anything more than asking the students to write the words "water cycle" would be beyond the scope of this activity. My ultimate question is: How do beginning teachers manage to sift through these kinds of absurdities while they are desperately trying to learn how to function in the real world of the American classroom?

You want to change education? Here it is in a nutshell: *Get class sizes down to ten students working with a properly paid professional*. Only then can we achieve true "individualized" instruction, which at the present time is nothing more than a catch phrase designed for public obfuscation.

I have long been intrigued by what seems to be universally accepted as the proper way to learn a musical instrument, i.e., one-on-one "private" lessons between a teacher and a student. I realize this is a direct outgrowth of the age-old tradition of apprenticeship where one learns a skill or trade while working alongside a "master." It is certainly the way I learned carpentry from my father, and it is the way similar skills have been passed down from generation to generation through the ages. Therefore, wouldn't logic dictate that this be extended to all other aspects of education? Of course we know we will never have one-on-one instruction for every student in every subject, but we can take tremendous strides towards this ideal if we limit classes to ten students.

I was recently reading about the latest advances in neurological research.[13] Apparently, by monitoring infant brain reaction to language stimuli, it may be possible to determine which children are susceptible to developing reading or speech disabilities later in childhood. It is being suggested that this may help diagnose processing problems early and better provide for individualized programs. If we are heading into this kind of "brave new world" to determine and accommodate the individual learning needs of each and every child, we had better start providing a school environment better suited to addressing these specific differences. What is now being offered almost exclusively to "special education" children may well have to be available to all. In the environment created by a ten pupil classroom, it actually would be possible for a teacher to accommodate individual learning styles while children work and develop at their own pace.

I have taught in this kind of an environment and know the success that teachers of high school advance level courses have in these smaller classes. My wife's Level V high school class is a perfect example. Consisting of mostly seniors, they read and discuss literature, do student generated reports, presentations, and PowerPoints, and they engage in discourse on a wide range of topics. While high school advanced classes of this kind tend to be homogeneous, it would still be possible to achieve the goal of individual progress in broadly leveled heterogeneous classes as long as they numbered no more than ten students.

This would engender "real" school reform; an antidote to those grandiose initiatives that look good on paper but are just another scheme to gull the public into thinking change is occurring. Since my first year in teaching I have known that class size is the primary obstacle facing teachers. Unfortunately, it simply isn't "sexy" enough to warrant serious consideration by the educational reform movement. Simply reduce class sizes? How do we possibly make something so mundane sound like a major new initiative? But it is, in fact, the key to everything!

Funding

How could we possibly afford a change like this? First, drastically reduce the bloated administrative bureaucracy that pervades every school system. Secondly, as per Recommendation #1 in Chapter 5, have every employee, except custodial and clerical staff, directly involved in the teaching of students. That's *everyone*, from the first year teacher to the superintendent! Finally and without question, it will require a substantial influx of funds. The current method of funding public education primarily with local property taxes is archaic. It simply exacerbates the disparity between wealthy and poorer communities—something which supplemental state and federal funding can't possibly bridge.

Then there are absurdities like the one that occurs in the town where I teach. This upper middle class community happens to be in an area saturated with vacation homes. Every time there is a budget referendum, the wealthy owners of these properties fly in to vote "No" on the education budget. It has nothing to do with whether or not they can afford to pay the taxes to support the town school system; it's simply a matter of not wanting to pay additional taxes for schools they don't use. Even if these vacation property owners do have kids, they go to school in whichever town they call home. And then there is the perennial issue that besets educational funding in every town: What about the individuals who don't have children or perhaps have just one child? Is it fair for them to be paying the same amount of property tax as a family with five children?

During a brief period of time in the 1980s, my wife and I owned a multi-family building and experienced the nightmare of being landlords (another book's worth of stories there). We paid a set amount of taxes on the property regardless to whom we rented—people with no children or the Brady Bunch. It wasn't until we rented to a family with five children that I realized the absurdity of the entire school funding system. During that time period I was paying approximately $5,000 per year in property taxes, while the average yearly cost to educate a child was $3,500. While my property taxes didn't change one iota, the town incurred a $17,500 tab to educate five more children. And it didn't cost the parents a penny more than the rent they paid me.

The current system of school funding needs to be completely revamped on a nationwide level. With one in every 100 citizens of this nation currently in jail, the highest ratio in the entire industrialized world, perhaps it's time to contemplate which is a better use of money. It costs upwards of $30,000 per year to keep a person imprisoned, whereas the average yearly per-pupil expenditure nationally is approximately $4,000. Regardless, the legislature in Florida recently chose to cut school funding in order to build more prisons! This is in spite of the fact that their educational system is already considered dysfunctional. Has anyone given serious consideration to the idea that a better educated overall populace might reduce incarceration rates?

Here's a bold idea that Ronald Reagan first floated back in the early 1980s: Eliminate the department of education at the federal level. I'd go one step further and dismantle the departments of education in every individual state. It is so easy to forget that the U.S. Dept. of Education was created in 1980, not a hundred years ago. Please show me the vitally crucial educational improvements that have occurred since the ED's inception. My 34 years in teaching have shown that these state and federal institutions do very little to ease the plight of classroom teachers or improve the delivery of instruction to children. They are basically massive, bloated, bureaucratic labyrinths that churn out a never-ending stream of mandates and initiatives that further encumber the educational process while consuming billions in taxpayer funds. Let's take all of that money and put it directly into America's classrooms. Just think what this could achieve! As an added bonus, this action would greatly reduce the highly disruptive resume building initiatives (see chapter 11) that are instituted by school administrators specifically seeking advancement to these state and federal levels.

I've been intrigued by the recent propositions by oil magnate T. Boone Pickens, imploring the nation to support alternative energy sources. Apparently he intends to invest millions of his own money and has a plan for everyone to participate in this crucial endeavor. This is exactly the kind of funding effort that is vital to addressing the needs of American Education. In promoting his new book "Hot, Flat, and Crowded" (2008), New York Times columnist Thomas Friedman has repeatedly asserted that the country which leads the world in the development of innovative energy technologies will emerge as the dominant 21st century power. If this is indeed the case, isn't it time to pour all possible resources into creating an educated populace to achieve this goal? That's what I'm proposing, *real* educational reform: A full and vigorous commitment from all levels of government, business, private enterprise, philanthropic foundations and ordinary individuals to provide the necessary funding for properly paid teachers and fully outfitted schools.

Recommendation #3: Grade Leveling

Assume for a moment that the nation adopts this reduced class-size initiative. Even with ten pupils per class learning at an individualized pace, we would still be mired in the unwavering length of the school day, coupled with whatever number of days constitutes the school year; progressing year after year until completing the prescribed quantity necessary for graduation. Therefore, to counteract the oppressiveness of this "disincentive," my third major proposal is to *eliminate grade leveling*. If the goal is to truly champion individualized instruction by allowing kids to progress at their own rate, the removal of grade levels would end the stagnation of moving from kindergarten to grade 1, 2, 3, etc., on a year by year basis. Allowing each child to move through the prescribed curriculum at his or her own pace would provide the ultimate incentive for students to work harder and progress faster.

My best evidence for the viability of this proposal comes through witnessing what some friends, acquaintances, and former students have achieved through "home schooling." In every case, these kids were able to pass the state standardized tests and fulfill all of the local school system's curriculum requirements for a high school diploma well in advance of arbitrary grade levels. However, because they had to adhere to the prescribed K-12 format, by the time the children reached age 15/16 they were filling time by taking courses at local community colleges. One child had accumulated close to 40 credits by the time he officially received his high school diploma.

If we eliminated grade levels and allowed children to progress through the curriculum at their own pace, measuring mastery via a variety of evaluative tools that included standardized tests, they could receive a diploma whenever they completed graduation requirements, regardless of age. Combining this with ten student class sizes, all students at all levels would be assured a proper "individualized" educational program. Now that would be true educational reform!

Recommendation #4: College Reform

A key component for enacting these reforms is the complete reformation of the college institution as it currently exists. If students are going to be completing high school graduation requirements at a younger age, we have to allow them *full access to college degree study at whatever point they qualify*. Virtually none of the credits that my "home schooled" students had accumulated at local community colleges were accepted to offset course requirements at the four year colleges/ universities they chose to attend. In actuality, they should have been well on their way to a college degree.

During my son's childhood years, as I watched college costs skyrocket, I quietly anticipated a public backlash. As average yearly tuition rates rose from $20,000 to $30,000 to $40,000, I fully expected that a tipping point would be reached where people would just say no and absolutely demand cost control. Alas, it was not to be. As a result, my wife and I find ourselves living paycheck to paycheck as we did when we were first married. Retirement should have been three to five years off but, in order to pay back college loans, it is now ten. While we are thrilled that our son was able to attend the best college for which he qualified and is now doing very well, we are in debt up to our necks. In addition, he is saddled with a number of college loans himself. I do not know how parents of two, three, four, or more children manage to afford this. There are now a steadily increasing number of universities that are topping the $50,000 mark! When does it stop? $100,000 per year? Just as gas prices have finally sent Americans scrambling for more fuel efficient vehicles, there must be a point where the same will be true for college costs. Perhaps the current economic meltdown will be the proverbial "straw that breaks the camel's back."

Reports of increasing student dropout rates due to financial problems are on the rise.

My son readily admits to something we all know is true: In four years of college, he applied himself more fully to his studies only during the final two years when he could focus specifically on his major area. That's a lot of money spent on "the college experience"—pledging to "Tappa Kegga Dey" and training for the WSOBP (if you're over 25, see references). It's not like they didn't do plenty of partying before college (who's kidding whom), and he certainly isn't living the life of a monk right now; it's just no longer 24/7 like it was during most of college.

Even as they are drowning in debt, I still hear parents spouting the familiar line of how important it is to be "on your own" at college; apparently waxing nostalgic about their own college experiences. The major difference, of course, is that "boomer's" college costs, adjusted for inflation, were about one-tenth of what they are today. I guess it boils down to convincing yourself that this incredible sacrifice is somehow worth it. What I want to know is, if we are giving tacit approval to the fact that the majority of college time is given over to the "experience" rather than the "education," isn't it time to rethink this whole thing? I guess only time will tell.

Intrinsically tied to this college cost issue is the need for colleges to stop the practice of including a multitude of general education courses that only serve to extend the time necessary to complete degree requirements. I've known since my own college days that, if one were only required to take courses in their actual degree area, they could probably finish in two years. What's the point of making students retake courses they already completed in high school, other than to double the length of time it takes to get a college degree so that the college can collect more money? Should tuition ever reach that seemingly indefinable saturation point, perhaps the general populace will finally start demanding such action.

I remember taking a tour of a major northeastern university during the summer after my son's junior year in high school. Aside from encountering a person sitting outside one of the dorms casually smoking a joint, my most memorable moment occurred when this student "tour guide" began describing her previous semester's course load. In order to fulfill some of her general education requirements, she had taken one course in horseback riding and another in wine tasting. All of us, including the student, chuckled at the absurdity. I couldn't help but think: Somebody sure is laughing all the way to the bank with that $32,000 per year tuition! It's long past time to eliminate this type of "gen. ed." insanity.

College courses must become more reality-based and superfluous graduation requirements need to be eliminated. In addition, if we are ever to institute the kind of changes to public education I am proposing, it will be absolutely necessary to *make college accessible to younger students*. When one considers the proliferation of online courses available for master's and doctoral degrees, it's not that great of a stretch to begin to offer the same opportunity at the bachelor's level. In fact, I've noticed that a handful of schools have already started providing online options for undergraduates. Knowing that some on campus work will always be required, in the event that commuting from home is not possible, a more closely supervised dormitory situation could be devised for younger students. The possibilities are endless, but the structure of undergraduate college needs to be radically transformed.

Essential Sidebar: An Overview of Grading and Evaluation Initiatives

1) Letter Grades

Most individuals age 30 or older will remember the traditional use of letter grades to evaluate student progress:

A - Outstanding
B - Above Average
C - Average
D - Below Average
F - Failing

Now, welcome to the "new" 21st century format for letter grades:

A - Average
B - Bad
C - Catastrophic

In all seriousness, rampant grade inflation has made the traditional grading system meaningless. Kids are basically getting "A's" for doing "C" work. Mind you, this is nothing official. Everyone continues to pretend the grades are based on "C" being "average," but let's get real! In my school, 87%, I'm not joking. . . 87% of the students make honor roll every marking period, and a full third of those are high honors! And to top it all off, each and every one of those over 500 names gets listed in the local newspaper every time! Believe me, this is *not* an isolated occurrence, it's happening in school systems everywhere!

Rather than the parents realizing that the whole thing is a farce, they incomprehensibly push for even higher grades! My colleagues and I can only assume it's an effort to avoid the humiliation of being among the 13% who don't make honors. I am simply amazed that in this day and age of "positive self-esteem" and "feel-good" mentality, a parent hasn't sued over the public degradation experienced by their kid for being one of the handful not on the list. Although there has been an ongoing push by a number of parents, with the enthusiastic consent of the teachers, to do away with the honor roll completely, nothing will happen while there are still a sufficient number of parents who wish to wallow in the self-deception that it has meaning.

I recently came across a fascinating statistic: Over the past ten years, the average scores of high school students on the various state academic achievement tests have remained virtually unchanged while their grade point averages have increased 23%. With absurd grade inflation like this, the need for an objective evaluative tool becomes all the more pressing; which only fuels the rush to standardized tests as the only viable means currently available. Sadly, my personal experience has repeatedly confirmed that parents tend to emphasize grades and test scores over any concern with actual learning. The long-term effect of such narrow priorities is most alarming. For example, material that I used to teach to fourth graders ten years ago, I am now having difficulty teaching to sixth graders!

Somewhere during the late 1980s, the push to change the grading system received widespread administrative support. If ever there was a perfect example of "reinventing the wheel," this was it. Rather than to focus on the real issue of student learning and achievement, we get sidetracked into exploring different ways to inaccurately report their lack of it. As with most educational reforms and initiatives, all of these began at the elementary level and died a slow death in middle school where they were ultimately deemed "unworkable." Needless to say, this pattern creates extraordinary frustration for elementary teachers who know, after one or two months—six at most, whether the new reform that's been thrust upon them is working or not. The administration, by virtue of the fact that they can completely avoid any practical daily experience with these initiatives, is able to continue "beating the dead horse" for any number of years.

The main reason that so many of these schemes die in the middle school is simply because a different educational "model" is being used. Whereas the elementary model consists of a self-contained classroom where the same 25 kids stay with the same teacher for most of the day, the middle school model is very similar to high school where students pass from teacher to teacher, period to period. Therefore, middle school children see multiple teachers each day and may have classes with as many as eight to ten teachers on a regular basis. It is the complexity of the model that saves middle school teachers time and again. Because high schools are always treated as completely separate entities, those teachers are usually immune to most of these matters. Instead they are inundated with continual "curriculum" reforms, which is more than enough interference and distraction in and of itself.

2) Numbering System

Allow me to elaborate on a few changes to the grading/evaluation system that particularly stand out in my memory. The first of these plans was the product of a long-standing committee made up of teachers, administrators, and parents. I heard a statement years ago that made such an impression: *Forget committees. Nothing of any lasting value has ever resulted from a committee. It has always been the hardworking and talented individual who has been responsible for great innovations.* As if to substantiate the truth of this assertion, the fabulous new "plan" that emerged from this committee was the replacement of letter grades by numbers:

1 = meets or exceeds expectations
2 = developing the skill
3 = skill not yet exhibited

There it was for all to see; the blueprint for the future "dumbing-down" of the entire grading system. Even though this was only being piloted at the elementary level, anyone (except, apparently, this committee and the administration that instituted it) could instantly see the ramifications to the entire letter grading system which was still in use at the middle and high schools. As every teacher knows, there is a world of difference between "meets" and "exceeds." There is no way they can be evaluated with the same grade! Therefore, I immediately began to use 1+ to delineate outstanding work, with the remainder divided fairly evenly between 1 and 2 and the occasional 3.

Because I was teaching fourth and fifth grade at the time, it took several years before students accustomed to this system reached my grade level. I will never forget the first time I received a phone call from an irate parent concerning a "2" I had given her son. "It was the first time ever, in any subject, in five years of school, that her son had received anything below a one," she bellowed! I honestly thought she was kidding and may have nervously chuckled at the absurdity of her statement. "The number "2" denotes *developing the skill*," I tried in vain to explain. The mother made it quite clear she understood. "You mean to say you have never questioned your child getting all "1's" in everything for five years?" I asked, "He has never been 'developing the skill' in any subject, ever?" The answer was an emphatic "No!" And then it became crystal clear that she actually believed a "2" meant her son was a dismal failure and now had no hope of ever going to Harvard!

Fortunately, it didn't take too many more of these incidents before I learned that I needed to amend this numbering system for my own survival. So, while parents continued to receive the same three explanations listed on the preceding page, my personal system became:

1+ = exceeds expectations
1 = meets expectations
1- = developing the skill
2 = skill nowhere in sight
3 = brain scan needed to detect signs of life

It quickly became apparent that I was not the only teacher at my grade level to be experiencing this parental fury. As a result, a number of my colleagues adopted my system. In order to avoid further unneeded parental wrath, 99% of the time I used 1+, 1 and 1-. Even though the report card still stated "meets or exceeds expectations," parents easily figured out the meaning. As I'm sure you can guess, I did indeed get phone calls complaining about the 1-. Consequently, by the time the students moved to sixth grade at the middle school, it's easy to see how an "A" became "average."

Here's a question to which I would love to have an answer: In the history of American Public Education has there ever been one recorded instance where a parent has contacted the school to complain that a grade was *too high*? In all my years, I have never known or heard of a single occurrence. If anyone has ever experienced such a thing, it would be truly inspirational to learn about it. If such a parent exists, he or she should receive a presidential citation.

3) Portfolios

Over the course of time, whether or not it had anything to do with the inadequacies of this 1, 2, 3 system, the superintendent imposed an additional "new" evaluative tool: The Portfolio. I have no idea where this initiative came from, but I know colleagues in a number of other school systems also had to endure this debacle. The concept was to collect representative tests, reports, worksheets, etc., in every subject area from each year of a child's schooling. This was to follow him/her to graduation. Apparently, by the time each kid reached high school, the administration would provide them with a personal baggage handler to drag this thing around. Again, those of us with experience at middle and high school knew that this would never fly at that level, but woe to the poor elementary school teachers—they were the guinea pigs!

In case I haven't yet sufficiently explained the overwhelming difficulty of teaching kindergarten, just guess where they started this portfolio business? You Bet! As with all administrative "initiatives" of this nature, the public hype is the most important thing. Dealing with the mess of trying to institute it becomes the teacher's problem. Once part A is done, the administration could care less about part B, unless it happens to have some impact on part A. There is rarely any protocol for application to existing conditions.

The program began with the first group of kindergartners and, because it wasn't the least bit clear what should actually go into this bulky 24x30 inch portfolio, by the time this group went to first grade, each child's folder was a bulging, five pound heap of papers, tests, artwork, worksheets—you name it! The response to this situation, of course, was to establish another committee! True to form, this committee dissected, inspected, rejected, and infected for six full years! At every stop along the way, classroom teachers had to deal with countless meetings and never-ending "suggestions" from this committee.

At long last that first "pilot" group finally hit sixth grade and, as so many of us had predicted, it was absolutely impossible to continue this nonsense in the middle school model. At the elementary school, the classroom teacher could be singularly in charge of the portfolio. At the middle school, the issue immediately became: Which of the eight to ten teachers the child sees on a regular basis was supposed to be in charge? And, if the portfolio was bulging in first grade, what did it start to look like in sixth? Fortunately, for six years the portfolio committee, for no other reason than physical practicality, kept reducing what was expected to be in the portfolio. And all this, only to meet its inevitable demise in middle school.

Now, we need to take a moment to think this through. The sixth grade teachers had to deal with this portfolio business for at most one year but were rewarded with the joy of killing the beast. Fifth grade teachers dealt with it for two years, fourth grade teachers for three years and, if you continue to count all the way back, the poor kindergarten teachers had to deal with this for *SEVEN* years!   Have I mentioned how difficult . . . . . ?

4) Narratives

With the demise of the portfolio, and the blatant inadequacy of the 1, 2, 3 system becoming ever more apparent, the administration decided that the next best way to offer parents a more detailed evaluation of each child's progress was the narrative. This involves the classroom teacher writing at least a one paragraph summation on each child, every marking period. Once again, woe to the elementary teacher! Because they have the same 25 kids for the whole year, this was their baby. Interestingly, the administration made absolutely no pretense that this would ever be extended to the middle or high schools. Perhaps they were banking on the tendency for parental interest to wane as children get older and school becomes more "routine." Regardless, with student loads that range from 80 to 120, it would be totally impractical for a middle or high school teacher to write this many narratives. But with only 25?

Now, I actually think the narratives are a great idea! It gives parents a detailed, individualized evaluation of their child's academic, social and emotional development in school. The problem is: Just think about the amount of time this takes! Are teachers given release days each marking period to write these evaluations? Of course not! It's just another thing to do on nights and weekends on top of everything else.

At the middle and high schools we continue to use good old-fashioned letter grades. We supplement these with comments that are listed on a computerized sheet: #67–shows improved effort, #118–progress has declined, # 232–kid is a complete pain in the ass (okay, can't one dream?). Even though we have to give grades to a lot more students than elementary teachers do, with 250 comments to choose from, teachers usually find the five to ten that most pertain to their subject area and many times will give 35 or more children the same comment. And, I can tell you without the least bit of hesitation that parents universally hate these computerized comments. I know I certainly did when my son started getting them.

In an effort to help rectify this situation, last year I volunteered to revise the comment code. With the enthusiastic blessing of the assistant principal, I categorized the comments by subject area and general topic, eliminated duplicate comments, and attempted to add missing concepts. Ultimately, the entire effort was stonewalled because the computer grading program wouldn't allow for any comment with more than 28 characters (both letters and spaces). I readily admit I am a complete technophobe, but, in this day and age of advanced computer technology, I find it absolutely inconceivable that we are restricted in this manner. In addition, it only adds to parental frustration to get these little "snippets" for comments. With ten pupils in a class it would be possible to write extensive narratives at all levels, kindergarten through high school, thereby eliminating all of this comment nonsense. Of course, to accomplish this task, release time at the end of each marking period would be an absolute must. (I can't help but notice that my comment #232 would fit within 28 characters by removing the "a" and "the." I'll have to run this by the administration.)

5) Rubrics

We are currently enmeshed in what is perhaps the most frighteningly stringent, narrow, and unenlightened form of structured evaluation I have ever experienced: Rubrics. During the early 1990s, when this concept was first thrust upon us, I thought they were saying "Rupricks," which caused for moments of extreme levity as we recalled Steve Martin's character from the movie "Dirty, Rotten Scoundrels." If only it were so, because at least it would be funny. This current initiative is anything but.

Rubrics entail writing out the exact course requirements that need to be fulfilled in order to receive certain letter grades for evaluation. To get a "C" you must accomplish certain criteria. If you want a "B" there are certain additional tasks to perform. Basically, the exact expectations to obtain each evaluative grade from "A" to "D" are spelled out in detail. While on the surface this may seem like a good idea, what shakes veteran teachers to the core is the realization that we are essentially diluting education down to "hoop-jumping." If you perform this exact task you will get this grade.

Most veteran teachers have been battling constraints like this for years! We want to encourage exploration, creativity, curiosity, experimentation, and innovative inquiry; all of the essential elements for true ownership of the material. Rubrics take that away. Instead, we have a narrow, machine-like exactitude that basically removes thinking from the equation: "Just tell me what to do and I'll mechanically do it." What kind of an imaginative workforce or enlightened general citizenry is going to result from something like this? Most alarmingly, because younger teachers have spent their entire schooling enmeshed with rubrics, they seem incapable of functioning outside of this stringent model. Everything needs to be spelled out in black and white so that it can be presented to the students exactly the same way. Great teaching requires ingenuity and spontaneity. Expecting all teachers to robotically do everything identically could be accomplished by feeding all classrooms with a single video lecture. If our goal is to shape innovative minds for the challenges of the 21st century, I simply shudder!

Let's examine one major unintended consequence of rubrics. Many kids, especially at the high school level, are simply deciding that they only want to work towards a certain level. If you set out the exact requirements for a "C" and the student decides that's good enough, what grounds does the teacher have to push the child to do better?

I vividly recall an incident from my own high school education that perfectly illustrates this concern. My physical education teacher was apparently a ground breaking visionary because he essentially created a model rubric for an instructional unit in gymnastics. He told us exactly what skills we needed to master in order to get an "A, B, C, or a D." One of my friends and I were evidently equally visionary because we decided that a "D" was good enough. Each PE class it took us about two minutes to run through the necessary expectations for a "D": forward and backward somersault, controlled bounce on the trampoline, and a few other minor tasks. Then we would hang-out for the rest of the period and watch the other kids who were trying to get an "A," or "spot" at the trampoline. Not surprisingly, the gym teacher was livid! I remember how he kept scolding and berating my friend and I for not pushing ourselves to our abilities. But, clearly defined rubrics like these remove working to capability from the equation. Student achievement simply becomes a question of whatever level the student chooses. Plainly, this teacher was unable to comprehend the unintentional consequences of laying out exact expectations the way that he did.

So there you have rubrics in a nutshell—yet another top-down initiative that teachers are forced to implement. However, even more than the preceding grand ideas, I am hoping against hope that this one will quickly disappear. Whereas the others were simply ineffective or impossible to execute, rubrics have dire educational consequences. If our goal is to create a thinking, resourceful citizenry, capable of full participation in all aspects of a functioning democratic society, we need to run away from "rubrics" as quickly as possible.

Recommendation #5: The Development of a Comprehensive System of Evaluation

The most insurmountable challenge to the adoption of these recommendations may not come from administrative/legislative resistance or lack of funding, but from overbearing parents. In an ideal world, parents would fully understand the benefits of allowing their child to move at his or her own pace; embracing the opportunity for the child to fully master the material. However, as long as today's parents think their child's grade in kindergarten is going to determine whether or not they get admitted into Harvard, the pressure for accelerated advancement will be unrelenting. I can picture it now: Phone calls about why that other student moved ahead to book II while my Sally still has three pages to complete in book I; or conferences in the principal's office about why your class is so difficult when kids in Mr. Smith's class progress faster (accompanied by demands to have their child switched to his class). Then my personal favorite: The parent who unrelentingly drills the material at home and subsequently reports that their child did it fine and therefore you should pass them.

Therefore, in order to maximize the educational benefits of having ten pupils per class, pursuing true individualized instruction, moving at their own pace, unhindered by the constraints of grade leveling, *a comprehensive, broad-based standard of evaluation must be developed.* This evaluation process needs to incorporate a variety of methods to accurately assess student progress, knowledge, development, and overall "ownership" of the material. It requires something far beyond our current antiquated report card system; a process that *eliminates the use of letter grades entirely* and substitutes concrete "whole-child" evaluative tools that include all school work (tests, worksheets, reports, presentations, etc.), plus standardized and aptitude testing, as well as social, emotional and character development.

Because rampant grade inflation has rendered the current letter grading system essentially meaningless, teachers must work to develop an innovative alternative evaluation system which is not dictated by the government, legislature, board of education, or school administration. This design needs to be of the teachers, by the teachers, and for the teachers to thoroughly evaluate the overall progress, achievement and development of the entire child. Most proficient teachers already use these broad-based evaluative tools on a daily basis. It is simply a matter of making the process more universal— finding a balance between objective and subjective evaluative measures. While standardized tests, regents, etc., serve an important function, it is the individual evaluation from a teacher who is intimately aware of the child's learning traits, skills and development as a living, breathing human being, that is certainly of equal value.

Ultimately, teachers must become the main architects of the entire evaluative process, including standardized tests. No more "No Man." The greatest consequence of the unmitigated reliance on standardized testing dictated by the "No Child Left Behind" legislation is that emphasis has been drawn away from teaching the whole child to creating mechanical test takers. Ensuring that every child is capable of answering every question the exact same way has become the focus. If all efforts are designed to produce universally proficient test takers, how can we lament the loss of creativity in our students?

I was not surprised to hear on the news that a "blue ribbon" panel of college admissions directors had just completed an in-depth study concerning the correlation between SAT scores and the success rate of students in college, which concluded that performing well on the SAT is *not* an accurate indicator of future achievement. They found that taking into account all aspects of pupil performance during high school was a much more reliable barometer. This extensive study merely substantiated what outstanding teachers have been saying for years—you have to look at the "total" child. Standardized tests can certainly measure factual knowledge, but many argue that these tests mostly indicate how well you can take tests.

As adults, the only time we take written exams is for a pursuit that requires accreditation or licensing. But, does passing the bar exam, for example, automatically mean one is going to be a great lawyer? While it provides a profoundly rigorous evaluation of each individual's command of the subject matter, does it in any way assess the ability to actually practice law; how one will perform in a courtroom, interact with people, or operate with honesty and integrity? It is not that written tests don't have value, it's just that they must be combined with other skill and aptitude assessments.

Getting a driver's license is an excellent example. Aside from a written test, one has to actually demonstrate proficiency by getting behind the wheel and driving. While the written portion certainly assesses knowledge of the rules of the road, it is the subjective evaluation of the examiner accompanying the driver in the car that judges driving ability. That's the way it is in teaching—the teacher evaluates applied skills. Would you want a surgeon to operate on you if they had only completed written tests but had no practical expertise? Hands-on experience is also essential for police, firefighters, electricians, barbers, or any other profession that requires licensing.

Just like the behind-the-wheel portion of a driving test, direct human interaction is essential to an in-depth evaluation. The only way this can be achieved in school is through small classes that provide ample opportunity for a one-on-one connection between teacher and student. By overemphasizing the importance of standardized tests, we make the evaluative process so one-dimensional that it loses its value as an accurate barometer of overall knowledge, skill and development.

On the other hand, until very recently, one area where most educators agreed excellence found true measurement, was in the high school Advanced Placement Test (APT). My wife has long championed this test as an immensely comprehensive evaluative tool. Every year she encourages five to ten seniors from her level V classes to take the APT. Two years ago, however, the test was completely revamped, making it absurdly and discouragingly difficult. My wife speculates that many *college* seniors would have trouble getting the top score of "5" on this new test. Because the APT is not required for college admission, many students are opting out rather than risk having something on their transcript that could be perceived as a negative. Just as with the SAT, efforts to discover who is responsible for these "new" APTs have come up empty. And, don't get fooled into thinking that the revised exam "raises the standards." Changing a test that teachers considered excellent into something that discourages the participation of top students is the height of futility. In a few years, when the "invisibles" who created this exam come to their senses, the APT will be revamped again. This time, let's involve the most important group of people: Teachers!

This just in. . . .

Federal Arithmetic and Reading Test [14]

In response to the federal "No Child Left Behind" Act (NCLB), it is proposed that students will have to pass a test to be promoted to the next grade level. In the hope that this proposal will be uniformly adopted by all of the states, the new test will be called the "Federal Arithmetic and Reading Test," or FART.

All Students who cannot pass a FART in the second grade will be re-tested in Grades 3, 4 and 5, until they are capable of passing a FART score of 80%.

If a student does not successfully FART by grade 5, that student shall be placed in a separate program known as the "Special Mastery Elective for Learning Language," or SMELL.

If, with this increased SMELL program, the student cannot pass the required FART, he or she can still graduate to middle school by taking another one semester course in "Comprehensive Reading and Arithmetic Preparation," or CRAP.

If, by age fourteen, the student cannot FART, SMELL, or CRAP, he or she can earn promotion in an intensive, one week seminar known as the "Preparatory Reading for Unprepared Nationally Exempted Students," or PRUNES.

It is the opinion of the Department of Instruction for Public Schools (DIPS), that an intensive week of PRUNES will enable any student to FART, SMELL, or CRAP.

This revised provision of the student component of House Bill 101 should help "clear the air" as part of the "No School Left Standing" Act.

13. Pretend Education

Studies have shown that since 1970 over one-half of the new dollars devoted to education have gone to specific populations of students in categorical programs such as special education, Title I compensatory education, bilingual education, and remedial education. Most of these programs operate under federal and state regulations that prescribe how teachers may be used and students may be grouped. Anyone involved in school finance will tell you how indescribably expensive and bureaucratic these programs are.

During my childhood in the 1960s, the house in which I lived bordered on a State Regional Center for the Mentally Retarded. Because the facilities included the most incredible playground equipment we had ever seen, my friends and I spent a lot of time there; eventually becoming volunteers when we got older. The campus included numerous buildings which housed the children according to the severity of their disability, including one geared to residents who were preparing for assimilation into the regular school system and town community at large.

Residents of this regional center who went to public school were taught in "self-contained" classrooms. This meant that, while these children attended the same school as everyone else, they were placed full-time in a separate classroom specifically outfitted and staffed for their individual needs. When I first started teaching in the mid 1970s, this model continued to be in vogue. As a result, the impact of special education children on the overall school atmosphere was minimal.

However, during a visit to my childhood neighborhood in the early 1980s, I was astounded to learn that this expansive regional center was completely shut down and that, due to various federal legislative acts, the closing of these types of facilities was occurring nationwide. The result was that, from the mildly impaired to the most severely emotionally, socially and physically disabled, *all* were being sent to the public schools. The collective consequences of these federal mandates have caused the most critical changes in public education I've experienced during my 34 years of teaching.

Legislation

Trying to provide a concise overview of these federal acts is perhaps the most difficult task I've encountered while writing this book. I have sifted through mountains of information and talked to numerous individuals directly involved with implementing these mandates. Anyone interested in more detail on any portion of what is discussed here, will be astounded at what a simple Internet search on any one of these topics will reveal. In fact, if you have never tried to read an original piece of governmental legislation, I highly recommend taking the plunge. Never again will you wonder why as a nation we always seem to be mired in bureaucratic stagnation.

The first federal mandate on public education that specifically addressed the "disadvantaged" was the Elementary and Secondary Education Act (ESEA) of 1965. One provision in this act provided that reauthorization must occur every five years; the most notable of which were the Educational and Consolidation Act (ECA) of 1981, the Improving America's Schools Act (IASA) of 1994, and the No Child Left Behind Act (NCLB) of 2001.

The most significant directive of the original ESEA was "Title I - Improving the Academic Achievement of the Disadvantaged." The purpose of Title I was to ensure that all children have a fair and equal opportunity to obtain a high quality education. This mandate specifically addressed the educational needs of low achieving children in high poverty schools, non-English speaking children, and children in need of reading assistance. The overall intention was to close the achievement gap between high and low performing children, especially minority vs. non-minority students.

While the "Title I" portion of the ESEA focused mainly on the "disadvantaged," it was the "Rehabilitation Act of 1973" that specifically centered on the "disabled." While mostly geared towards providing job opportunities and training to handicapped adults, this Act contained one single paragraph which was to have unmitigated consequences on public schools: "Section 504." This section stated: "No otherwise qualified individual shall, solely by reason of his or her handicap, be excluded from participation in, be denied the benefits of, or be subjected to discrimination under any program or activity receiving federal financial assistance." Serious repercussions from the gross lack of specificity in this statement continue to have a substantial impact on education to the present day.

In 1975, in an attempt at clarification, congress passed the Education of the Handicapped Act (EHA) which provided educational funding for children suffering from severe disabilities to ensure that they receive an appropriate public education. This federal standard has been amended numerous times since; the latest being the Individuals with Disabilities Education Act (IDEA) of 2004.

Consequently, starting in 1975, Congress recognized that, faced with the absence of adequate educational services in the public schools, "families are forced to find services outside the public school system, often at great distance from their residence and at a significant personal expense." This resulted in a mandate that all children with disabilities must be afforded the same equality of opportunity as their non-disabled peers to fully participate in the educational process in public schools. IDEA states that each child with a disability must be provided a Free Appropriate Public Education (FAPE) that prepares them for further education, employment and independent living.

One can plainly understand how all of this lead to the closing of facilities like the regional center in my neighborhood.

Implementation

Throughout this entire "individuals with disabilities" discussion, there is nothing more important than understanding the truth of the following statement as it pertains to socially, emotionally, mentally, and physically handicapped students in public school; all of whom fall under the general category of Special Education:

Government legislation sets the policies,
Lawsuits decide how the policies get implemented.

As previously stated, when special education students first started to attend public school they were housed in specifically equipped and staffed "self-contained" classrooms. This proved to be particularly appropriate as the most severely handicapped were being transferred in. However, as federal mandates were amended and parents became more educated as to their children's rights, implementation policies began to change.

The first major policy shift occurred with the institution of "Mainstreaming" in the mid 1980s. Under this concept, special education students were still housed in self-contained classrooms but joined their regular education peers during specific time slots as deemed developmentally appropriate. The amount of time, subject area, etc., was based on the individual child's ability to handle various situations. The importance of this stipulation cannot be overstated, because emotionally/behaviorally disruptive children and the severely mentally/physically handicapped did not attend regular classes. Therefore, the impact on the standard classroom, while still substantial, was basically manageable.

In due course, as legislation was further amended and landmark court decisions ensued, mainstreaming underwent a drastic transformation into what became known as *The Inclusion Model.* This format aligned with the principals of Least Restrictive Environment which state that any student with a disability should have access to the same curriculum, extracurricular activities, and any other school run programs as non-disabled peers. As a result, self-contained special education classrooms were eliminated and *all* children, regardless of severity of mental, physical, social, emotional, or behavioral handicap, were placed *full-time* in regular classrooms.

This impact this had on the conventional class environment was monumental. Special education teachers and instructional aides were sent to work with their pupils in the midst of standard classroom instruction. Children who required more intensive instructional sessions, or received speech and language therapy, occupational and/or physical therapy, and social work, were removed from class for these services. Ironically, because the designated self-contained spaces were eliminated, the hallway became the only regularly available area for individual work with special education students. Therefore, desks and tables lined the halls for a number of years. Interestingly, in our school system, it was the Fire Marshall who put an end to this safety hazard and a designated area to conduct these individual services was reinstated under the title "Study Center."

One of the special education teachers in my building has been incredibly helpful in guiding me through the quagmire of legislation and lawsuits that have had such an incredible impact on American public education. She asserts unequivocally that lawsuits drive the policy. "If all parents had a full understanding of their legal rights," she says, "schools would be paralyzed." She especially enjoyed my comparison of the situation to my neighbor's dog. Almost anyone who has installed an "invisible fence" in their yard knows that you must train the dog as to where they can go without getting zapped. Otherwise, the dog will end up like Bruno, who, because he has no idea where he can go without getting shocked, just stands motionless in the middle of the yard every time he is let out of the house. Soon, all of us in education will be in the same boat; unable to function for fear of getting "zapped" with a lawsuit.

If you think I am overstating the impact of lawsuits on how educational policies are implemented, a quick online search will reveal the myriad instances where any discussion of "Individuals with Disabilities in Education," or "Least Restrictive Environment," or "Free Appropriate Public Education" centers on case law. Whether it is the 1989 "Daniel R." decision or the famous 1993 "P.J." case, lawsuits have unilaterally driven how every legislative mandate has been instituted. By the late 1990s, this resulted in the full implementation of the Inclusion Model and the ramifications have been enormous.

I feel compelled to reiterate something I mentioned in chapter four concerning the difference between public and private schools. Not only can private schools weed-out the disruptive, non-academic students but, because they do not receive governmental funding, they are not required to abide by these federal and state legislative mandates and case law decisions. Advocates of school vouchers should give this careful consideration: Once governmental funds are allocated for use at private schools, lawsuits stipulating compliance with Title I, 504, IDEA, and similar governmental decrees are sure to follow.

Special Education "Modifications"

Throughout my years in teaching I have been subjected to countless workshops and teacher training seminars on every imaginable topic. The state legislature mandates ongoing teacher training, but implementation (both cost and content) is left up to the individual towns. While finding a meaningful one-size-fits-all solution for teachers of widely varying grade levels and subject areas is virtually impossible, I have never once been provided with one drop of training concerning special education students. All of a sudden they arrived in my classroom and I was expected to deal with it.

I know this runs counter to "politically correct" orthodoxy, but attempting to assimilate most of these children into regular education classrooms is basically "promotion by age." We have fifth and sixth graders in my school who can't read, period. Regardless, we are mandated to "pretend" that they are working at grade level with all of the other kids.

The root cause of this situation is that special education students are subject to "modifications" of standard requirements:

> Modifications refer to changes made to curriculum expectations in order to meet the needs of each "identified" student. Modifications are made when *the expectations are beyond the student's level of ability.* Modifications may be minimal or very complex depending on individual student needs and abilities. In short, Modifications are changes in *what* is to be learned (content).

In my experience, the varying degrees of modification that each special education student may require basically translate into lowering the standards of expectation; in many cases, years below grade level. At a recent meeting regarding sixth grade special education students, child after child was evaluated as "reading at first grade level," "math skills at second grade level," "overall skills at kindergarten/first grade level,"—on and on it went. I simply cannot understand for the life of me what can possibly be gained by this approach.

Regardless, it is the ongoing disciplinary issues that I find to be the most trying and exhausting part of the entire special education mandate. We have reading specialists, speech therapists, social workers, school psychologists, physical therapists, instructional aides, and the attending special education caseworkers attempting to assimilate these children into regular education classrooms. In spite of this, the classroom teacher is still spending extraordinary amounts of time, effort, and energy quelling continual disruptions. All of this, of course, detracts from the time, effort, and energy that could be expended on the "regular" kids.

Let me clearly state that I am not in any way against properly educating special needs children. My concern lies in the impact of these policies on the quality of education for *all* students. Nowhere is the chasm between policy-makers and those forced to do the implementation any more pronounced than in special education. Here's a sentence from a recent parent e-mail that puts the entire issue into concise perspective: "We make sure our special education kids have special teachers catering to them all day while our gifted and talented kids are forgotten." This is my point: We need to equally and appropriately provide all students with optimum educational opportunities. Unfortunately, all efforts seem to be committed to moving in the opposite direction. My wife tells me that the administration in her school system has decided to remove *all* ability leveling next year—including the high school. As a result, everyone, from the valedictorian to students with the most severe mental and behavioral disabilities, will be grouped together.

It has been made abundantly clear that state law requires every teacher who works with an identified "special" student to be responsible for all of the material contained in that child's file. Just this one factor should be enough to send any new teacher running for the door. Having 12 of these identified kids this year alone, I have examined these files, many of them close to two inches thick. Some children even have two files. Fortunately, the assigned special education caseworker usually supplies a synopsis for every teacher, highlighting the really important points. Still, you wouldn't believe what some of these modification sheets look like. Each child averages three to six pages. The chart on the following page illustrates the standard modifications that teachers encounter most frequently.

Individual Education Plan (IEP)
Program Modifications

Materials/Books/Equipment	Tests/Quizzes/Time
___ Alternative Tests	___ Modified Tests
___ Simplified Assignments	___ Limited Multiple Choice
___ Tape Recorded Assignments/ Responses	___ Alternative Tests
___ Consumable Workbook	___ Extra Time on Tests/Projects
___ Supplementary Visuals	___ Shortened Tasks
___ Modified Worksheets	___ Hands-on Projects
___ Large Print Text	___ Rephrase Test Questions/ Directions
___ Provide Manipulatives	___ Simplify Test Wording
___ Use of Calculator/Computer/ Spell Check	___ Open Book Tests

Grading	Organization
___ No Spelling Penalty	___ Provide Study Outlines
___ Base Grade on IEP Modifications	___ Give One Paper at a Time
___ No Handwriting Penalty	___ Provide Daily Assignment/ Homework List
___ Modified Grades	___ List Sequential Steps
___ Use of Pass/Fail Option	___ Post Routines/Assignments
___ Grade Effort Only	___ Extra Space for Work
___ Employ Lesser Performance/ Evaluation Standards	___ Provide Special Folders for Work
___ Evaluate Progress by Alternative Means	___ Assign Partner

Behavior Management	Instructional Strategies
___ Modify Rules/Expectations	___ Provide Extra Drill/Practice
___ Daily Feedback to Student/Parents	___ Multi-Sensory Approach
___ Collect Baseline Data/Chart Progress	___ Visual Reinforcement/Pictures/ Charts
___ Preferential Seating/Proximity to Teacher	___ Highlight Key Words/Concrete Examples
___ Create/Monitor Behavior Contract	___ Pre-teach Content
___ Structure Transition/Break Between Tasks	___ Review Directions/Repeat Instructions
___ Provide Clear Work Area or Study Carrel	___ Frequent Oral/Visual Reminders
___ Parent/Guardian Sign Homework	___ Provide Lecture Notes
___ Parent/Guardian Sign Behavioral Chart	___ Create/Use Personalized Examples

Believe it or not, a chart like this regularly serves as the cover for modification packets that can include numerous additional pages of written specifications on one child alone. Just try to imagine the extraordinary additional effort that any *one* of these modifications requires on the part of the teacher. Then consider that, while the average special education child usually totals around ten modifications, I have seen as many as 36. Could anything better illustrate the futility of what is being asked of teachers? By law, the teacher is required to attend to each one of these expectations. Please keep in mind that there can be multiple "identified" children in any given class, each requiring the teacher to incorporate a completely different set of modifications. Just attending to these kids alone would be sufficient for any teacher, but then you have the other 20-plus "regular" students that you are still expected to teach. As if this weren't enough, contemplate for a moment how all of this impacts the current infatuation with "common assessments." If I have five special education kids in a class and someone else has none, how can we possibly be evaluating all of the children the same way? Then try to consider how one would ever factor any of this into an achievement based "merit pay" system.

In essence, these modifications are what allow us to pretend the special education student is doing the same thing as everyone else. This is possible because anything involving only paperwork (tests, reports, worksheets, etc.) can be "fudged." Kid writes 2+2=5. You have him come up to your desk, use some manipulatives and, if he shows a modicum of understanding, you can both pretend the concept is mastered––kid passes. The fact that many states allow all pupils defined as "special education" to either be exempt from standardized tests or *not* have their scores count towards overall school evaluation, makes the task that much easier. Interestingly, our state has just instituted a simplified test for special education students. While this test *is* expected to be included in overall school rankings, the special education teachers tell me it's a lot simpler than they presumed.

The only discernible advantage to this whole inclusion activity is that the regular education students have learned such extraordinary tolerance. By assimilating children with varying physical, mental and behavioral handicaps into the regular classrooms, students are accepting of situations that many of us would find disconcerting. For example, last year we had a sixth grader who regularly exposed himself in the middle of class. While the other kids definitely took in the show, they hardly reacted. It just became part of the regular course of things. I've also experienced numerous instances where the class bursts into spontaneous applause over some minor achievement attained by a special education student. Although these displays of support and empathy can be most gratifying, this tolerance is only displayed towards the most severely handicapped. The "regular" special ed. student is subject to the same antics and needling as everyone else.

Because my wife has taught upper level and Advance Placement classes for much of her career, she has been insulated from the special education experience. However, due to her administrators deciding that everyone should "teach across the curriculum" regardless of subject expertise or instructional ability, my wife is now teaching two sections of Level I that include special education students with specific modifications. Consequently, she is now embroiled in all of the challenges of teaching special education children.

As a conscientious teacher, my wife has been having a terrible time accepting the idea of giving students grades they haven't earned. One particularly difficult parent stated in a meeting that she would be perfectly happy if her child received "C's" straight across the board in all classes. It has taken my wife five months to accept that, regardless of the child's failing performance, if she just gave the kid a "C" (as most of his other teachers have already done) all of her issues with this parent would simply disappear. Fortunately, this particular child is not a behavior problem like many of the other special education students with which she is struggling. Therefore, I was intrigued when she recently said to me: "All these years I've been thinking that your "pretend education" postulation was an exaggeration. Now I know, if anything, you have been understating the situation." When a teacher of my wife's caliber acknowledges this reality, rest assured that the state of affairs is grave indeed.

Cost

The financial burden of these mandates is equally significant. If a family with a severely handicapped child moves into town, it is immediately the town's responsibility to shoulder the expense of assimilating the child into school, regardless of the town budget. While some state aid may be available, many times the cost to the town can run into the tens of thousands of dollars.

A special needs child named Margaret arrived under these circumstances and proceeded to turn the building inside out. For an entire month, the special education caseworker, one-on-one aide, school social worker, school psychologist, and assistant principal were consumed with this girl. At minimum, $200,000 worth of staff was being devoted to this battle. To call this child highly volatile was an understatement. She screamed bloody murder, hit, punched, kicked, and completely destroyed any sense of order wherever she went. Finally, they were able to achieve some semblance of normalcy by getting her "meds" properly adjusted. Still, the same personnel, minus the assistant principal, are regularly required to attend to this girl.

Here's a little secret that parents and the general citizenry need to know. No matter how carefully the administration, board of education, and town officials try to properly budget for the extraordinary expense of funding special education, cost overruns are a regular occurrence. Almost without exception, come January of any given school year, approved budgets are frozen in order to pay additional special education bills that have arisen. This means that, even though there are six months left in the school year, any allotted instructional funds that teachers have not spent are taken away. Therefore, the quality of educational opportunity for the entire student body is drastically impacted by expenses incurred to serve a small minority. Because this occurs every year, one might think a smart teacher would plan ahead and spend all of his or her allotted funds by Christmas. But, no matter how well a teacher tries to plan in advance, it is virtually impossible to foresee every single instructional need for the entire year. The consequence of this sudden shortfall inevitably results in teachers investing personal funds in order to continue to have functioning classrooms. In my estimate, 95% of teachers are intimately acquainted with this experience—having spent their own money on numerous occasions where circumstances made it impossible to do without.

Not surprisingly, the closing of state facilities like the regional center in my hometown, gave rise to a cadre of privately run institutions specializing in various disabilities: psychological, behavioral, severe physical handicaps, etc. I became keenly aware of this a few years back when Clement, a special education student with behavioral characteristics alarmingly similar to Margaret, had to be "out-placed" to one of these facilities. While totally disrupting the entire school does not necessarily get you removed, Clem's crowning misstep was to make comments like "I'm going to kill all of you" while making gun shooting gestures with his hands. This was the tipping point that finally warranted out-placing him to one of these special private schools.

On the other hand, *actually* attempting to poison a teacher apparently doesn't qualify. A few weeks ago, one of our more temperamental special education children decided to put cleaning fluid in a teacher's coffee mug. Fortunately another child witnessed the act and informed the teacher. The perpetrator was somehow able to convince the administration that this was just a practical joke and that he had every intention of owning-up before the teacher took a sip. So, after one day of in-school suspension, he was released back to the classroom. As an 18 year veteran, the teacher had the wherewithal to refuse to have this child back in her class. So they found a second year, non-tenured teacher who, having no job protection, felt compelled to take the kid. This is a perfect example of why the educational hierarchy is so hell-bent to get rid of tenure. They need to have people around whose job security is so tenuous that they are willing to do anything the administration asks—even at serious personal risk.

I had this child in class last year and he basically acted with impunity. Even though he had a one-on-one aide, he arrived at class when he felt like it; shouted out, stamped feet and argued while he was there; and walked out whenever he wanted. On top of that, we were all required to "pretend" that the aide wasn't specifically assigned to this child (even though everyone, including all of the kids, knew it). Therefore, rather than to intervene in any way, the aide just sat there like a bump on a log, or chased after the boy at a sufficient distance to perpetuate the "not being assigned to this kid" charade (I'm *honestly* not making this up). It seems the sole purpose of the aide was to intervene *only* if the child *physically* endangered himself or other children. Total disruption of the classroom did not warrant the slightest consideration! (In case you are wondering where the aide was during the cleaning fluid incident, it was decreed at the beginning of this year that this boy no longer needed one.)

The hesitancy in making the decision to out-place students essentially boils down to the fact that this comes at an enormous expense to the town; often in the $50-60K range. We currently have five pupils in our school system that require this kind of out-placement. In addition, the town must provide round-trip transportation to and from the child's home. Although this is a significant expense, it is much less than the cost for a child to live full-time at one of these schools. Depending on the severity of the disability, the full cost with room and board can be over $100,000 per year.

We have six special education children in our building who have one-on-one instructional aides specifically assigned to them for the entire day. System-wide, we have twenty-three pupils receiving this kind of attention. Without a doubt, these are children with the most severe physical, mental and behavioral problems. Nonetheless, that's twenty-three adults! Even though they are "aides" and not fully certified teachers, it's a significant expenditure of funds to serve only twenty-three children. If by law and lawsuit we are providing one-on-one instruction to the lowest achieving students, why is it unreasonable to provide one-to-ten instruction for everyone else?

Once again, I am not by any means minimizing the need to properly educate these most unfortunate and deserving special needs children. My concern pertains to the *appropriate* part of FAPE (Free and Appropriate Education). Is it appropriate to have children in sixth grade who can't read? Because the entire issue of special education is treated with such extreme caution, I fully realize the likelihood of offending sensibilities by engaging in such a candid discussion. Even so, I feel compelled to make an attempt to bring this issue, which has had such a drastic impact on public education, into the light of honest deliberation. Any principled discussion of the issues facing American education must involve a forthright review of special education policies. At minimum, *all* federal education mandates should be financed entirely with federal funds. The same should be true for mandates by individual states. Local school systems should bear none of the expense for implementing programs that are imposed upon them.

I recently watched a discussion on TV concerning the fact that the United States has the highest per-pupil expenditure of any country in the world, but our student achievement, especially in the areas of math and science, ranks 19th. The ensuing conversation involved all of the usual consternation about raising standards, making schools and teachers more accountable, creating more charter schools, giving parents school choice, etc. I was most impressed that one individual actually raised the issue of the role that parents should play— that schools can't do it alone. Even so, there was no mention of the huge outlay of federal, state, and local education dollars that go specifically to special needs children. My question is: Do other countries allocate these same resources to this particular population of students?

Perhaps it is appropriate to clarify how "per-pupil" expenditure is calculated. First, the entire outlay of educational dollars in any given school district—local, state, and federal funds included—is bundled together. That sum is then divided by the total number of students in that district. However, the resulting per-pupil figure can be highly misleading. For example, if the district is spending $250,000 to out-place five special needs children and $520,000 to provide one-on-one instructional aides for twenty-six more, these amounts are getting figured into overall per-pupil costs. Having 31 students receive a combined $770,000 means that these individuals account for an average per-pupil outlay of $24,839 each, not to mention the cost of accommodating all of the other diagnosed special education children in the district. So, if a school system has a total of 1725 students, for example, based on the national median of $4,000 per pupil, the district budget should be $6,900,000. However, after deducting the $770,000 spent on the 31 special needs children, the average expenditure on the remaining 1,694 students is down to $3,618. Clearly, when one factors in the *entire* special education budget in any given district, the per-pupil outlay for the "regular" students may be well below what is being reported as "average."

The same is true for student/teacher ratios. Because these figures are calculated by taking the total number of students in a district and dividing it by the total number of teachers, the resulting ratios are highly misleading. Not every teacher is assigned to a full student load. Special education caseworkers, social workers, psychologists, department coordinators, computer, math, and reading specialists —the list goes on and on—may serve only a handful of students. Averaging these individuals into the overall student/teacher ratio for an entire school district results in a figure that is deceptively lower than actual class sizes. Now you'll understand why your child is in a classroom of 25, while your school district is advertising a student/teacher ratio of eleven to one. For some inexplicable reason, the educational bureaucracy apparently finds it advantageous to mislead the public on both per-pupil expenditure and student/teacher ratio.

A friend of mine recently returned from a trip to China where he spent considerable time observing classes in a variety of schools. Unabashedly, the Chinese put the best and the brightest in the front of the room where the teacher expends most of his or her time and effort. The lowest achievers are placed in the back of the room and are basically "on their own." Anyone to whom I mention this, gasps in horror. Yet, in our public schools, gifted and talented programs are cut while a disproportionate amount of funds are allocated to the lowest achievers. Because a classroom teacher's time is consumed with the demands of working with these children, the brightest kids are sent off to work "on their own" in the library or computer lab. Curiously, this does not seem to elicit statements of concern. If Thomas Friedman is correct that the country which harnesses the development of energy technology will be the dominant world power, ask yourself which nation is applying its resources to the students who are most likely to achieve this goal?

504 "Accommodations"

The other major component of the children with disabilities mandate is "Section 504" of the "Rehabilitation Act of 1973." Whereas a special education diagnosis results in specific modifications to the child's learning expectations, a 504 plan involves "accommodations" based on *a physical impairment that impacts learning.*

> Accommodations refer to the actual teaching supports and services that the students may require to successfully demonstrate learning. Accommodations do not change any curriculum expectations as to what the child should be learning. Accommodations change *how* the content will be taught (delivery and evaluation of instruction).

While special education calls for definitive changes in curriculum, 504 requires adjusting the delivery and evaluation of standard instruction to the child's individual needs. Evidently, because special education modifications are more specific and 504 accommodations are more generalized, the opportunity for lawsuits pertaining to 504 students is vastly increased. Consequently, there is an undeniable sense of caution prevalent in every conversation. A simple e-mail asking the social worker to list the top ten 504 diagnoses goes unanswered. In fact, absolutely no specifics get put into written memos, notes, or e-mails whatsoever. All information is kept in a special cabinet in the main office that contains the files on each one of these "diagnosed" 504 students. Once again, by law, every teacher who works with one of these children is responsible for all of the information contained in each one of these files. Our school principal couldn't have made the seriousness any clearer than when she said, "I treat any e-mail to the parent of a 504 student as if it is going directly to the lawyer."

Although the possibilities are limitless and new "ailments" are being added regularly, some examples of 504 disabilities are:

> Attention Deficit Disorder (ADD)
> Attention Deficit Hyperactive Disorder (ADHD)
> Pervasive Developmental Disorder (PDD)
> Obsessive Compulsive Disorder (OCD)
> Clinical Anxiety
> Generalized Anxiety Disorder
> Mild Anxiety
> Perthes Disease (affects sitting and movement)
> Behaviors that interfere with social and emotional
>   functioning with peers
> Sensory Integration Disability
> Impulsivity
> Distractibility
> Central Auditory Processing Disorder (CAPD)
> Depression
> Hearing Loss
> Stress-induced Asthma

While the list goes on, hopefully this is sufficient to give you the general picture. My absolute favorite is "Mild Anxiety." This could pretty much apply to any one of us on any given day. With categories like this, one can see how easy it is to meet a 504 qualification. For example, how many people do you know who exhibit "behaviors that interfere with social functioning?" Perhaps you may have noticed that the disabilities can involve made-up conditions such as, "Impulsivity."

While many of the accommodations for 504 students are similar to what was listed on the earlier sample "IEP Program Modifications" sheet, in almost every case, weekly contact with the child's home and regular meetings with various school support personnel are required. In addition, the remedy for these disabilities can sometimes be unfathomable. Recently we had a hearing impaired pupil for whom a large amplified speaker was installed on the ceiling of the room and a portable microphone was clipped onto the teacher's collar as if she was on a talk-show. To accommodate this one child the volume on this speaker was so loud that you could clearly hear the teacher in all of the adjacent rooms and across the hallway. Shutting classroom doors did not block out the sound.

So, why couldn't this child simply wear a hearing aid? Because he didn't want to! He had one that he wore whenever he was outside of the classroom (PE, art, music, lunch, recess, bus, etc.), but he "preferred" not to wear it in class. That being the case, why couldn't he have a smaller speaker set up at his desk instead of the huge speaker on the ceiling? Because he didn't want to be "singled-out" as the kid with the hearing problem!

This kind of unconscionable action is what happens when parents know their rights and everyone in a position of authority is afraid to say "no" due to the threat of litigation. But why not disturb the learning of four to five classrooms of kids to accommodate one child? Impacting all of the students to comply with governmental mandates and case law decisions that pertain to only a small minority is what happens all the time. Welcome to the "real world" of education.

14. Creative Hydrodynamics

One of the boy's lavatories in our building consists of three floor-length urinals and two regular toilets in separate stalls. The doors on these stalls are in various states of contortion due to the kids' irresistible urge to hang from them and swing back and forth. In the middle of the floor is a six inch drain strategically placed for the "rare" event of an overflow. However, within the constraints of the school atmosphere, that drain quickly becomes a fixation for the "behaviorally challenged." One basically knows that spring has arrived when the water starts flowing. There is perhaps no better example of passing applied knowledge between "master" and "apprentice" than through the exploits of these boys every April.

The basic design of this water harnessing project consists of placing five to six wet paper towels flat over the drain in the center of the floor. Additional paper towels must be similarly placed over the drains at the bottom of each urinal. Then, just like a seasoned safe-cracker, one must correctly jiggle the flushing handles on each urinal so that the water keeps flowing. If your towels are properly placed, you simply stand back and watch your mini "Lake Mead" develop.

This yearly ritual runs its course until the novelty wears off, normally within two weeks. This is despite every imaginable administrative effort to prevent it. But, no matter how many different sign-out sheets they devise, or teacher/administrator patrols, or custodian checks, the activity continues until the students lose interest. One year the administration even tried locking the boy's room except for designated times. That was very short lived, undoubtedly because of numerous phone calls from complaining parents, and the violation of I can't imagine how many health and sanitation regulations. Despite all of the hand-wringing, the only way you can possibly intercede successfully in a situation like this is to place an adult monitor in the lavatory full time.

In any event, the *real* excitement occurred about three years ago. Around the same time that the boys began to tire of their yearly ritual, the directly adjacent girl's lavatory began flooding. Because there are obviously no urinals in the girl's room and there was absolutely *no* evidence of the toilets being stopped up, the only logical conclusion was that there had to be a leak of some sort. Despite numerous suggestions to this effect, the administration immediately re-instituted all of the failed policies of the boy's room flooding but with an additional sense of urgency. Not that a few of the girls weren't willing to abet the hysteria by placing paper towels over the drain in *their* lavatory. Oh, but for the heightened subterfuge.

Since there were no readily visible signs of a leak, and a closer inspection would have required getting down on the soaking wet floor to look at the various plumbing connections, this went on for well over a week. Because the front office refused to consider any possibility except student misbehavior, the town maintenance crew was never contacted. Finally, the night custodian brought in a pair of fishing waders from home, put on some rubber gloves and got down on the floor to thoroughly inspect behind the toilets. Lo and behold, there was a crack in one of the tanks that caused the water to flow down the back of the toilet and spread onto the floor in a manner that effectively hid the source. So, despite the frenzied intercession of two administrators who collectively earn well over two hundred twenty-five thousand dollars, the problem was solved by a person making just over minimum wage.

15. The Disconnected

Limiting class sizes to ten students and offering a true opportunity for individualized instruction and progress, completely devoid of the constraints of grade levels and set years of schooling, would benefit students across the academic spectrum. With high school dropout rates as high as 50% in many rural areas of the country, plus the well documented problems in urban schools, urgent action is required. I am proposing that *all* students receive the same individualized attention that we currently administer to special education students without moving kids along from grade to grade arbitrarily. We would no longer have to deal with children in sixth grade who can't read because there would be no sixth grade. Classes of ten students would allow children to progress individually within very broad-based ability grouping. Although we certainly want to avoid a strict homogeneous alignment, we also don't want any hint of the current inclusion model. In short, we need everyone engaged in ability appropriate instruction, learning, and progress.

My main focus at this point is that vast, amorphous area of "struggling" students who are not achieving academically but do not qualify for special programs. Contrary to common misconceptions, when we talk about children on the lower end of the academic spectrum, we are not necessarily speaking about a lack of ability, creativity, or work ethic. We are often discussing kids who simply can't connect to the school experience and become lost amongst the multitudes. This brings to mind two students who epitomize this situation. I met them both through their participation in the community based educational program that I directed.

Let's start with Jeffrey, an extremely creative, hard working kid with incredible common sense and an uncanny ability to figure things out, who was failing miserably in school. The confinement and unyielding regimentation ran contrary to his innovative nature. Much of what we do in school is arbitrary busywork and, if Jeff could not find a meaningful reason to do something, he'd have no part of it—and there was absolutely no way you were going to get him to do otherwise. In fact, the more you pushed, the more he dug in. Like so many children, his independent spirit did not lend itself to sitting at a desk all day long. However, because he was basically quiet and didn't disrupt class, despite the never-ending battle over schoolwork, he managed to trudge through elementary and middle school and finally entered high school.

As a result of skills he had learned from working with his dad on various projects, Jeff found work outside of school doing odd-jobs, minor repairs, and handyman work for a number of individuals. By the time he was 16 and able to drive, he found himself working on the estate of a well-known fashion photographer. Before long he was basically functioning as "foreman" of the grounds. This man could have hired anyone he wanted and certainly wasn't employing Jeff out of generosity towards some kid who was struggling in school. Jeffrey simply did the job better than anyone else.

One achievement that stands out in particular was the renovation of a garden pond fountain system. Evidently, the owner had tried more than once to get "experts" to solve the problem, but to no avail. So, Jeff strapped on scuba tanks, plunged into the murky waters and, in no time, analyzed a situation that had confounded all of the others. Before long, he had cleared the system, run new pipes, and repaired walls and terraces; the result being that the entire system, which had been non-functional for years, now runs like clockwork. Fountains are splashing, waterfalls flowing, streams of water are spouting from the mouths of all the little cement cherubs, and the whole recirculation system is functioning perfectly.

Despite his ongoing difficulties in school, Jeff finally reached the point where the only requirements he needed to complete for graduation were English and PE. As a logical thinker, he simply couldn't understand why he wasn't allowed to just come into school for those classes and then leave. While the teachers found no issue, it was the front office that dug in their heels. No matter how absurd, rules are rules: rigid, inflexible, and arbitrary. Jeff simply wasn't going to adhere to something that made no sense. Therefore, instead of coming to school at the prescribed time and sitting in homeroom and study halls until the scheduled English class, he simply came in for English class. Consequently, he was marked tardy and given detentions. He didn't attend the detentions, and they accumulated to the point where he was repeatedly getting suspended. The final straw occurred when the school administration decided that the only solution was to out-source Jeff to a regional "reform" school. So, here we have the foreman of the estate of a world renowned photographer being sent to a school for juvenile delinquents because he is tardy to school. The parents had to threaten legal action to get the administrators to back off and allow Jeff a "flex" schedule.

Another student, Steven, simply *never* connected to school at all. Throughout his elementary years his dad had to physically escort him into the school building every day. Whereas kids like Jeff can find a way to just sit and survive, children like Steve have a horrible time assimilating into school. Because his birthday is in November, his parents chose to wait a year to start him in kindergarten, which meant that he was a year older than most of his classmates throughout his schooling. Therefore, when he got to high school he was able to get his driver's license early in his sophomore year, whereas most kids are juniors when they start to drive.

Like Jeff, Steve was a hard working, outdoors kind of kid who was soon involved in his own lawn care business. Being an excellent self-starter and a great worker, his business soon expanded to year round. By his junior year, Steve had earned enough money to start buying some of his own equipment. He purchased a snow plow and built a huge contraption in the bed of his pickup truck for vacuuming up leaves. In short, he was a successful businessman.

Wisely wanting to finish his high school diploma, Steve found himself in a situation very similar to what Jeff had experienced; simply needing to complete a few basic courses to fulfill the requirements for graduation. Fortunately, his school system was a bit more flexible than Jeff's, and it *only* took Steve's dad several months of unrelenting effort, but no threat of a lawsuit, to finally get the administration to allow Steve to come into school just for the needed classes.

Due to his outstanding work ethic, Steven's business grew to the point where he was hiring other kids to work for him. At one point, Steve's dad got laid off from the local aircraft plant and went to work for his son! I enjoy imagining Steve the "boss" giving his dad the necessary instructions about what needed to be done so that Steve could run over to the high school for his required classes.

As these two examples clearly demonstrate, it is just as essential to create accommodations for the "non-academic" students as it is for those who have special needs, are college bound, and everyone in-between. Therefore, I'm proposing that we institute evening course offerings as part of standard public education. A program like this would meet the needs of the multitude of students like Jeffrey and Steven who only need to finish one or two specific classes for graduation. Even more importantly, we could counteract the dismal prospects for dropouts by making it easier for older students to return and finish degree requirements. Although evening classes are often instituted as part of adult education programs, it is usually to gain a High School Equivalency Certificate (GED). I'm proposing that evening classes become an integral part of the regular school curriculum so that returning students can receive a full High School Diploma.

When it comes to high school dropouts, the crux of the matter is this: What is to be gained from further "punishing" young people who, for whatever reason, have never had an adult in their lives who could "save them from themselves" and have fallen victim to their own youthful short-sighted stupidity? I say this repeatedly: No matter how obnoxious, infuriating or downright incorrigible teenagers may be at any given time, they are still just *KIDS!* Have we all forgotten when we were 17 and knew everything? Guiding children from their own ill-advised instincts requires *real* parents. If good parenting is absent from the lives of young people and they fail to connect with another responsible adult as a mentor, where do they turn for guidance? More often than not, it is to their peers—and the downward spiral simply accelerates.

As a society, we need to be doing everything possible to help bring these young people back into the fold. At whatever point they finally "come to their senses," the opportunity to continue their schooling and help them towards productive, fruitful lives must be available. If we truly believe that an educated populace is essential to a functioning democracy, the public should be clamoring for such programs. In fact, this just might be the answer to alleviating some of our frightful incarceration rates. Evening programs would also diminish the gross under-utilization of our school buildings. These facilities ought to be as vibrantly active at 8:00 in the evening as they are during the day—weekends too!

I am continually flabbergasted by the standard "status quo" solution for our problems in education, i.e., longer school days and longer school years. If what we are presently doing isn't working, how will doing *more* of the same make it better? While we bemoan current dropout rates, will we reverse the trend by asking "marginal" students to spend *more* time in school? Let's try a "less is more" approach by allowing all students to move at their own pace through meaningful, ability appropriate instruction within a flexible school format designed to accommodate their individual needs. Considering the instantaneous access to information that is currently available through computer technology, isn't it long past time to look at a complete revamping of the rigid school configuration? Rather than persist in recycling the same tired ideas of the past 40 years, let's try some *real* educational reform.

I was recently enjoying my regular encounter with a sixth grader named Colby. He tends to join me on my morning duty to chew the fat. Colby is another superb example of the kind of kid who does not fit the mold for which school is designed. Large, outgoing, and gregarious, he was telling me about the weekend he spent installing a new septic tank with his dad on the farm on which he lives. Although he is only 13 years old, he was evidently driving the pickup truck from which a chain was wrapped around a huge boulder he and dad were trying to pull out of the ground. This effort required multiple attempts because, to hear Colby tell it, the rock was the size of Gibraltar.

The entire time Colby was recounting this story—loud, larger than life, arms a-flailing—I couldn't help but think about the fact that in a few minutes some poor teacher would be trying in vain to have him sit quietly at a desk, in a row, in a class of 25 pupils, and intently engage in the task at hand. Can you picture this exercise in futility? Colby is just the type of kid for which the individualized, non grade leveled, progress at your own pace, small class size program would be ideal!

16. Blind-sided

Hello, you've reached the automated answering service of your child's school.[15] In order to connect you to the correct staff member, please listen to *all* options before making your selection.

- To lie about why your child is absent - press 1
- To make excuses for why your child did not do his or her homework - press 2
- To complain directly to the principal about some half-truth your child told you about his or her teacher - press 3
- To ask why you didn't get needed information that was already enclosed in your newsletter and several bulletins mailed directly to you - press 4
- If you want us to raise your child - press 5
- If you wish to complain about how we are doing it - press 6
- To request another teacher for the third time this year - press 7
- If you wish to yell, curse and treat your child's teacher or any other figure of authority, rudely and disrespectfully - hang up.
- If you realize that this is the real world and your child must be accountable for his or her own behavior, class work, and homework, and that your

child's complete lack of effort is not the teacher's fault, *thank you and have a nice day!*

I recall a meeting with a hostile father during my first year of teaching public school. Because I was young and single, I had no qualms about allowing the job to dominate my life. So, rather than to simply use the official quarterly report card, I developed my own comprehensive progress report which I sent home to parents *monthly!!* At that time, prior to the onset of political correctness, a rating scale could simply state "good, satisfactory, or poor." This man's son, by making no effort whatsoever, was performing miserably in all areas. As a result, he earned a "poor" in each category of the progress scale.

So, in comes the father, slaps the report on the table and announces, "This is Bullshit!" Now, as a basically novice teacher, I got quite flustered and tried to deal with this man in a civilized manner as he proceeded to behave as rudely, disrespectfully, and obnoxiously as humanly possible. In reflection, it was providential that this occurred so early in my career, because I was blessed to be surrounded by a marvelous veteran teaching staff which I wisely sought out for counsel on a regular basis. I received extraordinary advice and insight from them which has served me ever since. However, I have often fantasized about a replay of this encounter. Father: "This is Bullshit!" Teacher: "I'm glad to hear that you so emphatically agree but, unfortunately, I'm not allowed to use that category on the form."

I cannot begin to describe how devastating it is to teachers, especially novices, to be confronted by a belligerent parent. Absolutely nothing is ever mentioned about any of this during college or subsequent teacher training workshops, so handling a situation like this becomes part of on-the-job training. The first incident basically hits you like a train—completely *blindsided!* Over the years, experienced teachers may develop a more protective shell, but events like this are always gut-wrenching.

I don't believe I will ever understand why some parents feel entitled to treat teachers so disrespectfully. We are living, breathing human beings just trying to do our best to treat students with fairness, dignity, and respect. The nature of our job requires us to be attuned to the fragility of the human psyche. Because the "calling" is at the root of who we are, rude, disrespectful parents can cut us to the core. Denigrating us as teachers is synonymous with denigrating us as individuals.

I can't count the number of sleepless nights I have endured after a parent has verbally assaulted me. It took me years to realize that, by engaging in this kind of behavior, parents are able to "get it off their chest" and usually forget about it. But the teacher is left with a sick-to-your-stomach feeling that is extremely difficult to shake. In addition, he or she is basically expected to "take it on the chin." Anything approaching an in-kind response can result in administrative reprimand.

Unfortunately, these encounters can cause resentment and have a devastating effect on a teacher's general spirit and overall approach to the job. However, it is essential to remember that, when you harbor deep-seated anger towards *any* individual, who is the only person being adversely affected? It's certainly not the parent who is more than satisfied with having "vented." The fact is, you are only hurting yourself. I have found the following expression to be incredibly helpful in these situations:

Harboring anger or resentment towards another person is like setting yourself on fire and hoping the smoke will bother them.

A child from another state moved into one of my classes early last year. It takes a while to discover the strengths and weaknesses of a new student and evaluate the level of proficiency they had acquired at their previous school. Oftentimes, their transcript will show, or they will personally claim, to have covered material about which they clearly have no understanding. Because the teacher is aware of the trauma that can result from a move to a new school, he or she basically "walks on eggshells" while trying to assess the student's capabilities.

Thankfully, this new girl seemed to acclimate quite well. She made friends and appeared to have a good grasp of appropriate grade level concepts. Although she was doing fine, I had the sense that she wasn't reaching her full potential. My efforts to gently challenge her with more difficult material were unsuccessful. She did the required work quite adequately and showed steady progress, but nothing more.

In December, I got a phone call from her father requesting a conference. On the phone he wouldn't give a hint as to his concerns, which caused me a bit of angst as the meeting approached. Not unexpectedly, he came in with both barrels loaded. "Since September," he said, "my daughter has felt like she is not being allowed to progress fast enough." My attempt to explain my repeated efforts to address this exact issue fell on deaf ears. When I tried to move the conversation towards what we should start doing to improve the situation, he stated, "It's too late to do anything now, she's too turned off." My immediate inquiry as to why he didn't come to see me earlier in the year rendered no response.

Things quickly went from bad to worse as he tried to shift all blame towards me. He neither acknowledged nor accepted any responsibility for not rectifying the situation back in September and, as he became increasingly agitated and caustic, my years of experience helped me to expediently conclude the meeting. While it would have been so satisfying to simply say "bad parenting" right to his face, I actually began to think about how helpless a novice teacher would have felt when exposed to this hostility. I so much want to say to these types of parents: "If behaving so uncivilly and spouting such poison makes you feel better as a human being, then I'm glad to have been of service."

Many parents with two or more children understand that, despite all of the same environmental factors, siblings can often be total opposites. The hard working, conscientious, responsible child is offset by one who exhibits none of these attributes. Unfortunately, because this parental understanding does not seem to extend to the school environment, some of my most shocking instances of getting blind-sided have come from working with siblings.

My first experience of this type occurred with the parents of a highly achieving, very successful first child, who were effusively supportive. Because it is usually the unhappy parent you hear from regularly, it was wonderful to experience such enthusiasm. Then, just two years later, along came the polar opposite sibling and virtually overnight I became the world's worst teacher. Their attitude toward me became one of total disparagement. Here you are the same, hopefully even better teacher, actually looking forward to having another child of these wonderful parents, now getting denigrated so unexpectedly. The consummate shock and dismay is impossible to describe.

It can also be equally disillusioning when it goes the other way. If the first child was the non-achiever, and the parents were outspoken, letter-writing critics, you understandably have trepidation at the thought of having another of their children. While it is certainly a relief when, in the eyes of these parents, you have suddenly become a skilled purveyor of knowledge, it is incomprehensible that they think their "change of heart" fixes everything. Even when I have openly suggested that it would work wonders if they expressed this newfound enthusiasm to the very administrators to whom they were previously complaining, *never once* has a parent made the effort. Accordingly, the administration has no knowledge of this turnaround, and telling them yourself simply doesn't carry the same weight. It is so sad how the negative gets shouted from the rooftops while the positive is held so close to the cuff.

I guess I should be satisfied that at least the parents expressed their changed feelings to me.

Over the years I have found it necessary to hang-up on abusive parents three times. In each case, when the parent became overly agitated, I calmly stated, "I'm concerned about the direction and tone this conversation is taking—perhaps we should continue at a later time." Surprisingly, this statement seemed to be like pouring gasoline on a fire. In all three instances the verbal abuse reached the point that I needed to state multiple times: "I'm going to have to hang up now," and finally follow-through. The last time, which occurred about five years ago, I immediately informed the principal so she would be prepared if the parent called. To my astonishment, she began to suggest better ways I could have handled the situation, which basically amounted to my lying down and taking whatever the parent was dishing out for as long as the parent desired. At that moment, I realized why the parents had so little respect for her.

It is a fact of life that the only way to effectively deal with bullies is to stand up to them. Because these individuals always suffer from low self-esteem and extreme cowardice, I have never experienced an instance when the bully hasn't backed off, never to disrespect me again—as was the case with this parent. Actually, as time went on and he became more aware of my skills as a teacher, he did a complete about-face, which resulted in a wonderfully complimentary encounter at a year-end event. I am convinced that the foundation was laid with the respect I demanded during that initial phone conversation. Nonetheless, it is so exhausting to have to prove yourself to these types of parents year after year.

During my childhood, I was ever fortunate to have teachers with whom I developed the type of close mentoring relationship that is so essential in the lives of young people. One was with my extraordinary sixth grade teacher with whom I was doubly blessed to develop a lifelong friendship.

Very early in my teaching career he shared a wonderful piece of advice for dealing with belligerent parents who threaten to call the superintendent. My friend's suggestion was to reply, "Here, let me give you his number." Make no mistake, this requires an abundance of confidence and is, therefore, very difficult for a novice teacher to employ. But, parents who engage in this behavior are only trying to intimidate you, and want to hear the panic in your voice when you beg them not to make the call. It stops these parents dead in their tracks to discover that their bullying subterfuge is not working. I am delighted to say that each time I have employed this tactic, no parent has ever followed through with the threat.

At the beginning of every school year there is an "open house" night when parents come to school, follow their child's class schedule, meet the teachers, and hear brief overviews about what goes on in each subject. Because I've been doing these for a number of years, I have developed a very pleasant presentation that offers the necessary information in an enjoyably lighthearted manner. It is so disconcerting to stand in front of 30 or more smiling, laughing parents while two or three sit there looking miserable. There is no question that it requires a diligent effort to approach life, with all of its attendant trials and tribulations, in a positive, well-adjusted manner. On the contrary, being miserable and infecting everyone and everything around you with the same attitude is relatively easy. I know it sounds terribly cliché but, because the only person we can change is ourselves, by doing this, each one of us could eventually change everything. Wouldn't it be wonderful if we could at least start with parental interactions with teachers.

17. The Most Important Job in the World

Be grateful if you are one of the few American families that bear some resemblance to the perfect Norman Rockwell ideal; where mom, dad, and kids all live together in one harmonious unit; where everyone understands and fulfills his/her role in a nurturing atmosphere of mutual respect and selflessness. Homes where there is no alcohol or drug abuse; no physical, mental, or verbal abuse; where problems are resolved without yelling, screaming, fighting, or the launching of airborne projectiles. Homes where there is sufficient income, adequate food and clothing, and nominal material amenities. Households in which parents support instead of undermine teachers, coaches, referees, and other authority figures.

Unfortunately, the divorce rate continues to skyrocket, broken homes abound, and alcohol/drug abuse continues to rise *across* socioeconomic lines. While awareness of physical abuse has improved in recent years, emotional abuse continues to spiral. Family issues may be further exacerbated by the economic necessity for both parents to work or, in the case of single parent homes, where one parent works two or three jobs.

There is an inextricable correlation between good teaching and good parenting. However, whereas teachers undergo years of training and preparation to get certified, there are no such requirements for parenting. The mere act of procreation is all that's necessary. Ultimately, parents are left to "on the job training," with nothing to emulate except personal experience: their own parents, extended family, or possibly parents of a friend. Can you imagine what would happen if we certified teachers based only on their willingness to replicate whatever their teachers had done while they were in school?

Thus comes the inherent problem in parenting: One is basically left to "winging it" for the duration. There is no question that parents want to do everything possible to ensure success for their children. But, considering that teachers have a set curriculum to follow, what guidelines exist for parents? For the most important job in the world, there is no training or certification. Therefore, wouldn't it be in the best interest of their children for parents to work cooperatively and respectfully with highly trained teachers?

Some parents are fortunate enough to have had good parents themselves, or extended family and friends to call on for help and guidance—to share issues, ideas, and solutions. But what about the throngs who don't? I know people whose solution to any problem is to simply do the exact opposite of whatever their parents did. As the product of a family that took all of the "fun" out of dysfunctional, I must continually be vigilant to identify and reprogram instinctive actions and reactions that are ingrained in me.

I recall attending childbirth classes prior to our son being born. Typical of many organized educational programs, it took six weeks to accomplish what could have been done in one class. Still, it made me think: What if there were meaningful, ongoing parenting classes available to everyone without any fear of stigmatization? Not by court order or as part of some rehabilitation program, but open to all. A place where one could learn basic parenting skills, ask questions, receive information, concepts, and ideas in a safe, caring environment; free from fear of ridicule or repercussion. If we developed continuing evening education as an extension of free public schooling, a program of study in parenting would be of extraordinary benefit, not only to individual families, but to the success of public education as a whole and the stability of society at large.

Earnest parents who attempt to navigate the self-help section of a library or bookstore are barraged with mountains of information and opinions which are often contradictory. Imagine a course of study with the express purpose of helping parents to set a course of action grounded in solid, tried-and-true pedagogy. Due to the simple fact that the fundamentals of good parenting are identical to those of good teaching, almost any veteran teacher could successfully conduct such a program. Because successful human interaction at any level has trust at its fundamental core, nurturing child development through mutual respect, clearly defined boundaries of expectation, consistency, fairness, honesty, and integrity, is grounded in the creation of a climate of trust. The balanced application of all these elements is what makes parenting the most difficult task one can undertake.

The greatest failures I have witnessed occur when parents try to become their child's friend and ally, instead of the authority figure every child so desperately needs. Children need parents, not buddies. This ill-conceived style of parenting results in general disrespect for authority. It basically entails siding with the child at every opportunity when, in fact, the exact opposite response is required. E-mail technology has provided irrefutable evidence of this phenomenon. The teacher writes to the parent with a detailed account of what occurred during a particular incident—cheating on a test, inappropriate verbal or physical behavior, etc.—and the parent writes back with the child's "victimized" version. This usually includes instructions on how the teacher could have better handled the situation; which generally amounts to letting the kid do whatever he or she wants and placing the blame on all of the other students and/or the teacher.

A marvelous, highly respected veteran teacher once shared the key to resolving issues with these types of parents. She simply said to them: "You believe half of what your child says about me, and I'll believe half of what he says about you." This always causes "buddy" parents extreme consternation. The very thought of their kid saying anything derogatory about them is simply inconceivable! What they don't understand is, by abandoning their proper role, they have only increased the chances that their child is telling tales out of total disrespect for them. In addition, children learn to play parents against the teacher in a manner shockingly similar to how children of divorce play one parent against the other. The willingness of parents to believe the worst about the teacher is most dismaying. It doesn't serve their child in the least!

Isn't it ironic that, even from the youngest age, children will continually test authority because they have no rational understanding that they need limits? Picture a child in an enclosed backyard. He will kick, dig under, or try to climb the very fence that provides him safety and security. Similarly, a child will continually "push the envelope" of parental authority. Parents need to understand that every time they disrespect a figure of authority, in their child's eyes, they are ultimately undermining themselves. These children learn by example that it's okay to disrespect *all* authority. I cannot recount the number of times I have seen students openly ridicule their own parents. It seems the more "buddy-like" the parent, the worse the disrespect.

One of my favorite lines from "buddy" parents is the excuse: "He's *only* ___ years old." This is usually applied when the child has shown a complete lack of responsibility. For example, if you are calling because the child continually forgets his homework, the parent will say, "He's only 11 years old." The question I always want to ask is: "When is his age no longer *only?* 12? 14? 16?"

If parents could be taught anything from the outset, it would be this fundamental truth: Your child will adore you until the onset of puberty, at which point you will commence upon a steady decline towards complete mental incapacity. This affliction generally reaches its low point by the time your kid is 15-16 and tends to last into their early 20's, when your dementia is typically cured. The key to parenting a high school student can perhaps be best summarized as follows:

You are absolutely indispensable at one moment and a complete embarrassment the next.

Parents who have fostered an atmosphere of trust and respect find this period, while still extremely stressful and challenging, vastly more survivable than "buddy" parents, for whom any semblance of an appropriate parent/child relationship falls into complete shambles.

This is especially true for the "he's only___" parents. If you suddenly decide at age 15 that your child is no longer "only," it's way too late. Every stage of childhood should have defined expectations that are appropriate to that age level. This is certainly how standards are applied in school. If you are parenting correctly, you will never find yourself saying, "He's only ___."

It is in the extraordinary phenomenon of hovering "helicopter" parenting that the issue of "he's only" never ends. These are the parents who continue to bring forgotten homework into school for juniors and seniors in high school and end up giving their child a wake-up call every morning at college. Most interesting is the extraordinary effect pampered children like this are having on the workplace. When mom is coming in to meet with the boss about why her 26 year old isn't getting a certain promotion and absolutely none of the kid's peers see anything abnormal in this behavior, we are heading into frightening times indeed.

On the other end of the spectrum is an equally disturbing situation that became glaringly apparent when I was teaching high school. At the exact time when children need the stability of appropriate parental guidance more than ever, too many parents opt for abandonment. This is especially true of 'buddy" parents who tend to lose any sense of authority and are more than happy to turn parenting right over to the school. Real parents—those who have established lines of communication over years of meticulously building trust and respect—can still offer nurturing advice and direction in the face of all odds. Needless to say, it is extremely difficult to strike the appropriate balance between "helicoptering" and abandonment.

It was due to years of training and practical application with students that my wife and I were able to successfully apply balanced parenting to our own child. By no means am I implying that all teachers make great parents. Many times the best of teachers are unable to transition to effective parenting. Interestingly, these same teachers would probably be able to teach an excellent parenting class, because knowing *what* to do and actually doing it are not necessarily the same things. Losing weight is a perfect example. We all know that we need to eat healthy foods and exercise, but how many of us really do it? For my wife and me, coming home from an exhausting day of dealing with everyone else's kids, it was everything we could do to remember that the most important child on which to expend our energy was our own.

While it is inconceivable that parents don't receive even a modicum of practical child-rearing technique, there is hope in the fact that some high schools are beginning to offer "life skills" within the framework of existing coursework. Teachers are being asked to do more in terms of teaching these basic skills because less is being learned at home. However, rather than attempting to squeeze this into existing classes, schools should make instruction in life skills and parenting an integral part of the curriculum for high school and evening education programs. At the same time, we must start providing all students basic instruction in finances: how to manage credit/debit cards, use a checking account, pay household bills, deal with state and federal IRS requirements and, perhaps most importantly, introduce the fundamentals of sound financial planning. A cursory glance at the unmanageable rate of personal debt in our country clearly demonstrates the dire need for instruction of this nature. Classes like this might also help students to fully realize the importance of education to a sound financial future.

Perhaps you may recall the situation in Gloucester, Massachusetts that was splashed all over the national headlines during the late spring of 2008. Apparently, a group of teenage girls made a "pact" to get pregnant and raise their babies together. Subsequently, a raucous debate ensued about access to birth control, too much accommodation by the school for pregnant teens/teenage parents, hard economic times, children growing up purposeless, the influence of movies such as "Juno" and "Knocked Up"—the finger pointing was endless. My personal favorite concerned the "noble choice" these girls were making not to have abortions. *Of course* they weren't going to have abortions; they were *trying* to get pregnant!

This situation fits perfectly into my mantra for teaching high school: "Saving Students from Themselves." These kids are *children!* They think like children: "Won't it be fun to have a cute little baby?" It's so easy for kids to think a baby will bring unconditional love, happiness, meaning, and fulfillment to their angst-ridden lives. They're teenagers! Their lives are *supposed* to be filled with angst, confusion, and uncertainty. They aren't thinking about a lifetime of child rearing and all of the sacrifices it entails!

This brings me to a major issue I never once heard discussed: Where were the parents of these high school children? Somehow, either tacitly or directly, these kids had to be given the impression that their parents would support them in this endeavor. I saw the pictures of these adolescents walking their babies in $200 strollers. You can't tell me that, with the number of girls involved in the "pact" and the number of boys who had to be involved in getting these girls pregnant, *not one* parent caught wind of it? That kind of extreme parental disconnection is inconceivable!

When my son was a freshman in high school he tried to arrange a party at our house when he knew my wife and I were planning to be away at a conference. Before even six of his friends were contacted, we got the word from another parent. And this was for a single clandestine party, not a massive pregnancy pact! Truthfully, if the parents of all of the kids involved in this pregnancy ring were that out of the loop, adult parenting classes should be instituted in Gloucester immediately. Similarly, if they approved of this activity, immediate parenting classes should be mandatory. *Sixteen year olds should not be having babies!!!*

Because we all know this Gloucester incident is far from isolated, considering the absence of real "parenting" from the lives of so many high school children, the need for schools to institute comprehensive life skills education is urgent. Otherwise, I'm glad I will be long retired before this wave of "children of children" hits the schools.

18. NCLB

I was recently watching an interview with Margaret Spellings, former U.S. Secretary of Education, during which she espoused the wonders of the "No Child Left Behind" (NCLB) Act. In essence, this legislation evaluates student progress based on the results of standardized testing. Individual schools or school systems that don't meet certain arbitrary test score minimums or show significant progress towards those minimums are subject to various sanctions. These can include withdrawing federal funding, allowing parents to move their kids to other schools, or providing parents with funds to hire private tutors. Wouldn't it be logical, if a school is dealing with huge numbers of non-English speaking children, or students suffering from traumatic home environments, or gang violence, or large populations of students with special needs/disabilities, to give them *more* help instead of taking it away?

Because volumes have already been written about the consequences of NCLB, and I have previously discussed the topic of evaluation techniques that are narrow in scope, I want to focus on a few *parodies* of the "No Child" legislation that clearly underscore its huge deficiencies. In theory and on paper, the NCLB legislation may seem like a great idea, but applying it to living, breathing human beings is a whole different matter.

Perhaps the impact of NCLB on education can best be understood by applying its requirements to the game of football:[16]

1. All teams must make the state playoffs and all MUST win the championship. If a team does not win the

championship, they will be placed on probation until they are the champions, and coaches will be held accountable. If, after two years, they still have not achieved this goal, their footballs and equipment will be taken away *until* they win the championship.

2. All kids will be expected to have the same football skills at the same time even if they do not have the same conditions or opportunities to practice on their own. NO exceptions will be made for a lack of interest in football, or a desire to perform athletically, or the genetic abilities or disabilities of the players or their parents.

All kids will play football at a proficient level

3. Talented players will be asked to work out on their own without instruction, because the coaches will be using all of their instructional time with the students who aren't interested in football, have limited athletic ability, or whose parents don't like football.

4. Games will be played year round, but statistics will only be kept in the 4th, 8[th,] and 11th game. Every school is expected to have the same level of talent and all teams will reach the same level of proficiency.

IF NO CHILD GETS AHEAD, THEN NO CHILD GETS LEFT BEHIND

One of the essential arguments against NCLB's heavy reliance on standardized testing, concerns the narrowness of scope. These tests do little to evaluate a child's overall mental, physical, or emotional development, nor the ability to apply skills to actual life circumstances. Not long ago, I read a different NCLB parody called "No Cow Left Behind"[17] that humorously applied each of the basic tenets of this legislation to dairy farming. This parody points out the absurdity of arbitrarily testing cows in a manner that may not have any relation to the cow's ability to produce milk. Identical to the NCLB provisions that allow the state to take over schools that continue to fall below standards, if enough cows on a given farm didn't meet arbitrary "testing" requirements, the state might come in and take over the farm. In addition, it would be necessary to place a "highly qualified" farmer in each barn. Regardless of how many years one has been farming, every farmer would need to pass all of the legislative testing mandates to become certified. Also, disgruntled cows that weren't performing up to standards would have the option to move to another farm. Finally, all of the costs involved in complying with the "No Cow" legislation would be borne by the farmer, regardless of whether or not these expenses forced him into bankruptcy.

The most poignant parody I have encountered, applies the provisions of NCLB to a dentist in charge of school age children in a rural area plagued with a high incidence of tooth decay and generally poor dental hygiene.[18] Under the tenets of NCLB, the dentist would be held completely responsible for decreasing the number of cavities and increasing the overall oral health of all the children in his jurisdiction. Applying even a modicum of thought one will quickly realize that, regardless of the qualifications, training, or diligence of the dentist, success in meeting increased standards in dental health depends mostly on what happens at home. In addition to insufficient brushing, flossing, etc., if the child is eating inordinate amounts of candy and similar high sugar content foods, no matter how outstanding the quality of care provided by the dentist, oral health will not improve. Even though he or she may be offering students the most comprehensive instruction in proper dental care, a lack of follow-through at home will render most of the dentist's efforts wholly ineffective.

Thus we come to the greatest deficiency in the entire "No Child Left Behind" legislation: The total absence of parental accountability! All requirements for success lie entirely with the school. If, by following the provisions of NCLB, the home is to be completely exonerated from any responsibility for the success of a child's education, we might as well start transforming all public educational institutions into boarding schools.

19. Conflict Resolution

Mark, our school health teacher, was showing a DVD to his sixth grade classes dealing with the topic of "bullying." The segment on the dangers of name-calling became quite detailed, using specific examples which included the term "douche-bag." In the ensuing discussion, Mark was very clear that students were never to use these terms against each other, but also emphasized that they were *not* to be repeated outside of his class, period. As I'm sure you can imagine, one of our more sterling citizens started saying "douche-bag" in math class and immediately defended himself with: "We were taught that in health."

At the end of class, the math teacher went to the *office* to complain; never so much as giving a thought to discussing it directly with Mark. What made this especially ironic was that this particular math teacher was a champion complainer about parents who go directly to the administration with concerns rather than addressing them with the teacher first. Right on cue, the principal went to Mark to discuss the matter and to let him know how to better teach the lesson and deal with these sensitive topics, all of which, Mark pointed out, he was already doing plus a few more. This, of course, only caused the principal to continue with further admonitions to be more diligent, careful, sensitive, etc. Apparently, Mark had not yet learned that the most expedient way to deal with administrators in these kinds of situations is to silently defer to their wisdom. Attempting to have meaningful discourse will only exacerbate the situation.

Regardless, in the course of all this the principal was unaware that she had inadvertently revealed which teacher had made the complaint. As a forthright person, Mark went to the math teacher, explained what had really happened and tried to point out how much hassle would have been avoided if she had just come to talk to him first. The math teacher did a soft-shoe that would have made Mr. Bojangles proud and, when they parted, immediately went down to the office to find out why she was "outed." Not surprisingly, the principal claimed innocence and round and round it went. The upshot? Seeds of doubt were not only sown; but fertilized, watered, tilled, weeded, pruned, and harvested. Incidentally, it turns-out Mark was a very quick study—eventually coining the phrase "Nod 'n Do."

The point of this story concerns the inordinate amount of time we expend in education on the issue of Conflict Resolution. Naturally, this necessitates the usual "looks good on paper" teacher training workshops and excessive amounts of class time discussing it with the students. Ultimately, because all of this conflict resolution revolves exclusively around adult intervention, the children learn absolutely nothing about the most important element: *Learning to work it out themselves!* As a result, they are always running to the teacher: "Johnny called me a name," "They won't let me play in that game," "Sally is being mean." Then these kids suddenly find themselves in their twenties and "on the job" with absolutely no functional conflict resolution skills.

During the 1990s, I befriended the parent of a student that I had taught in my community-based program. One of our favorite topics of conversation concerned the demise of "garage bands" and all of the life skills they developed. Being of a certain age, we reminisced about the fact that when we were kids in the late 60s and early 70s, garage bands were everywhere. In my own extended neighborhood we had three or four operating at any given time.

The band I helped organize underwent many metamorphoses from seventh grade through high school:

personnel, styles of music, band names, etc. But, the most important result was the extraordinary experience that a bunch of teenagers had trying to put this together on their own. We had to decide who was in or out, schedule rehearsal times, pick which songs to do, and then try to rehearse them. Just imagine the issues that arose when each kid had a different idea of what constituted "doing it correctly!" Then we had the business end of it: trying to get chances to perform, deciding how much to get paid, was the gig any good? We had to work all of this out on our own.

Naturally, our parents purchased the equipment, drove us around, and put up with our rehearsals but, if you wanted to exemplify the true essence of conflict resolution, our garage band was it. We argued, got mad, broke up, got back together, let people in, kicked people out, and had *plenty* of "talk it out" smoking breaks. We chose a leader, bagged the leader, discussed chord changes, vocals, and decided about solos: which instruments, how many, and how long. The decisions were endless. The only parental involvement I can remember occurred when we accidentally swore into the microphones. The resulting degree of parental intercession was in direct proportion to the word choices.

In short, it was a kid-run operation. We worked it out on our own. Nobody's "mommy" ever called another parent to defend their little darling. Honestly, the very thought of involving a parent in that way was absolutely mortifying! Because our garage band experience was completely trial and error, the interpersonal skills we learned were without measure; something that today's generation of "play date" children can only imagine.

The good news is that during the past few years I have seen an increase of young people attempting to form their own bands. In this day and age I truly marvel at students who go through all of the work to learn how to play an instrument and try to put a band together. Especially when there is "Guitar

Hero" and "Rock Band" that make you sound like you are performing with Deep Purple at the flick of a switch. Don't misunderstand, I find this technology to be a blast. It's a great group activity for family gatherings that keeps the children occupied for hours. But, conflict resolution? It seems to be non-existent. If you make too many mistakes, the machine shuts you off automatically! There are no discussions and there is nothing to work out. The only decision-making involves sharing turns or picking the songs—no other resolutions are needed. And suddenly these kids are supposed to participate in group "cooperative learning" activities at school; solving problems, discussing issues, and creatively initiating and completing projects; pursuits that use every conflict resolution skill in the book. But, without the video game directing the show, the only alternative is the teacher.

Essentially, the more we talk about teaching conflict resolution, the more we seem to engage in policies that circumvent the desired outcome. The same is true for the parallel issue of "bullying." Increased adult intercession has done little to alleviate the matter. Although we are addressing this topic regularly, because we remove any opportunity for kids to "work it out themselves," the problem does not diminish proportionally. Then, what will happen when these students become adults in the workplace? We might wish to pretend otherwise, but the entire corporate structure is enmeshed in the practice of bullying. Whether it is employees trying to get ahead by using any and all possible means to outshine colleagues, or bosses using intimidation tactics on workers, the intrigue is ongoing. Successful human interaction requires individuals to be their own advocates. How is the continual intervention of parents, teachers, and administrators helping children to develop these essential life skills?

This incessant need for authoritative interference brings me to one of the most significant and disturbing observations of my adult life: The demise of the sandlot baseball game. In spite of the fact that my wife and I live in a suburban neighborhood full of children of every age, the first experience my son had playing a sport with other kids was at the age of six in the town-wide soccer program. In what seemed like an instant, there were coaches, assistant coaches, scheduled practices and games officiated by paid referees. The only positive element I could see was that girls and boys played together on the same team.

It took just one match for me to discover the root cause of much that ails our society. First there were the parents; screaming on the sidelines as if the outcome would decide the fate of all mankind. Fathers (and mothers I was astounded to see) yelling orders, admonitions and downright berating the kids, often in complete opposition to the instructions the coaches were trying to give. It was a feeding frenzy that increased in urgency as the game progressed.

Secondly, there were the coaches. Although they were often the parents of the players, I always found it wonderful that they were willing to undertake this awesome responsibility. However, the only training one needed to be a coach was saying "yes, I'll do it;" something I found myself doing on several occasions during my son's youth. The laxity in the screening process was revealed to me when my first assignment involved assisting a coach who smoked cigarettes during practices. Talk about a role model!

Because the most important child to any parent is their own, the coaches, completely contrary to the league rules which state that all participants must play equally, put their own kids in 90% of the time, regardless of their ability. In all fairness, I have to admit that the children of the coaches were usually pretty good, otherwise the father wouldn't have volunteered to coach in the first place. I mean he certainly couldn't have his future David Beckham being coached by any old parent.

The games involving the youngest children were refereed by seventh, eighth, and ninth graders who got paid a whopping $15 per match. To a kid this seemed like a pretty good deal, so my son gave it a try when he was in eighth grade. He officiated exactly four games before he said, "F--- this! No way is this worth the hassle!" My wife and I were really proud of him for lasting four games (verbiage was another thing). We had learned back when he was six years old that kid-refs received extraordinary abuse from screaming, bitching, and complaining parents, coaches, and (by example) players.

However, it was during the third game of that first year that I witnessed a stomach churning event. At the conclusion of the game, the coach of the opposing team started to rip into the 13 year old girl who was refereeing. Apparently this concerned some earth-shattering call she had made during this all-important match that involved a bunch of six year olds! We had just watched 30 minutes (two 15 minute periods) of youngsters moving as a pack, clustered around the ball, with no idea that they were supposed to spread out, despite coaches and parents screaming. And for that, this sweet thing was standing there getting verbally pummeled!

Unbeknownst to this coach, I had been videotaping the entire episode; watching as he worked himself into a lather. Just as I was about to intercede, he saw me with the camcorder and started to come toward me menacingly. Thankfully, he realized what he had done and stopped in his tracks. While lowering the camera I said, "That's right, the whole thing is on tape!" As he turned and walked away, I remember trying to say some words of comfort to the poor girl, who was obviously crushed. I'm sure she still shudders to this day every time this incident crosses her mind. It goes without saying that I never saw her referee again.

This is where the lifelong belligerence towards authority begins. Children learn from what they see and experience. Simply turn on the TV to *any* sporting event and watch the coaches beleaguer the referees. In the broadest sense, this behavior could be considered a natural reaction to the total dependence on authority figures that now permeates childhood—a rebellion against that which controls your life. By example, kids learn how to rail against referees starting at the youngest age. Is it any wonder that this has extended to authority in general?

When I was a kid, my house had a huge front yard where we played the most incredible neighborhood baseball games imaginable. Mind you, there was a rock garden between where the pitcher stood and first base, which, similar to second base, was a stone sticking out of the ground. Third base was scratched out in the middle of our long gravel driveway. There was a huge prickly rose bush in the middle of left field, and shrubs and more rocks in center and right—in other words: Perfect! As a precursor to the garage bands to come, life skills were gleaned on our little field. Was it a ball or a strike, fair or foul, were you out at first or not? Although many games ended due to lost balls, more often than not, a disputed call escalated to the point that one or more players would storm off in a huff, only to return again the next day.

No adults were ever involved except when the language got too colorful (I find it interesting that foul language seemed to be the only trigger for parental interference). We played these games for years, until we grew to the point that balls were flying across the street, hitting neighboring houses, and breaking windows. As a result, the games had to be moved to the local elementary school. Although this was about a mile away, it was never an issue because we rode our bikes *everywhere*! Over time the games became less frequent, but I still remember a few, even during my senior year in high school.

This brings me back to my son. Here he is growing up in this perfect little "Leave it to Beaver" neighborhood, and it just so happens that a small manufacturing firm on the next street has a beautiful, perfectly groomed baseball field complete with a backstop, pitcher's mound, base paths, and an outfield fence. And you know what? Not once, in all of his childhood years, did my son and the neighborhood kids put together a game over there. And year after year I ask my students in school, but the answer is always the same: Never! "That's what Little League is for!"

So, there you have it. A game can't be played unless it's organized by adults with official coaches, game schedules, and referees. Yet, we wonder why we have so much trouble teaching conflict resolution skills in school and why they are so hard to develop in adulthood; whether in the workplace, marriage, or any aspect of life.

I was recently perusing some brochures for children's summer camps and was intrigued by the repeated emphasis on learning autonomy and self-reliance through independent problem-solving. Most require that all cell phones, Blackberry's, etc., be left at home to discourage parental intercession. This brings me to the following familiar quip that I have adapted accordingly:

> People over 40 should be dead.[19] According to today's bureaucratic and parental regulations, those of us who were kids in the 50s and 60s probably shouldn't have survived.
>
> As children we rode our bikes everywhere!—without any need to "suit-up" as if we were about to play goalie for a professional ice hockey team.
>
> We rode in cars without airbags or seat belts, in the space under the rear window or in the "flip-up" seat that faced backwards. Riding in the back of a pickup truck was a regular favorite (trailing ropes out the back was an optional pleasure).

We drank water from the garden hose and shared a soda with four friends, from one bottle, and no one died.

We would play all day with no adult supervision; no cell phones or pagers.

On rainy days we had Monopoly and Risk tournaments.

We did not have PlayStations or X-boxes; no 50-inch flat screen TV's, 400 channels on cable, or satellite dishes; no Blu-ray Discs, DVD's, or surround sound; no computers, web pages, or blogs.

We had friends! We went outside and found them. We rode our bides or walked to a friend's home and knocked on the door, or rang the bell, or just walked in and talked to them.

We spent hours building our own tree forts out of scraps, by ourselves, high up in the trees.

We fell, got cut and broke bones and teeth, and there were no lawsuits from these accidents. They were accidents. Remember accidents? No one was to blame but us.

Our actions were our own. Consequences were expected. The idea of a parent bailing us out if we broke the law was unheard of. They actually sided with the law! Imagine that!

We had freedom, failure, success, and responsibility; and we learned to deal with it all. True Conflict Resolution!

20. Let's Get Physical

A number of years ago, a marvelous colleague gave me the following statement on the importance of play:[20]

> Play is the underpinning of all learning. How can we teach writing if children aren't immersed in pretending and expressing themselves in dramatic play? Children don't learn language by merely copying a sentence from a blackboard. It is the everyday give and take role playing and conversation with their peers that develops this ability. This flow of play energy is our greatest resource as we teach basic skills. Our formalization of what children know will drop in its tracks if we do not support their play.

I find the following quotes from the 1973 book "The Power of Play" by Frank and Theresa Caplan to be particularly meaningful:

- "Play is a voluntary activity which permits freedom of action, diversion from routine, and an imaginary world to master."

- "Play is the most dynamic childhood learning method."

- "Self-powered play embodies a high degree of motivation and achievement. It is a happy activity which begins in delight and ends in wisdom. Play is an autonomous pursuit through which each child assimilates the outside world."

- "Feelings of autonomy and competency help a child function effectively as an active agent in the environment, not merely a reacting one."

The advent of "play dates" and the proliferation of organized sports leagues, coupled with all of the safety fears permeating suburbia, have caused for the virtual disappearance of free outdoor play time at home. Therefore, it is left to school recess to fill the void. It has become the last holdout for kids to hone the true cooperative learning and conflict resolution skills that come from playing together independent of adult coordination! But what have we done in the name of "No Child Left Behind" and "Time on Task?" We're eliminating this essential part of childhood development from the school day too! In the staggering number of schools that have eliminated recess, a few have attempted to replace it with increased time in physical education class (unless your school is one of those that have eliminated *this* also). From a health, exercise and skill development standpoint, more PE is certainly advantageous, but in terms of immersion in the important life skills acquired on the playground, there is no comparison.

The most wonderful development I observed during my years of elementary school recess supervision was the complete transformation in the behaviors of female students. During the 1970s and early 1980s, girls would basically stand in groups and talk while the boys organized and played the games. During the 1980s, however, the gradual shift towards active female participation was a marvel to behold. By the mid 1990s the circle chats had virtually disappeared. I'm convinced that this metamorphosis was a direct outcome of the growth in female athletics that resulted from the Title IX legislation of 1972. In addition, organized youth sports leagues deserve credit for promoting equal participation for boys and girls, especially by allowing them to play on the same teams in their early years.

Because my school is one of those that inexplicably cut recess for fifth and sixth graders, the physical education teachers, in a marginal attempt to replicate the lost opportunity for unrestricted play, started to offer the kids occasional "free play" classes. They made sure ample playground equipment was provided and, in the absence of a structured lesson plan, the students were told to organize their own games and activities. The number of children who simply could not function in such an environment was astounding! The more they asked "What should we do?" the more the PE teachers understood the extraordinary need for this type of unstructured time. Unfortunately, some of the students went home and complained to their parents that they weren't doing anything in gym class and the parents called the principal. Concerned about the perception that the PE teachers were slacking-off, the principal suspended "free play."

I honed my skills at recess supervision very early in my teaching career: Set the parameters for safety, be vigilant that they are being followed, and *Let it happen*! Fortunately, in the late 70s and early 80's, kids were more self-directed, so that very little intercession was required. I learned from a wonderful fellow teacher how to foster self-reliance in children while, at the same time, making your own situation a breeze. When they came over to say "Johnny used a swear," or "Bobby won't give us the ball back," Glen would simply say, "Tell him I said to knock it off!" And away they would go, completely satisfied with this astounding piece of adult wisdom.

Over the years, it was incredible to watch the younger teachers, versed in all the various intervention techniques, make their lives miserable by inserting themselves into every possible situation. If a child came over and said "Johnny used a swear," before I could even take the breath to utter "Tell him I said to knock it off," the other teacher would respond "Tell him to come over here!" So, back come the kids with Johnny and it starts: "I did not," "Did to," "Did not" . . . and the teacher gets all tied-up in a no-win situation, vainly attempting to apply all of the approved conflict resolution techniques.

I spent years trying to demonstrate the Glen method, but to no avail. It became apparent that, from the younger teachers' viewpoint, I simply lacked the proper knowledge of current trends. So I quickly learned to back away as soon as I heard "Tell him to come over here," opting to view the drama from afar. No matter how many times younger teachers watched my system work, it was so counterintuitive to their ingrained skill-set that I'm sure they felt I was aloof or unsupportive when I refused to jump into the unnecessary confrontations they continually created.

Many times these misguided interventions would end up in the principal's office. This, of course, creates a big hassle for the principal, who eventually realizes: "Gee, having Jane on recess duty is a huge problem for me, while having Hank out there is a breeze." And thus comes one of the saddest truths of the teaching profession: If you show yourself to be adept at handling the difficult tasks and difficult kids, you are guaranteed that your job assignment will consist of nothing else. The teacher who is worth his or her weight in gold and can handle the tougher children, tasks, and job assignments, is doomed to the same year after year. Conversely, teachers who show that they have trouble managing the "challenging" students get rewarded with nothing but "good" kids.

This is where the entire concept of "merit pay" collapses. According to conventional wisdom, the teacher with the highest achieving students receives the extra pay when, in fact, it should be the exact opposite. The teacher who demonstrates the superlative ability to control, instruct, and connect with the most difficult and challenging students, should be rewarded accordingly. We affectionately call this "combat pay."

A few years back I taught with a fourth grade teacher whose outstanding control skills resulted in her being regularly rewarded with students for whom the term "difficult" would be an understatement. I will never forget doing a presentation with one of my classes that included a number of children from her room. At the conclusion, Louise approached me and said, "You deserve a place in heaven for getting results like that out of a group of convicts." While that memory always makes me laugh, I also cherish it as a priceless moment of recognition from someone who really understood.

Amazingly, when those students graduated from high school they placed their fourth grade class picture in the high school yearbook. We all groaned at the memory of what those kids had put us through, yet rejoiced at the touching tribute they had paid to Louise. The fact that, after all that time, those graduates remembered what an integral part Louise had played in their lives was truly miraculous. These are the moments that provide essential sustenance in this extraordinarily misunderstood profession called teaching.

Returning to the topic of physical exercise, the past few years have seen an explosion in hand-wringing consternation over the rising childhood obesity epidemic in our country. The numerous causes include: lack of sufficient physical activity, too much junk food, and too much electronic media (computers, video games, cell phones, etc.). As an individual who regularly exercises on a NordicTrack and has a son who is an exercise physiologist, one solution seems obvious to me:

Immerse children in comprehensive cardiovascular and strength training techniques from the youngest age possible.

Studies have shown the indisputable importance of maintaining these activities throughout adulthood, including octogenarians. If participating in a regular workout routine is essential to good health and longevity, shouldn't this be a cornerstone of physical education instruction for all children?

I have read about some urban schools that, due to their proximity to commercial fitness centers, have established arrangements for regular use of the equipment by school PE classes. Having access to the equipment has been the key to teaching proper physical training techniques. Although many high schools have weight rooms for athletes who participate in school sports, oftentimes these are not *fully* equipped strength training facilities. In addition, it is very rare to find a cardiovascular component in school work-out rooms (Stairmasters, treadmills, elliptical trainers, stationary bikes, etc.), and certainly nothing that is fully accessible to all K-12 physical education classes.

In addition to proper health and nutritional instruction, any comprehensive effort to combat childhood obesity and promote lifelong physical health is going to require a significant investment in proper facilities and equipment to realign school physical education programs towards these goals. Much of this equipment can be obtained very inexpensively, or even for free, from sports clubs, hospitals, colleges, and sports teams that regularly upgrade to newer models and discard perfectly functional machines. (We actually have a beautiful recumbent bike in our family room that was being discarded in just such a manner by a hospital.)

In spite of the fact that numerous studies have shown that physical exercise and accomplishment in the classroom are inextricably linked, it is baffling how many schools have eliminated this essential component for student success. Teaching children how to maintain physical health will not only increase their productivity in school but, if it becomes an integral part of their adult lifestyle, will produce a vastly healthier American populace.

21. School Survival Skills

I recently encountered a student in the hallway during a time he was supposed to be in math class, or some such place, and immediately realized that this was getting to be a frequent occurrence. To the complete astonishment of this twelve year old, I shook his hand and said, "Griffin, I must compliment you on having developed a skill which will serve you well in your remaining school years. It appears you have perfected this wandering the halls routine—very nicely done!" As the lad stood there with a dumbfounded, deer-in-the-headlights look on his face, I finished: "However, you really must get to wherever you are supposed to be." And off he scurried in a state of complete bewilderment.

Approaching a student in this manner catches them completely off-guard because I am breaching that indelible barrier separating "teacher world" from "student world;" that place where children perfect their survival skills and constantly push boundaries, always believing that teachers could *never* understand. If I had simply ordered Griffin to get his butt to class *tout de suite*, I would have been acting within my prescribed role. But, by letting him know that I know, I blurred the line and left him momentarily rudderless in the land of "kiddom."

The next time he comes to class it is essential to pretend nothing ever happened. No mention of the incident can be made. School life must continue with boundaries firmly in place. Of course, a teacher can only do this with selected students; the ones that are quietly playing the system. Attempting to engage the loud, obnoxious, class disrupters in such an activity would be flirting with anarchy. So, the "disrupters" are left to watch these "stealth" kids get away with things they couldn't begin to approach. Unfortunately, the disrupters will never understand that it is only by means of the constant distraction they cause, that the Griffins of the world can pull this stuff off.

This is how stealth kids make it happen. They do their work, don't disrupt class and, as a result, are able to take advantage of the innumerable distractions caused by the disrupters. Sometimes a disrupter will inadvertently rat out a stealth kid when he cries out in complete frustration: "How come Griffin always gets away with it?" At this point the teacher might express some degree of interest, tempered by a consideration of who is doing the complaining. This only forces Griffin to be a little more careful for a few days until numerous other distractions consume the teacher's attention and everything goes back to normal.

To be completely honest, as a teacher I have always admired the stealth kids because, during my own school years, I erred (to put it mildly) on the side of the disrupters. Therefore, I deeply empathize with their plight because, I too, was completely incapable of understanding why I never got away with anything. The fact that I was the loudest kid in the building never crossed my mind. However, as an adult I finally got the point, and it has served me well as I developed my own teacher survival skills. I can emphatically state that the benefits of staying under the radar far outweigh any drawbacks. Being perceived by the administration as a cooperative team player virtually assures a complete lack of interference. Of course, this must be coupled with all the elements of good teaching and classroom management. You can't be sending students to the office or constantly having parents calling to complain. It's a delicate balance.

This brings me to the most incredible group of all. Originally, this group was very few in number because of the true "chutzpah" involved. However, more and more students seem to be figuring it out. These children behave exactly like the regular stealth kids with one major exception: *They don't do any work at all!* I may be divulging a huge secret but, if a student attends class and does whatever is required while they are there—takes tests, pretends to pay attention, and, most importantly *doesn't misbehave*—they can stay in school until they graduate high school. They don't have to do a lick of homework, read a book, study for a test, nada. And, they will never get kicked out and never stay back. They will be promoted from grade to grade and yes, ultimately graduate!

If you are wondering how this could be possible, the answer lies in the "self-esteem" movement which now pervades all aspects of child rearing: school, parenting, and extracurricular/community based activities. It is simply too devastating for a child to be negatively singled out. We must promote positive self-esteem above all else. Everyone is going to Harvard and we will all play basketball like Michael Jordan. Many of us remember a completely different time, when a "C" was average as were most of the kids. A handful of very bright students were going to top universities, "non-academic" students were going to "blue-collar" jobs, and the rest of us were going to state/community college or straight to the business workforce. Actually, it's *exactly* like it is today, except that we've created a massive culture of pretending it isn't—pushing kids on from grade to grade no matter what.

Back in the day, children really *did* stay back. Most were for one year and it was usually to make up for entering kindergarten at too young an age. Then there were the Murphy boys. By the time I entered elementary school their nicknames were so firmly established that hardly any of us knew their real names. Teachers, of course, dwelling in their alien world, had to call them by their real names. In fact, I understand it was quite a hoot to be in class with one of these boys when the teacher called them by their correct name and none of the kids knew who the heck they were addressing.

The oldest brother was a huge, hulking boy who eventually became a lineman for the high school football team. Everyone knew him as "Tiny." The other two brothers experienced something that would be sacrilege today. The middle brother stayed back so many times that the younger brother actually passed him in school! Thus came the nicknames "Hi-Hi" and "Dodo" (if you can't figure out which was which, perhaps you needed to join Dodo for a bit).

For those of you who are gasping in horror, Dodo did become a very successful auto mechanic and eventually owned his own garage. He also enjoyed driving stockcars. I can remember seeing him at the local track—the crowd cheering as he sped around the oval. It would be nice to say he went on to become a star on the NASCAR circuit, but I really have no idea. I'd look for his name but, like I said, only the teachers (and his mother, I suspect) knew it, and I somehow doubt he'd be listed as. . . . .

Believe me; I thoroughly understand the inappropriateness of what happened to this kid. However, now the pendulum has swung so far in the opposite direction that students truly have no practical idea where they stand in the scheme of things. I hate to break the news, but all of you are *not* going to Harvard (legally blond or not). If we honestly want to examine the high teenage suicide rate, perhaps we need to look no further than the false self-esteem culture in which these young people dwell. At the point when they finally realize they've been lied to all of their life, similar to the way most practical life/survival skills are learned, each individual is left to figure it out on their own.

It is this current self-esteem culture that is responsible for pushing students on no matter what. Remember, all a child needs to do is attend class, be respectful, participate in whatever is going on and, most importantly, not be disruptive or exhibit bad behavior. The fact that they are doing absolutely nothing—no homework, no studying, failing tests miserably–

–won't get them kicked out of school. Here are the things that will: misbehaving, chronic tardiness, skipping school, fighting, blatant disrespect, etc. In the upper grades especially, rule violations of this sort will result in detentions. And, what happens if a child doesn't attend the detentions? They get suspended! This has always been one of my favorites: If a child skips school, he or she gets detentions; if they don't go to the detentions, they get sent home to skip school. (Seriously, is this kind of stuff a standard staple of Administration 101?) But, if they aren't doing a lick of work? No problema! They can stay right there, occupy a seat, and glide along.

My introduction to this "glide-along" phenomenon occurred when I was a student in high school. One of my friends attended class, did seatwork, and took tests, but never did a lick of homework, read a book, wrote a paper, or did any assignments whatsoever. Because he was very bright, he managed to maintain what essentially amounted to a "D" average and kept being promoted. Then, in the fall of his senior year, he took the Scholastic Aptitude Test (SAT) and scored a perfect 1600 (on the "new" SAT that would be a 2400).

Suddenly this boy was a National Merit Scholar. The SAT people came to our building and held a school-wide assembly to honor him. The administration tried to say complimentary things while grappling with the issue of why this student was doing so miserably in school. Obviously, the SAT people were also aware of his low achievement but, a perfect score is a perfect score regardless of school work or grades. It was the first time a student in our school system ever scored a perfect 1600. Apparently it is pretty rare, as I've only known of two others in all my years in teaching.

Now, fast-forward to current times, factor the positive self-esteem movement with rampant grade inflation, and one will clearly understand how much easier it is to play the glide-along game. Unlike my childhood friend who had to rely on his innate intelligence in order to maintain a "D" average, nowadays, if you attend class and are basically cooperative, there's *no way* you're failing. The passing grade is yours for the taking.

Ultimately, everyone in school is developing and refining their individual survival skills. Acquiring these skills is perhaps one of the most indelible lessons learned in school, yet you won't find this topic in any curriculum, lesson plan, administrative directive, or governmental initiative. Survival skills—one of the most important things a child can learn—aren't taught anywhere! Each individual is left to his own devices.

22. Why We Don't Brush Teeth In School

All my life, I have heard the importance of "Brushing After Every Meal." Any viable program of dental health revolves around this basic tenet. Therefore, wouldn't it make sense to brush after lunch at school? You would be hard pressed to find anyone in an "official" position who wouldn't support this basic component of dental health. However, similar to many educational initiatives, were it to be enacted as mandatory in school, it would look *fantastic* on paper and be an *absolute disaster* in practice. Consider the logistics, then factor the inherent time-wasting mentality that defines student protocol, and you've got a recipe for catastrophe.

Considering that most school classrooms are too small to begin with, add-in the general paucity of counter, cabinet, and storage space, and the first question becomes: Just where would we put all of these toothbrushes? Then, of course, because the toothbrush always ends up touching the opening of the toothpaste container during application, each child would also need their own tube of toothpaste. Since most school lavatories have two or three sinks at most, even if you have those half-circle models with the foot pedals, how many children can be in there brushing their teeth at once? And, due to all the spit splashing, direct and indirect, unintentional and on target, should the kids wear protective gloves or full-body hazmat suits? In addition, just who is going to monitor this activity? More instructional aides? Fire department? EPA? With 200, 300 or more students per lunch wave, this could easily turn into a 45-60 minute activity.

And the complications don't end there. Toothbrushes don't last forever. Who is going to determine when each child's toothbrush needs to be replaced? What happens when he or she forgets to bring a new one from home? Does the school provide an "interim" toothbrush or does the kid just go without brushing? Who contacts the parents to remind them? If the parents don't follow-through and the school is responsible to assure that brushing occurs, are parents entitled to sue for negligence if their child gets a cavity? By this standard, could the school be held responsible for *all* dental bills? What about when the student runs out of toothpaste? If, by chance, he or she uses someone else's, considering all of the current concern over blood-borne pathogens, can the parent sue for child endangerment? And, if the toothbrushes are being stored in those little tubular cases, who makes sure those stay sanitary? If the kid comes home at vacation or at the end of the school year with mold inside his toothbrush holder, can't you just imagine the urgency of the phone call to the law offices of Dewey, Cheetham and Howe?

If one considers the magnitude of the disruption that could result from an initiative that looks so good on paper and is as seemingly simple and well intentioned as brushing your teeth after lunch, and applies it to all of the other initiatives and mandates that teachers are expected to enact on a regular basis, you will begin to understand the extraordinary effect that outside forces have on the "reality" of the classroom.

23. Duties

It wasn't until Fred became my principal that I fully understood how often administrators treat supervisory duties as if they were the most important function of a teacher's day. Naturally, the front office will deny this, but the *only* issue throughout my years that has regularly resulted in entanglements with the administration has concerned duties. You can be sitting at the computer sending e-mails during class time, but don't you *dare* be late to a duty!

Duties are also known as monitorials. I find it fascinating that the first definition of "monitor" in my Random House Dictionary is "A pupil appointed to assist in the conduct of a class or school, as to help keep order." It is not until we get to definition #10 that we come to the general: "to observe, oversee, supervise." A *pupil!?* How does this even vaguely imply that the person assigned to the job needs to have four years of college plus a master's degree? From a teacher's perspective, duties can range from the most stressful to the most aggravatingly mundane part of the school day. They include:

- Lunchroom/Cafeteria
- Bus Loading and Unloading
- Parent "Pickup" (parents who drive their child to and from school instead of using the bus)
- Recess
- Homeroom

- Before School (overseeing an area where the students congregate before the opening bell. This can occur in a variety of venues including the cafeteria, gym, outdoor blacktop, etc.)

- Study Hall

- General Hallway/Bathroom (the term "Lavatory" is gone with the wind)

- After School Detention

- In-school Suspension

I challenge anyone to find me a teacher who believes doing duty is a valuable use of their time. During the years that I was assigned to recess duty there was no way you would ever get me to proclaim that I liked it, especially when freezing to death during the winter. Still, my distaste towards this absurd use of my time was always tempered by the fact that I found recess to be so essential to student development. However, none of these "duties" require a college education. They can easily be done by any competent individual hired on an hourly basis. The lunchroom/cafeteria experience at the elementary schools in which I have taught, provides an excellent illustration.

Lunch Duty

In the course of a school day, there is no overriding concern quite like student lunch. It is the one area of unstructured time that includes high numbers of children during which problems arise on a daily basis. In order to provide a little background on the lunch supervision issue, I perused several teacher contracts and each of them includes a statement to this effect:

> Although the Board views the lunch period as
> an ongoing part of the instructional program,
> it realizes the additional tensions incurred
> by staff members in supervising this activity

> could potentially detract from other portions
> of the instructional program. Therefore all
> *elementary* school teachers shall be exempted
> from such duty.

What has always confounded me about this policy is, if the first sentence is true, why would the second sentence apply *only* to elementary school teachers? What on earth makes supervising a middle school or high school lunch period any less tension-filled or potentially detracting to other portions of the instructional program? If anything, it is even more so!

Regardless, by contract, elementary teachers don't have to supervise the kids in the lunchroom, but get to monitor recess instead. Because our school system recently adopted a 5-8 middle school format, elementary school now encompasses only grades K-4. Consequently, fifth and sixth grade students no longer have recess. It simply baffles me that, just because these two grades are now part of a middle school instead of an elementary program, the same age children who had been getting recess for years suddenly don't need it. Insane!

During my elementary experience, as many as 150 kids would eat together under the supervision of two hourly employees. Generally these individuals served as paraprofessionals/aides during the remainder of the school day; working one-on-one with special education students, doing clerical work for the office, or covering classes when substitute teachers weren't available or didn't bother to show up. I've been close friends with one of these "paras" for years, and I can't believe how competently she handles anything that is thrown at her, particularly when you consider that she has no idea what she will be doing when she comes to work each day. Although her regular job assignment is to work with special education students, the administration simply puts her wherever they need coverage that day. It is a good thing that she finds it interesting and challenging because almost everyone

I know agrees that they could never handle not knowing in advance what they were going to be doing every day.

The policy in the elementary lunchroom was that the supervising aides would raise their hands when they needed to quiet the students down for an announcement, dismissal, etc. At this point the kids were also supposed to raise their hands and stop talking. As might be expected, this worked perfectly for the first few days of each school year. Then, the amount of time it took for the children to quiet down gradually lengthened day by day. This is where the aides inadvertently began to teach a valuable lesson in mathematical fractions. As all teachers know, the first time you try to get the attention of a group of students, it is basically a warm-up exercise for your vocal chords. The second time, the most conscientious, straight "A" pupils might hear you. The third time, a few more, and on it goes; except that experienced teachers use numerous admonitions, cajoles, incentives, disincentives, etc., to expedite the process.

Apparently, these aides had perfected a "counting system." They would raise their hands and, after a pause, shout, "One!" At this point the decibel level in the cafeteria would immediately plummet from somewhere around 90 all the way down to $87^1/_2$, accompanied by a few of the best students raising their hands. After about five to ten seconds: "Two!" A few more hands would go up along with a similar marginal reduction in noise. "Two and a half!" Now, a good 50% of the children start to pay attention. You see, they have learned from experience that everything up to this point didn't count, which is why they were ignoring it in the first place. "Two and three-quarters!" the aides would bellow, "We're getting serious!" The kids always *loved* that one. Evidently the aides were just kidding up to this point.

Over the years I heard every division from $2^1/_4$ to $2^7/_8$'s. Sometimes $2^5/_8$'s would come after $2^3/_4$'s; a definite faux pas. Recess served a very valuable purpose in this situation. The threat of time being deducted was a huge incentive to behave. For many students, along with PE, recess was the best part of the day!

At the middle school where I am currently teaching, there is a 30 minute lunch period during which 325 pupils are monitored by four to five teachers. The kids generally finish eating in about ten minutes, which gives them 20 minutes in which to fool around, disrupt life, get in trouble, and generally drive the duty teachers nuts! Because the administration and board of education have eliminated recess at the middle school, there is no longer any unstructured "blow off steam" time after lunch. Therefore, not only do students miss all the valuable opportunities of free play, but the major incentive to behave during lunch has also vanished.

At the high school level where my wife has taught her entire career, cafeteria duty is the only place where she has regularly experienced major student behavioral issues. In her classroom, she has complete control. However, during lunch duty, student behavior ranging from lack of cooperation, to swearing, fighting, and being totally belligerent are common. I've never been able to understand how this doesn't meet the contract criteria of "additional tensions." And, why does my wife get this duty year after year? Because she has shown she is good at it! That's how it works in school; show you're good at the difficult assignments and that's all you'll get. Interestingly, since she has been doing lunch duty for so many years, my wife now prefers this assignment because it provides her with an additional opportunity to "connect" with the students. Isn't she something?

Due to the level of serious behavior being encountered, many high schools have begun to hire security guards or policemen for lunch monitoring. It's getting to the point that you need someone with that level of authority (firepower?) to maintain order.

Bus Duty

Another monitorial I have regularly endured throughout my teaching career is bus duty. In the morning this involves recording bus identification numbers on a clipboard as they arrive and supervising the kids as they enter the building. Morning tends to be a little less hectic because the busses arrive sporadically. In the afternoon it's more complicated because all the busses are lined-up along the curb and large numbers of children pile out of the building all at once. Since the busses are never in the same order from one day to the next, students either need help finding their bus or they have to be sent back into the school because their bus hasn't even been called. In addition, end-of-the-day tension release is more apt to result in running, pushing, and shoving, as opposed to the morning when the kids are groggily shuffling, in varying states of consciousness.

I simply marvel that *anyone* takes the job of school bus driver. Not only do these individuals have to drive these humongous vehicles, but they have 40-60 screaming kids behind them to help ease the tension. Think about what it sounds like to have two to five children in the car with you when you're driving to a soccer game and then multiply it a few times. In addition, it's the 21st century and many school systems *still* don't have seat belts on these things! Laws for private vehicles basically require that kids under 18 years old be strapped in like they're on a mission to Mars. The adult driver is flirting with something close to lethal injection if they get caught with children who are not wearing seat belts. But on the bus? No problema! The kids jump around, yell, punch, intimidate, and bully; and the poor bus driver is supposed to monitor all of this through that silly little mirror above the sun visor—while trying to *drive!* Basically, what we have is a big yellow box of lawsuits on wheels!

In my opinion, in addition to seat belts, every bus should have an adult monitor on board to handle all of the discipline issues (and make sure that the children actually *use* the seat belts). This would enable the bus driver to do what he/she is supposed to doing: Safely transporting the kids to and from school. I guess it's probably cheaper to pay the insurance premiums to cover the lawsuits than it is to outfit buses with seat belts and supervisors. However, it was a direct result of these exact circumstances that led to one of my more memorable "bus duty" stories.

One morning a student was getting off the bus when he suddenly remembered he had left something back on his seat. As he turned around and jumped back up the steps, the driver was apparently so startled that she took her foot off the brake and the bus rolled into the overhang at the front entrance of the building. Because I was the only one assigned to this duty, I was busy monitoring the arrival of several busses and did not directly witness the incident. Still, the damage was so minor, basically a bent gutter, that I thought the bus driver could just "call it in" and be on her way. Silly me!

In a scene reminiscent of Arlo Guthrie's "Alice's Restaurant," it became the biggest "crime" of the past dozen years! Two police cars showed up, as well as an ambulance and a fire truck! The bus wasn't allowed to move, pending a full investigation. Consequently, the entire school driveway was blocked for the remainder of the morning which disrupted all school traffic, other busses, deliveries, etc. It wasn't until I was called out of my second period class to come to the principal's office to help fill out the official incident report, that the gravity to which the administration had elevated this situation became clear. The principal even went so far as to imply that I could be held liable for this event since I was the one "in charge" of that area at that time. When I pointed out that she had actually created this unsafe situation by assigning only *one* person to this duty area, the rhetoric immediately subsided.

Almost everyone possesses the ability to retain "snapshots" of past events in their minds—memories that can resurface as clearly as if one were viewing a photo album. I have two pictures associated with this event: One is of the bus wedged against the bent gutter, and the other is of the grave look on the principal's face as we discussed the situation in her office. Just the thought that I could be held legally responsible for an event in which I had absolutely no culpability, was simply mind-boggling! Here I am marking bus arrivals on a clipboard, a job that could be done by a ten year old, and I'm supposed to be responsible for driving the bus too?

This incident perfectly illustrates something told to me many years ago by a retired administrator:

"The primary purpose of every administrator is self-preservation"

I learned a very valuable lesson from this event. Whenever I am assigned to a situation that is the least bit unsafe or understaffed, I send the principal a written memo expressing my concern. This places the responsibility right back where it belongs—on the shoulders of the highly paid individual who created the situation.

A colleague in a neighboring school system was on afternoon bus duty in the K-6 school in which she teaches. One youngster was struggling to get on the bus with a large project, so Ann decided to help her. While Ann was on the bus, a large sixth grader saw some friends through the bus window and decided to go charging off the bus to talk to them. Being keenly aware of her surroundings, as teachers tend to be, Ann noticed some kindergartners coming up the stairs who were about to get trampled by this older kid. Quickly, Ann grabbed him by his backpack and directed him to go back to his seat, citing the fact that bus rules clearly state that once students get on the bus they are expected to stay there. Defiantly, the boy told Ann that she couldn't touch him and stormed back to his seat in a huff.

Because Ann stopped this child by his backpack, she actually never had any physical contact whatsoever. And she certainly didn't tackle, lasso, or hogtie him. She simply kept him from possibly hurting some little kids. Ann rightfully felt she had expediently prevented a potentially harmful event.

The next day, Ann was greeted by the principal who promptly informed her that the mother was filing a lawsuit. Physical restraint of students is a hot-button issue in education. Was the danger sufficiently imminent to warrant restraint in the first place? Was the amount of restraint justified? Was this child being singled out for other reasons? Since so much is subject to interpretation, the second-guessing can be endless. Thankfully, there are some general protections for teachers against getting sued individually for an incident of this nature that occurs in school. But what about the nightmare Ann now has to endure; sleepless nights, constant agitation, and general upset—all because of "bus duty?"

One will quickly realize that this was a lose-lose situation for Ann no matter what she had done. Obviously, if she hadn't helped the little girl onto the bus with her project, she wouldn't have been up there in the first place. Then there's the possibility that the sixth grader barreling off the bus might not have hurt the kindergartners at all. However, if the boy's actions caused something bizarre to happen, like the bus driver taking her foot off the brake and hitting the building, Ann would have certainly been called on the carpet. And if the kindergartners had really been hurt? Imagine the lawsuits then!

Pickup Duty

My current after-school duty involves monitoring parental pickup of students who are being driven home from school. If there ever was a situation where a police officer should be in charge, this is it. The parents are supposed to keep their vehicles in a straight line along the side of the driveway and pull up as each group of cars is loaded. As teachers, our primary concern is child safety, as well as the expedient loading of the vehicles. Clearly, the faster we get this done, the sooner we can leave. Parents, unfortunately, are often focused only on the "expediency" part. In their agitation to get going, they will drive around cars into which students are loading, or park elsewhere and then call their kid across the driveway, totally oblivious to the moving traffic.

The adamant refusal of so many parents to follow the direction of the teachers on duty is the cause of many of the problems we experience with the students on a daily basis. Children learn by example, and these parents are teaching them incalculable lessons in defiance. And talk about "stress" on the teachers. This can often be the most challenging part of my day.

So, let's get back to that board of education policy concerning "additional tensions incurred by staff members in supervising an activity that could potentially detract from other portions of the instructional program." In other words, the board recognizes that the additional stress and distraction "duties" place on the teacher can affect how they perform in the classroom. And, just like the elementary lunchroom, most duties can be performed by hourly employees. If a more authoritative adult presence is required, security guards or policemen should be hired for the job.

When we compare American education to other countries, we should do an analysis of how much time their teachers expend on mundane tasks such as those described in this chapter. In Japan, for example, teachers instruct class during the morning and the remainder of their day is devoted to lesson planning, extra help, research, etc. If we want to improve American education we must stop inundating teachers with distracting, stressful duties and allow them to concentrate their energies on *Teaching!*

Just before this book went to print, my wife said to me: "With all of the initiatives that are currently being enacted at my school, I'm worried that your book may already be obsolete." To which I responded, "Really?"

- Has your salary been doubled and you're just keeping it a secret from me?

- Have your class sizes been cut in half?

- Do you have a full time clerical assistant?

- Has your superintendent, assistant superintendent, curriculum coordinator, special education coordinator, principal and assistant principal started actively teach classes?

- Have your special education students been assigned to an instructional environment that *truly* addresses their distinct needs?

- Have your monitorial duties been eliminated?

- Do you have a phone on your desk?

- Have you been assigned to a true linear career path as a mentor/master teacher with the corresponding salary, benefits, and recognition that you so justly deserve?

- Have teachers been put in charge of creating educational policy?

- Has grade leveling been eliminated and students allowed to progress at their own rate? Has a comprehensive "whole child" evaluative tool been created to facilitate this process?

Although my wife can actually answer "yes" to having a phone on her desk (a definite rarity in public school), when she realized that the initiatives being enacted at her school are essentially more window-dressing, she commented, "It would be great if there was a spot in your book where all of your recommendations were listed together." Good idea.

24. Lawsuits and Legalities

Remembering Ann's horrific ordeal, it is essential to discuss a problem that, if it remains unchecked, will bring the functioning of America's public schools, if not American society as a whole, to a grinding halt: *The proliferation of lawsuits!*

It is so sad that the legal system, which should only be used to resolve the most extreme cases of purposeful malfeasance, has been abused by a "sue over anything" culture. The increase in frivolous lawsuits has so hampered every aspect of our society that individuals with legitimate grievances have become trivialized. I believe this entire phenomenon can be traced to the "get rich quick" mentality that permeates American society. The notion that everyone is going to become a multi-millionaire manifests itself in widely varying schemes, both legal and illegal, in which lawsuits have become an integral component. If the vast majority of American citizens had *any* idea how vulnerable they are to being sued while simply carrying out the most mundane daily activities, perhaps a national uprising would result in monumental reforms.

Do you have a swimming pool in your backyard? If you knew how susceptible you are to being sued, you'd probably fill it in. Do you think you're safe because you put the required fence around the pool? If someone hops the fence or breaks the lock and injures themselves in any way while "illegally" swimming in your pool, you can be held liable. If they drown? Heaven help you! Go ahead, take a look out there at your children and all of their friends having a wonderful time! If one of them gets hurt, you're getting sued! Hosting a child's birthday party and believe you've covered all of your bases by hiring a life guard? Fat chance! And you don't even want to think about when they get older. Some weekend when you're away, they'll come home from college and a bunch of underage kids will be out there having a "kegger." You had no idea, you say? That will fly like a lead balloon if one of those drunken fools gets hurt.

I know a number of parents who have openly allowed minors to drink at their houses and many more who had no idea their house was "party central." The differentiation is really insignificant if someone gets hurt or killed driving home. You are liable, either way! While his son was away at college, a friend of ours had the pass code on his home security alarm changed and didn't tell the kid. Sure as can be, the boy came home one weekend when he knew his parents were away, and there were loads of party-goers parked in the driveway, on the lawn, and in street before he found out that he couldn't get in. The parents, of course, learned all this from the neighbors. Thankfully the kid had enough smarts not to try to break-in, and the pre-party crowd didn't push the issue. Post-party would have been an entirely different matter. Inebriated people don't tend to consider that security alarm violations will likely alert "guests" of a different kind.

I've said for years that if you want to curb the population explosion, just give pre-conception parents a 30 second glimpse of what life will be like when their child is between the ages of 16 and 20. Zero population growth would commence immediately! Prospective parents seem incapable of looking past the "bundle of joy" stage. My mother-in-law has a favorite saying:

Younger children disturb your sleep, older children your life

A fellow teacher told me about the time his college-age sister and a group of her friends broke into his parent's vacation home and held a blowout bash. This property was a good six hour drive from where the parents lived, so they had absolutely no idea this was happening, until the police called.

Almost all of these kids were underage and my colleague's parents were held responsible for enabling minors to drink on their property (in lieu of the only other option, which was to have their daughter arrested for breaking and entering).

When my mom turned 70, my wife and I hosted a wonderful surprise party at our home. Although a few of her friends had to travel an hour or so to get here, they made the effort and mom was delighted! Unfortunately, for my wife and me the event turned into an invaluable lesson in legal liability. Upon her arrival, one of these older women tripped on a small step between our family room and kitchen and fell into another woman whose hip fractured. My sweet wife followed the ambulance to the hospital and spent the next six hours sitting with this person until she was finally settled in a room for next day surgery. In the meantime the party went wonderfully, but my wife, who had spent weeks planning this event, missed the whole thing!

We went to the hospital to visit this woman a number of times post-surgery and during her rehabilitation at the nursing home. Every visit she expressed her gratitude for all of the attention we bestowed on her—how it was above and beyond, etc. Ironically, when we got home from what turned out to be the last visit, there was a message on our answering machine from the company that holds our homeowners insurance: She was suing us!

Eventually, the insurance company settled for an undisclosed amount of money, but I'm sure you can imagine the consternation my wife and I endured in the process. The claims adjuster visited our house and indicated all of the places that bars and handrails needed to be installed in order to be in compliance with the codes for hosting elderly people. Mind you, this is not only for a party, but anytime an elderly person enters your house. And, don't get fooled that it's just the elderly. It can be a child's birthday party, a Christmas gathering; anytime you host anyone in your home you are liable if someone gets hurt, no matter what the reason. Think your friends won't do it to you? Think again. People have this bizarre attitude that the insurance company will pay and it won't have any effect on you. The truth be told, many insurance companies ascribe to a two or three year "window" from the first claim. File a second claim during that period and you can lose your coverage. This is especially true for automobiles. If you don't believe me, check it out yourself. The following example should remove all doubt.

A friend of ours had her house burn down while she was away for the afternoon. It was a total loss! The inspectors eventually discovered that the source was one of those night lights that turn on automatically when it gets dark. Apparently, during that afternoon, the sun kept going in and out due to passing clouds which caused the night light to turn on and off a sufficient number of times that it became overheated. Because she was fully insured, the insurance company paid for the complete rebuilding of her house; even allowing some improvements the original structure didn't have. After enduring the devastation of a disastrous fire which was intense enough to melt all of her jewelry, our friend was delighted! Unbeknownst to her, she was in for an incredible surprise.

When the job was completed, the insurance company canceled her policy! Why? That's just what they do. I have no idea if it's in the fine print or what, but there wasn't a lawyer who would touch it. She went without insurance on this beautiful new home for six months before she could find a company who would even give her a skeletal policy.

My point in a nutshell is this: While the insurance industry as a whole remains on very solid financial footing, insurance companies use lawsuits as an excuse to continually raise premiums, deny coverage, or cancel policies. Even a legitimate claim like my friend's house is not exempt. It is easy to place the blame (undoubtedly well deserved) on lawyers who prosecute frivolous cases but, the individual citizens who pursue litigation in the first place are more than equally accountable. At any given time, the vast majority of our public schools are involved in legal proceedings of some sort. It has become standard operating procedure. And the result is that rising insurance premiums are added to overall school costs, and city/town property taxes increase.

When I was in high school, a good friend broke his two front teeth on the school trampoline during gym class. Even though there were so-called "spotters" all around the rim, when a jumper lost control, instead of putting their hands up to keep the person from falling off, the spotters would back away. Because this was prior to pads being placed over the springs and rim, my friend came straight down onto the metal bar. While the school insurance definitely paid for his dental bills, did his parent's sue for negligence? Of course not! This was back in the days when accidents were considered a normal part of being a kid.

Owing to the high rates of injury, I don't see many trampolines around schools anymore. Insurance companies won't cover them or, if you can get coverage, the premium is prohibitively expensive. Nonetheless, I see them all the time in backyards. My insurance agent explained that, as long as your insurance company hasn't told you to get rid of it, the trampoline is covered. However, if the insurance agent comes out to your house for any reason and sees the trampoline, or the Pit Bull, or a diving board on your swimming pool, you'll be told to remove them. If you don't and someone gets hurt––woe to you.

Recently a girl was running on the school blacktop. She managed to trip on a large piece of air, fell flat on her face, and the parents sued. Absolutely nobody else was involved in any way, so what were the grounds for a lawsuit? And why on earth this girl decided to break the fall with her face instead of her hands, none of us could figure out. But, this is the way it goes in school in the 21st century; any little thing can result in a lawsuit! I'm most disturbed to discover that the elimination of recess in numerous school districts is not merely the result of a shortsighted fixation on increased instructional time. It's due to lawsuits! And furthermore, in order to decrease the risk, a number of schools that still have recess have actually banned running!

I recently learned that the elementary school at which I taught for a number of years removed a wonderful playground structure because our insurance carrier would no longer cover it. Evidently, after lawsuits occurred in other towns due to scraped knees on playground equipment, the apparatus was deemed too risky. It's astonishing how the very individuals who file these repugnant lawsuits seem to have no inkling that *their* actions are causing these results. I suggest that before you sue McDonald's for causing your child's obesity, think about the fact that your last lawsuit resulted in the elimination of recess at his school. Wait a minute . . . maybe you can re-sue the school for making your child obese by eliminating recess!

Occasionally, when an opportune moment presents itself, I take a yardstick and, while tapping it on the palm of my hand, say to the kids: "Back in the good old days if you did something like that you would get sent to the principal to have your knuckles rapped with a yardstick." I demonstrate the motion of the ruler towards the back of my hand for dramatic effect and, as their mouths hang open in disbelief, I continue: "And you know what would happen when you got home? Your parents wouldn't call their lawyer—they would give it to you double!"

Blurring the Line Between Home and School

It seems the ultimate cruelty that, on top of all the challenges inundating teachers' lives, the Internet adds a whole new set of issues. My wife and I recently attended a workshop on Cyber Bullying. As I looked around the room, all of us appeared to be in the 40-plus category with the exception of a smattering of younger "twentysomethings." At one point, I couldn't help but express my astonishment that these younger teachers weren't running for the doors. In essence, the line between parental and school responsibility has become so blurred that it is virtually nonexistent. Apparently, if *while at home*, a child is chastised, badmouthed, or made fun of in any way while "online," and that child is visibly upset or expresses a concern to any adult at school, it becomes a "school issue" that needs to be dealt with as if it had occurred in school! The reasoning is that these incidents may have an adverse affect on the child's successful school/learning experience and disrupt the educational process. Of course, the ramifications of this kind of thinking has extended to *anything* that occurs to a child at home; from not eating breakfast to serious verbal/physical abuse. If it affects learning, it is now the school system's responsibility to address the issue.

A major concern that I have not yet seen analyzed is the all-consuming need amongst young people, especially teenagers, for the entire world to know every intimate detail about them. Conversations with students at all levels have convinced me that, when they pour all of their personal information onto My Space, Facebook or the like, they think only their friends are viewing it. They are oblivious to their vulnerability, but then the school ends-up having to deal with the outcome. I am hoping to find definitive studies that address this self-exposure phenomenon. Are we all so desperate for our "15 minutes" of fame that there is no limit to the lengths we will go to get it?

As a teacher, my life is plenty public enough. I don't care to have my privacy compromised any more than is absolutely necessary. This is why I have never lived in the same town in which I have taught. I make the commute precisely to maintain my privacy. I constantly hear stories from other teachers about how they are trapped into mini-conferences in the grocery store. This stems from the notion that teachers are "on the job" 24/7: correcting papers, making phone calls, writing recommendations, doing lesson plans—all at home. Why shouldn't that extend to your grocery shopping? Not for me, thanks.

One of the traits that have made my wife such a successful high school teacher is the incredible empathy that enables her to connect with students on a personal level. Because they trust her as a confidant, they talk to her about *everything!* Gaining a student's trust is the key to all good mentoring. Just like my wife, many teachers are almost surrogate parents to the kids, especially if the children don't have that kind of relationship with their actual parents.

In order for mentoring to be successful, students must feel free to talk without fear of repercussion. Up until very recently, teachers could simply use their discretion to separate the significant from the mundane. Unfortunately, either because of litigation or the desire of legislators to do everything possible to protect children, new laws have made this impossible. Teachers are now under a legal imperative to report any and all student comments pertaining to even the slightest possible abuses. Because there are no absolutes as to what is or is not considered "abuse," we are simply instructed that, in order to protect ourselves, *everything* should be reported.

While these laws may be well intentioned and are ultimately designed to protect both teachers and students, they are having a highly detrimental effect on student willingness to talk freely. Because my wife interacts successfully with a large number of inner city youths, she is continually navigating a vast sea of serious issues. Over the years she has been able to help kids resolve any number of situations via the trust they develop with her. Even the slightest perception on the part of the students that this trust may be violated can have significant ramifications. Many times children simply need a place to "vent" without worry. Sadly, these new legalities are having a devastating impact on an essential element of student development: A strong mentoring relationship with a caring and empathetic teacher.

In fact, the similarities between what my wife is currently doing with the minority students at her school and our earlier discussion concerning the movie "Freedom Writers" are uncanny. Because she possesses the same extraordinary compassion and empathy as Erin Gruwell, my wife is able to connect with these pupils at a level which has lead to the principal dubbing them "her" kids. It totally defies conventional wisdom that this middle-aged white woman could achieve this level of trust and understanding with students who are bused from the inner city. Mind you, unlike Erin's situation in "Freedom Writers," my wife does not have all of these individuals in one class. Many are spread throughout various classes and the others she sees only as part of the Diversity Club she started.

It is truly heart-wrenching to experience firsthand the challenges faced by these young people. They regularly attend funerals of friends and acquaintances who are victims of gang violence. They have witnessed incidents and live under a "fear" that most of us can only guess at. While we celebrate shows like "The Sopranos," these children live under the threat of gang violence on a daily basis. In truth, once you join a gang you can *never* get out. Move to another town or state and they will track you down. Imagine if your parents and other members of your immediate or extended family are gang members. How limited are your choices? I now understand the dire consequences these kids will suffer, gang members or not, if they talk to the police or display even the slightest appearance of disloyalty. The vicious circle of these life circumstances is frightening.

It is solely as a result of my wife's experience with these students that I now fully understand why 40 years of school integration hasn't worked. Through her efforts, my wife has developed a thorough understanding of the many cultural qualities that are unique to the life experiences of these young people. Even though there are 36 of these students trying to integrate into a total school population of 450, the school administration still resists holding school-wide assemblies or workshops to forge an understanding between cultures. In essence, their attitude is that these kids are expected to "be white" while in school. As anyone with experience in these matters will tell you, the absurdity of this approach is incomprehensible. So, it basically falls to someone like my wife to try to bridge the chasm on an individual incident by incident basis, which is frequent and ongoing. Under the circumstances, what she is able to accomplish is remarkable.

I've learned through the years that, totally contrary to widely accepted perceptions, family stability in the higher economic strata can be as alarmingly unstable as any other socioeconomic group. While the majority of divorced children live full-time with one parent, the explosion in shared custody has created a substantial number who split their time evenly between both parents. Inevitably, with bedrooms in two places, school materials are constantly being left at one place or the other. However, this scenario is a model of stability compared to what happens when each parent starts having a relationship with a new partner. Being divorced with kids tends to result in a parent partnering with someone who is also divorced with kids. Therefore, when they move in together, along come the children from both sides.

I can't tell you the number of students I've had through the years who, along with their siblings, spend one week at mom's house with her boyfriend's three children, and then spend the next week at dad's house with his girlfriend's four children. Think about it: What are the chances all of these people are going to get along? In most instances the kids are miserable. Additionally disconcerting is the number of times the new living arrangement finally gets stabilized and there's a breakup. How about if mom gets remarried and has more children with the new husband? Then *they* get divorced? And further down the line, mom gets a *new* boyfriend and they move in together?

Just think about what happens when both parents are mirroring these same scenarios simultaneously. Now, factor in that most divorces are far from amicable, and the result for children can be both physical and emotional upheaval. And, should the child express upset over any of this at school, *it becomes an issue that the school must address!* This is why we need to be staffed with full time social workers, psychologists, counselors, and school nurses, to deal with the constant turmoil generated by these extraordinarily compromised home situations. Then, regardless of how ill-advised parental judgment may prove to be, barring irrefutable evidence of extreme neglect or abuse, parents still have final veto power over *any* decision the school makes! So, despite the best intentions of lawmakers, the school is ultimately mired in a no-win situation, not to mention the poor child who's stuck in the middle of all of this.

False Molestation Accusations

Even in the most amicable of divorces, numerous difficulties can face parents who are attempting to develop new relationships while dealing with the fragile psyches of their children. The chances are slim that children are going to welcome a stranger into whatever semblance of "normality" they feel has been established in their home. This is especially true of teenage daughters and their mother's boyfriend. Even if he is the greatest thing since sliced bread, all of the pent-up anger they feel about the divorce in general, and perhaps towards their own father in particular, is likely to be aimed at the "new guy." As almost any parent can tell you:

"Hell hath no fury like a pissed-off teenage girl!"

Depending on the degree of wrath the daughter harbors, the consequences can be devastating.

A few years ago, there was a news story about a teacher who developed a relationship with a divorced woman who had a 17 year old daughter. Sadly, like too many girls her age, she was angry with her parents, home life, and authority in general. In a moment of blind rage, she told her father that this man had molested her. Being one of those less than amicable divorces, the father couldn't notify the authorities fast enough. Reports are that it took only three weeks for the girl to realize the gravity of what she had done and recant the whole story. But, once it was "in the system" it took on a life of its own.

I've known of other situations that confirm the fact that once the District Attorney's office gets involved, there's no turning back. Do you remember the case of the child beauty queen JonBenét Ramsey in Colorado? It took *twelve years* and the mother's death before the DA apologized for the agony they had put the Ramsey family through. I remember the news commentators saying how unusual it is for a DA's office to admit they are wrong. So, in the case of this teacher, we have an innocent man who lost his job, reputation, and, even if he is able to retain his teaching license, he may never get hired again.

We continually lament the paucity of male teachers in public school, but when you consider the dire ramifications of false molestation charges, it is a wonder that any man takes the risk. A few years ago, news of a sixth grade teacher that had been accused of molestation by a student headlined our state news reports. Although he adamantly proclaimed his innocence, in the course of defending himself, he lost his job, family, home, and ultimately had a complete nervous breakdown that required long term hospitalization. When the girl reached her early 20's, she finally summoned the courage to admit the accusation was false and that she had made it in a fit of anger. However, as a 12 year old, terrified by the uproar and publicity that surrounded her allegation, she became mortifyingly afraid to admit the truth. So, as the result of a complete falsehood, a man's life was ruined and, aside from guilt and remorse, the accuser got off scot-free.

Meanwhile, as this event unfolded, I was in the midst of teaching high school. A portion of my student assessment process included individual evaluations that I conducted in a separate office area connected to my classroom while the remainder of the class worked on something else. I will never forget the day I was sitting there with one of those "angry at the world" 17 year old girls, when the gravity of the extraordinarily vulnerable position in which I was placing myself suddenly struck me. I distinctly remember the dread that fell over me as I realized that this girl, who didn't like me that much to begin with, could ruin my life in an instant! As I praised the girl to the hilt, I immediately ended that session and suspended evaluations of that type forever! To this day, I am very careful to never be alone in my room with a female student.

It is for this very reason that I have long been an advocate for security cameras in classrooms. I consider this the ultimate protection against all manner of false accusation. Of course, the operative word here is "security." These recordings would *only* be viewed by school personnel or during a conference with parents held to specifically address an issue that allegedly occurred in class. Any thought of making this into a live "webcam" broadcast, streaming into every home, would be absolutely out of the question.

Security cameras would also be a boon to classroom discipline. All pupil misbehavior would be recorded, thereby offering indelible proof in every situation. In the early 1990s, I had a student who tormented all who had contact with him. He was a textbook example of a kid who had "mom" wrapped around his finger. Anything he told her, she would believe as gospel. Therefore, he knew he could act with impunity. One day, in a stroke of genius, I set up a video camera in the corner of my room. Once this boy realized that everything he did would be recorded, rendering it impossible to continue manipulating his mother, he *never* misbehaved in my class again. Now I'm hearing that my use of video for this purpose could result in legal proceedings for "violation of privacy" or some such thing. It's a public school for heaven sakes!

Those teachers who have concerns about security cameras in the classroom need not worry. The cost will make it prohibitive. This reminds me of a quip I heard from comedian Jay Leno: "Have you ever noticed that convenience stores have $20,000 worth of cameras guarding $20 worth of Twinkies?" Wouldn't it seem reasonable that, given the current paranoia over school safety, the security of our students, teachers, and staff would at least be worth an equal expenditure?

It is perhaps providential that, as I'm writing this, an offer for Educators Professional Liability Insurance has arrived in the mail from one of the education associations to which I belong. The policy offers to cover legal bills and judgments against teachers that may not be covered by school insurance. Two million dollars worth of liability coverage per occurrence at a cost of $136 per year seems reasonable. Of course, you've got to love that "per occurrence" thing. After you've had one claim you can bet the insurance company would drop you like a hot potato. It's important to note that teachers are generally covered under school liability insurance as an "agent of the school board." In addition, the teachers' union provides coverage in case, for example, the administration or school board wishes to take legal action against a teacher because a bus driver hits the building.

I find it interesting that it has only been during the past four to five years that these supplemental policies have been actively promoted. It's a sad statement on the times. It is also truly incredible the kinds of things that are covered. Some, such as "injury to students under your supervision," might be expected. But just look at a few of these others:

- Improper placement of students
- Failure to educate
- Failure to promote students or grant credit
- Violation of student rights

Failure to educate? This is one I've been anticipating for years; especially since the implementation of the inclusion model for special education. If we're promoting the misconception that all of the students are doing wonderfully, it's only logical that a proliferation of lawsuits should follow when they don't get into Harvard!

"Violation of student rights" has become an area rife with litigation. "Illegal" searches of student lockers are a perennial favorite. The kid gets caught with dope in his locker and the parent files a lawsuit over "illegal search and seizure." Even though the locker is clearly not the child's personal property, by law, school personnel must substantiate reasonable grounds to justify the search. Are we honestly getting to the point that we need to start obtaining search warrants to check lockers? It seems a permanent police presence in school is becoming a true necessity.

And what about the Internet? This has opened up a whole new world of discussion regarding student rights. I've read of innumerable "free speech" charges filed by parents in response to disciplinary actions imposed by schools on children who have written defamatory comments about school personnel on their home computers. Think about this: Under the protections of "free speech," a child can write whatever he or she wants about the school, but then the school is responsible for addressing the needs of the child if they come to school upset about what some other kid has written about them! And we wonder why there is a teacher shortage.

School Lockdown Procedures

One would be hard-pressed to find a more preposterous policy than the school lockdown procedures that were instituted in reaction to the 1999 Columbine High School tragedy and similar school shooting incidents. And, there is perhaps no better example of the cavernous gap between public perception of a school policy and the reality of its implementation.

A quick check at the National Center for Educational Statistics website reveals that homicides and shootings that occur at school *are so rare* that estimates from school crime and safety surveys are not reported. Regardless, school shootings have served as the primary impetus for instituting school lockdown drills. So, if there are 49,800,000 students in America's public schools and 26 students have been the perpetrators of homicidal school shootings since 1990, this means a total of .0000004% of public school students shoot other students. As a consequence, 99.9999996% of the students, plus 3.3 million teachers, not to mention teacher aides, clerical and custodial staff, are subjected to school lockdowns!

Aside from the 2006 shootings at Platte Canyon High School in Colorado and the Nickel Mines Amish school in Pennsylvania, all of the other 24 school shootings since 1990 have been committed by students. However, the way school lockdowns have been designed, one would think that all school shootings are the result of outside perpetrators. Let's think this through: If 92.5% of school shootings are carried out by students who attend the school where the shooting occurred, and *all* of the students in every school are subjected to lockdown drills, wouldn't the fact that potential shooters have an intimate knowledge of the lockdown procedure actually make the students *less* safe? It seems the administrators and boards of education that institute these policies haven't given this a thought. Nor has the public for that matter, who totally acquiesce to the idea that these procedures are really making their children safer.

I have learned that the lockdown procedure in the school system in which I teach is similar to ones in other systems, but I am absolutely certain that the way my principal introduced it was unique. At a faculty meeting devoted to the official presentation of our new "General Lockdown Procedure," we all received brand new *green* folders which contained the detailed, step by step directions. Like most administrative directives, it became glaringly clear from the outset that this procedure was to be entirely conducted from the main office. In the event of a "Lockdown," all instructions would be delivered by the principal via the intercom. Consequently, if a perpetrator simply took over the office, the entire plan would be null and void.

Regardless, in the event of a "Lockdown," the first announcement would be:

"Attention All Staff: Please Follow Your YELLOW Schedule"

Since this Lockdown policy was also to be followed by all substitute teachers, one poor soul raised her hand and logically suggested, "Wouldn't it make sense to have the Yellow schedule be in a Yellow folder?" There was this wonderfully pregnant pause before the principal ripped into her: "NO! It's going to be in this *green* folder!" I wish you could have seen the entire staff sitting there with our mouths agape, as if we had all been instantaneous recipients of full frontal lobotomies. It was a wonder to behold!

I'm not going to list the entire four page procedure but, suffice it to say, it is filled with enough contradictions to have kept us entertained for hours. One of my favorite directives states that the children are supposed to sit on the floor in an area least visible from the hallway or outside doors and windows. Yet, at the same time, we are instructed to keep the blinds open and the room visible from the outside! Another dictate stipulates that classroom doors need to be closed and *locked* by the teacher. Because this can only be done with a key, and substitute teachers don't have keys, it is further noted that "the principal or his/her designee will lock the doors of classrooms in which there are substitute teachers." Try to picture the building under siege by armed gunmen, and the principal (isn't he/she supposed to running this show on the intercom?) or some poor "designee" is calmly walking around locking doors.

The ultimate absurdity comes at instruction #12: "Disregard all bells, including fire alarm, unless danger is imminent." At this initial meeting, even though we had just witnessed the "yellow folder" questioner getting fried to ash, another teacher asked, "Do you have any suggestions as to when we decide danger is imminent?" At this, the assistant principal bellowed, "You *NEVER* decide *anything!* We [the administration] will tell you what to do!" In the ensuing days we had tears-in-our-eyes fun with this one. When is danger imminent? When you smell smoke, see fire, or when the first kid bursts into flames?

Almost equally absurd is the provision on page four instructing the physical education teachers to return to the building immediately if they are outdoors with their classes. Why in heaven would you want to return to a building that is under siege!? At the time this was first presented, my classroom had an outside door that opened directly onto the field on which outdoor physical education classes were held. The PE teacher and I had our own lockdown plan: Run for the woods, arms a-flailing optional!

My wife and her colleagues at the high school level especially enjoy the provision that requires all students assigned to study hall in the cafeteria to huddle together in the middle of the room. Remember, because virtually all school shooters are students of the school at which they do the shooting, these potential perpetrators will have an intimate knowledge of all of these procedures. Therefore, if they want to easily fire on a large group of kids all clumped together, they'll know just where to go: The Cafeteria. Speaking of which, the plan in my school for what to do *during* lunch, which would also seem a prime time to achieve optimal carnage, is even more bizarre. The 325 kids that constitute each lunch wave are instructed to calmly walk up a single, four foot wide staircase to congregate in two upstairs classrooms that couldn't possibly hold this many children. Under the calmest of circumstances, it would take at least ten minutes to move this many kids up that narrow stairway, never mind during the panic of an armed attack! In addition, I can't believe that the Fire Marshall has signed off on a plan that supposedly places 325 students in two rooms that couldn't possibly hold more than 200 kids total, even if they were stacked like cordwood. I'm guessing that the *real* plan is, if gunmen attack during lunch time, they'll be instructed to come back later.

Be that as it may, there is one final question that has not been answered in any of this discussion. When I became a teacher, where did I sign up to put my life on the line? Unlike police officers, I am not allowed to carry a gun, nor am I trained in firearm usage. Despite this, it seems that as far as administrators and boards of education are concerned, my "right to life and self-preservation" is totally in their hands. I'm sorry, but the moment that assistant principal said "You never decide anything" is when I resolved that all determinations regarding my physical life will be mine. Of course, I will do absolutely everything possible to keep the children in my charge as safe as I will my own self. However, when discussing the absurdities in this lockdown procedure, unlike other equally ridiculous administrative edicts, this one has life and death consequences. Allowing administrators to decide how I'm going to die is where I draw the line.

25. Tales of Misadventure

As "fired-up," "go-getter" teachers, my wife and I have organized and led countless overnight trips through the years; I, all over the country, and she, to Europe. This is in addition to innumerable daylong field trips from school. Unfortunately, as the threat of litigation loomed ever larger and the economy soured, my wife took her last school trip to Europe in 2002, and my last youth trip was a cruise in 2004. In essence, these excursions serve as a detailed travelogue of our years in teaching.

In the latter half of the 1970s, driving students around in our personal vehicles was something many teachers did with impunity. Believe it or not, for many of those years a bunch of kids would pile into the back of my pickup truck and I would take them home from an after school event or on some similar shorter excursion. Can you imagine anything like that today? Regardless of new laws, parents would be reaching for their lawyer's number before I even shifted the vehicle into "drive." The simplicity of this former lifestyle allowed for such wonderful, informal interaction with pupils. We are now at the point where, just last week, my wife's principal scolded her for making a bag of microwave popcorn for a group of kids who were hanging around her room waiting for the late bus. The paranoia about food allergies combined with new rules prompted by the obesity epidemic, have made a simple bag of popcorn an issue!

Nevertheless, the significance of these marvelous trip experiences for both students and, in my case, the parents who were encouraged to join us, is substantiated every time we encounter a former participant. These journeys were not only outstanding educational experiences; they also provided students with some of the most memorable moments of their childhood years. Whether it was swamp tours in the bayous around New Orleans, viewing giant Redwoods in California, strolling South Beach in Miami, romping through a vast field of sunflowers in Spain, raising the flag at Fort McHenry, or experiencing the delight on a child's face when they saw the Wright Brothers plane at the Smithsonian in Washington, D.C.; these moments more than compensated for whatever effort was involved in getting there. However, these trips also served as fodder for some of the most incredible "stories" imaginable.

This began during my very first year of teaching when I was working at the parochial high school I mentioned earlier. Two of my third period students would occasionally skip their second period study hall, go outside to smoke a couple of joints, and come to my class stoned (*that* study hall teacher was certainly asleep at the wheel!). Because there were only 12 kids in this class, it was rather impossible not to be distracted by the equivalent of 16.5% of the kids sitting there with glossy, bloodshot eyes, desperately trying to pretend they weren't high. It didn't take more than two or three of these occasions before I decided to take these two boys aside after class for a chat. I made it emphatically clear that, in addition to my concern about their need to get "high" in the middle of the morning, this activity was obviously very disruptive. In short, I just didn't want them coming to my class stoned. So, as they were giving me all of the "Gee, Mr. Warren, what are you talking about?" nonsense, I simply reemphasized that, while I was not turning them into the office or calling their parents, if they continued to come to my class stoned, I definitely would.

Thankfully, this seemed to do the trick; until we went to do a presentation at an elementary school later in the year. Whether it was because life was simpler back in 1976, or that this was a parochial school, I am still amazed that no school busses were involved in making this trip from the high school to the elementary school. Not only was I allowed to drive children in my car, but students who had licenses were also allowed to drive and take other kids in their cars with them! I found it curious that none of the other students wanted to ride with these two boys and, just as I feared, they showed-up at the elementary school eyes a-blazing!

At the conclusion of our activity, I told them how disappointed I was that they had violated our agreement. Amid a flurry of the expected "What do you mean?" gibberish, I told them that I was going to use the overnight to mull what action to take. Now, wouldn't you think these guys would clean out, scrub, and sanitize the inside of that car at the mere *thought* that I might turn them in? Apparently not! After class the next day, I explained to them that, because they had chosen to blatantly disregard my request, I was turning them into the office—a decision that dramatically changed my life at that school.

Not unexpectedly, the principal went out to check the car and found a substantial amount of marijuana. The two boys got suspended and were forced to enroll in a mandatory drug education/rehab program. In addition, I became the most hated "narc" in the school. Kids I didn't even know hissed at me. Evidently, even in the eyes of the "good" kids, I had egregiously crossed the line! Fortunately, it was very close to the end of the school year and I somehow managed to survive. However, I took with me a lesson that I have remembered to this day. When it comes to drugs, I pass my concerns surreptitiously to school councilors, social workers or psychologists. An interesting thought just crossed my mind: If that 1976 incident transpired today, the parents would probably be calling their lawyer over "illegal search and seizure."

Very early on, my wife developed a fantastically innovative way get students to pay attention during guided tours on trips. During the visit we would formulate questions about key pieces of information that were being presented. While we were in the gift shop that invariably ends every tour, my wife would buy some inexpensive trinkets to use as "prizes." Once we were back on the bus and en route to our next destination, we would ask the questions over the PA system and give out the prizes to the correct respondents. Even the high school kids participated enthusiastically. You'd think we were giving out winning lottery tickets! Incredibly, something as simple as this "game" removed 90% of behavioral issues from tours.

Of course, any teacher who has attempted these kinds of trips knows the other side of the coin; experiences so entirely angst-ridden that they can only be laughed at after much time has passed. One memory which still makes me shudder after 15 years involved an excursion to New York City during which we attended the famous Christmas Show at Radio City Music Hall.

Because my group's seats were spread out over a large section of this gargantuan hall, the chaperones and I decided we would all meet in the area by the gift counter in the main lobby at the conclusion of the show. When that moment arrived, after all of the head counts and list checks, it turned out that four students were missing. As the terror that swept over me escalated by the minute, I can still picture myself leaning on this huge gift counter, praying: "Lord, if you return these kids to me, I promise there will be no strangulations." After a 15 minute eternity, word came that a parent had found them outside. Apparently, inspired by the "Home Alone" movies, these kids had decided to walk on their own to nearby Rockefeller Plaza to view the Christmas tree.

As I took a moment to catch my breath, it immediately became quite clear that these children were oblivious to the danger of their little escapade. So, I asked them, "If some well-dressed person in a tie and jacket had come up to the four of you and said, Are you with the Youth Group at Radio City? I'm supposed to take you back in this car; what would they have done?" Once they realized that their idea of an abductor was basically that of a homeless person, the thought of falling prey to a professionally dressed person in a nice car caused their faces to blanch. I had the opportunity to take two of these students on numerous subsequent trips and they were models of responsibility.

It only took one overnight trip for me to learn that the travel industry standard of one chaperone to every 20 pupils is *woefully* inadequate. Therefore, I began to encourage parents who were willing to pay the trip fee to join us. Because the trips were so comprehensive, well organized, and cost effective, it didn't take long before entire families started to participate. This not only ensured phenomenal student supervision, but provided invaluable opportunities to witness parenting skills. Suffice it to say that parental notions of "oversight" run the entire length of the spectrum. For example, the number of parents who would allow their kids run wild through a hotel was simply astounding. My personal favorite was allowing them meet, prior to bedtime, in the sitting areas of the hotel lobbies to "talk." As any experienced chaperone knows, the concept of "talking" for a group of 12-15 year olds begins at a volume normally associated with an exorcism and escalates from there. Add to this the fact that most hotel lobbies have the sound proofing of an echo chamber, and the immediate result is a phone call from the front desk to the trip director: Me!

Attempting to quiet children of this age who are just "talking" is a unique challenge. First you get them seated and quiet and calmly explain the need to keep it down. This, of course, elicits comments like: "We weren't doing anything," "What are you talking about?" "This is so unfair," etc. And, it's not that they are being totally disingenuous. To them, they *were* just "talking." However, if you've ever watched these tweens and early teens, "talking" involves continual movement. Even when they start out seated, in an instant they have gone somewhere else. And, naturally, this perpetual motion is accompanied by the insatiable need to handle and touch everything in sight. Now, add in the noise level and you've got a lobby that is completely unusable by anyone else, and a front desk staff with apoplexy.

After all of your efforts explaining, discussing, and dissecting the situation, you establish a time frame for the kids to return to their rooms, say 15 minutes, and attempt to depart. Unfortunately, you don't get halfway to the lobby elevators before the whole thing is rebooting. But this time there's the added element of certain kids shouting "Quiet Down!" "Stop Running!" while they themselves run and shout. So, back you go to disperse them to their rooms, fully expecting that they will be wandering the hotel until whatever time their parents had told them to return. Amazingly, when you speak to the parents about this the next day, you discover that not one of them even thought to go check on the kids during the entire time they were out of their rooms.

In the interest of expediency I must save the plethora of "Europe" stories for another time. However, I simply can't resist divulging how we discovered that the McDonald's in Spain serve beer. During an overnight stop in Madrid, we happened to be staying at a hotel that was directly across from the "golden arches." I found it oddly curious that there seemed to be a constant stream of our kids heading back and forth across the street. It wasn't until I observed the *same* kids making multiple trips, that I decided a little investigation was in order. One would think that the lookouts would have sent warning of my approach, but apparently their attention was fully focused on the Spanish version of a "Happy Meal." Sure as can be, I walk into the McDonald's and there sit a dozen or so of our kids with Supersized Cervezas. I also discovered the reason for the continual trips. Beer was the only item on the menu not available for "takeout."

Out of numerous additional choices, I'll end with a distinctly memorable event from one of my trips. The hotel at which we were staying consisted of four separate buildings nestled along an access road that ran beside a major highway. There was a six foot high chain link fence that separated the hotel grounds from the access road. While there were plenty of walkways and paths within the hotel grounds, it was definitely faster to walk from the building that housed our rooms to the main building by walking down the access road sidewalk. This is how we discovered, by pure accident, that living in the bushes between the access road and the highway were a couple of homeless men.

One morning about ten of us were walking down this sidewalk to breakfast when these two guys seemed to appear out of nowhere to practice a little panhandling. I was about 50 feet behind the first kid who, after being solicited, decided to offer some employment advice: "Get a Job!" I heard him say. No sooner did I shout to him to "shut up and keep walking" than one of the homeless men turned towards him and said in a noticeably irritated and threatening voice: "What did you say little buddy?" Rather than heeding my advice, this boy decided that the situation necessitated his repeating, "I said, Get a Job!" Realizing the potential danger of the situation, I immediately implored the man to "just ignore the smart-ass kid—I'll take care of him later" and handed him a $10.00 bill.

That turned out to be one of the best ten bucks I ever spent. The homeless man, after a bit of hesitation, decided to back off. Perhaps due to the steam coming out of my ears, the boy quickly realized that, because he had no idea how unstable this man might be, his actions had been extraordinarily foolish. Needless to say, from that moment on we walked inside the fence. However, to this day, "Get a Job!" still echoes in the forefront of trip memories.

26. Tools for Living

Love, charity, selflessness, forgiveness, empathy, compassion, humility, honesty, confidence. These elements of strong spiritual health, and the resulting freedom from fear, anxiety, and self-degradation, are not the exclusive providence of organized religion, philosophical discussions, or 12 step/self-help programs. These are human character traits that need to be learned and practiced—they are *anything* but automatic. The happiest, most contented people I know, base their lives on these attributes. Any conversation is never about them, but always about the other person. True selflessness is the key to a happy life. My wife's ability to connect to her inner city students is solely the result of extraordinary empathy and compassion. Her knack for getting young people to open up to her with the most incredible tales of pain, rejection and downright agony, is a marvel to behold. Long ago, she demonstrated to me that the key to success at any social or business gathering is to simply ask people about themselves. What generally occurs is a conversation that flows (the only drawback, of course, is how to get away from those who find themselves endlessly fascinating).

Attempting to teach selflessness to young people is the most difficult undertaking one can imagine. Because the development of the sense of "self" is perhaps the most all-encompassing aspect of childhood, attempting to teach selflessness creates an undeniable dichotomy. In fact, the process of developing a healthy sense of self can last well into adulthood. However, it is through selflessness that one receives the positive responses, feedback and interaction so essential to achieving this goal. By stepping outside of yourself you learn how to expand your concept of self. It is learned by doing.

As I stand on morning duty every day, some students cheerfully say hello, ask how you're doing, or stop for a chat. But far too many children trudge in, completely self-absorbed. You say, "Hi, Tim" with no response. Good teaching mandates that you address this issue, and it requires due diligence. I have a friend who teaches at a middle school in one of the most impoverished inner city areas of our state. I find his approach to teaching basic life skills truly inspirational! For example, he stands at his door and as the students walk into his classroom they are expected to shake his hand, look him in the eye and say, "Good morning, Mr. Baker." Learning to respect others translates into self-respect.

In my daily interactions, I try to employ a concept I heard in a workshop some years back. The facilitator said that his approach to all human contact is to assume everybody likes him. If you approach everyone that you encounter with this attitude, you will find yourself being instinctively cheerful, positive, pleasant, and outgoing. In the business of teaching, where the vast majority of what you do involves human interaction, what manner could be better? Very early in the movie "Amadeus," the older Salieri says, "Everybody liked me—I liked myself." I always pause the tape at that point and say to the kids: "There it is, the key to it all." As they give me a puzzled look, I ask them to think: "Do you like yourself?" Invariably, I end up pointing out: "If there are things you don't like about yourself, only you can change them." I'm always amazed that most of the children have never thought about the concept of "self-like" in such specific terms. We all spend so much time trying to get others to like us that we completely forget the importance of liking ourselves first.

Virtually every day I find myself applying this concept to the broader perspective of dealing with the school environment in general. I explain to the kids: Most of what occurs in the course of the school day you have very little control over, but the one thing you can be in charge of is how you react and interact. I regularly point out that there is no such thing as a "bad day." There may be a bad moment or occurrence, but that only becomes a "bad day" if you allow it to. You have the power to restart your day at any moment; fifty times if necessary.

Because students don't have the knowledge of how to be less miserable—where to go, what to do—teachers become the conduit to resolutions. We are the role models for our pupils. This awesome responsibility that teachers bear is captured perfectly in the well known quote from Haim Ginott:

> "I've come to a frightening conclusion that I am the decisive element in the classroom. It's my personal approach that creates the climate. It's my daily mood that makes the weather. As a teacher, I possess a tremendous power to make a child's life miserable or joyous. I can be a tool of torture or an instrument of inspiration. I can humiliate or humor, hurt or heal. In all situations it is my response that decides whether a crisis will be escalated or deescalated and a child humanized or dehumanized."

Of the numerous keynote and motivational speakers I have encountered during workshops and conferences throughout my career, the handful who truly made an impact stressed this same message: The only thing you can significantly change about most of the circumstances life throws at you is how you react to them. One speaker in particular, Nina Spencer from Canada, builds her workshops and books around specific recommendations of things *you* can do to immediately change your attitude and how you interact and react to all of the people, issues, and situations in your life. Your action and reaction is the *only* thing over which you have complete control. I was finally able to take this message to heart only because I was at a point in my life where I was truly ready to hear it and take action.

Conducting yourself in this way requires real work and, sadly, many people are not ready to take this kind of control of their lives. It is *so* much easier to be miserable. As incredible as it sounds, I've come to realize many people prefer it that way. Of course, they would never come right out and say it. Self-deception is indeed a powerful tool. Overcoming it is astronomically difficult. How easy is it to grump, complain, and blame everyone and everything around you! Actually doing something about it—changing your attitude and approaching life's challenges in a positive way—requires vigilance and hard work! I recently heard this expressed so succinctly:

Issues are like Tissues; you take one out, and another pops up.

If you truly understand that you will never have an "issue-free" life, you'll be ready to do the work.

It was by pure happenstance that I came across information for "The First Tee" golf program for youth. A quick look at their website will reveal the most unique aspect of their program. They don't start off with all of the wonderful ways they are going to improve your child's golf swing or putting skills. Instead, their program uses golf as a vehicle to promote character development through nine core life-enhancing values: Honesty, Integrity, Respect, Confidence, Responsibility, Perseverance, Courtesy, Judgment and Sportsmanship. This reminds me of my wife's key phrase: "I teach young people; my subject is just the vehicle." I hope "The First Tee" flourishes.

We've all heard it said a million times, that if everyone incorporated these skills for living into all of their daily affairs, the world would be an infinitely better place. Sadly, for the vast majority of people it just becomes a cliché. But for the lucky few who honestly live them, a whole different world is opened. The dog eat dog, eat or be eaten, win at all costs, survival of the fittest dogma that permeates our society, is the basis for so much unhappiness. The idea that it makes no difference who you trample, backstab, or downright ruin to get ahead, often seems to be the cornerstone of our corporate society. How many of us know people who, when it comes to material success, "have it all" and still have found little contentment?

For me, the bottom line is "How do I want to be remembered?" After I leave the job, retire or pass on, what will people say about me? Ask yourself: Who are the people you remember most fondly? What characteristics did they possess? I suspect that your list will include many of the traits presented in the first sentence of this chapter and in the nine core values of "The First Tee" golf program. As you think back on the most influential teachers in your life, you will hopefully realize that their greatest gift was living by, and imparting to you, these essential principles of life. Teaching, by the very nature of its constant interaction with scores of students on a daily basis, requires all of these elements. The tremendous energy that a teacher must expend, all day, every day, in an attempt to have this positive affect on *each* of his or her charges, is something only those who have experienced life in the "trenches of teaching" will possibly understand.

So, I try to be sure to do something kind (hopefully a few things) every day and, after days, weeks, months, and years of this daily effort, perhaps build this kind of legacy. As a teacher, you'll never know which seeds you have planted will grow to fruition, but you keep on planting-away. Altogether too rarely does one have the kind of "Tuesdays with Morrie" experience of reconnecting with a student that I did this past January. I had not seen Richard since he graduated high school when he came into my room, now in his early thirties, and announced to his girlfriend in tow that I was: "The best teacher he *ever* had."

As I stood there astounded, I realized that I was experiencing one of those *"moments"* that teachers often refer to as "something that makes it all worth it." There's no denying it was wonderful and totally unexpected! As we chatted and I learned of his life experiences, he shared how much he remembered all of my little "quotes and sayings." At some point in the conversation I interjected that one needs to be cognizant of the fact that "life is what happens while you are busy making other plans." Instantaneously, Rich jumped up and, while gesticulating wildly towards me, exclaimed to his friend: "You see!? You see!? That's what I mean!"

I must admit that this reaction took me completely by surprise because I was just talking like I would normally during the course of my daily teaching routine. It didn't seem like anything all that incredible but, like I say, a teacher never knows what small thing, in a long day of small things, interspersed with occasional large and sometimes catastrophic things, may make a lasting difference. Success stories are not created by having children sit in rows and regurgitate information back onto a test. They are the result of individual teachers who take an interest in us; those who are willing to reach beyond the confines of the system and go the extra mile. Isn't it wonderful that so many of us have had that in our lives.

Of all the accolades bestowed during the passing of "Meet the Press" moderator Tim Russert, nothing was more impressive than hearing of the continual gratitude and recognition he showered on his teacher and mentor, Sister Lucille. The fact that he remembered and honored her throughout his life was, for me, the finest indicator of the character of this man. They say one of Tim's greatest attributes was that he never forgot his roots. What a poignant moment it was when his beloved teacher spoke at his funeral. Simply unforgettable!

Thus, I implore all who read this to:

> *Make an immediate effort to contact those teachers*
> *who made the most significant impact on your life.*

With the vast reach of the Internet, it becomes easier every day to find anyone, anywhere. Write, call, e-mail, get on My Space or Facebook; tell them what a positive affect they had on your life and say "Thanks."

I am deeply aware of the major hurdle that will hold many of you back: Fear! Perhaps this is coupled with a healthy dose of guilt. All I can say is: Relax! I mentioned "Tuesdays with Morrie" earlier. What happened when Mitch finally contacted Morrie after umpteen years? Did Morrie hang up on him? Swear at him? Contact Tony Soprano to rub him out? No! Morrie was thrilled! And what a life altering experience it became for Mitch. You too will be amazed at the welcoming response you will get. If you had a relationship with a teacher that results in your regularly thinking of them, even if 20 years has passed, your teacher will remember you. Teachers experience these contacts altogether too infrequently. I want that to change! Even if you were a huge pain-in-the-ass to the teacher, you'll find all has long been forgiven; especially now that you've made the effort to contact them (be sure to apologize anyway).

Wouldn't it be wonderful if this became a major movement! I would love for all of us teachers to be inundated with contacts. In addition, I hope that many of you will take the time to share with me the joy of this experience (see below). Of all the ideas and recommendations presented in this book, this is one that, while costing nothing, will bring priceless joy into the lives of untold numbers of teachers. So, before class is dismissed, be sure to copy this final assignment off the board:

GET GOING WITH THOSE CONTACTS!!

To share the joy of contacting former teachers, or for teachers to share stories of their own experiences, or if you have any comments in general about *It Simply Must be Said,* please go to **www.trenchesofteaching.com**

Let's Get the Dialogue Started!

References

The Reality of Teaching

[1]Adapted from *The Joy of Teaching*. via www. Author unknown.

Chapter 1: Would You Care To Speculate on the Assumptions Heard Thus Far?

Ross, Gary (Producer and Director). (1998). *Pleasantville* [Motion Picture]. New Line Cinema.

Connelly, Joe; Mosher, Bob (Producers). (1957-1963). *Leave It to Beaver* [Television series]. Republic Studios, Univeral Studios.

[2]Stengel, Richard (2008, July 21). Mandela, His 8 Lessons of Leadership. *Time, vol.172, no.3*, 43-48.

Forstater, Mark; Jones, Terry (Producers). Gilliam, Terry, & Jones, Terry (Directors). (1975). *Monty Python and the Holy Grail* [Motion Picture] Python Pictures, Ltd.

Chapter 4: Teacher Shortage

Grazer, Brian (Producer), Oz, Frank (Director). (1999). *Bowfinger* [Motion Picture]. Universal Pictures.

[3]Wallis, Claudia (2008, February 28). How to Make Better Teachers. *Time, vol.171, no.8*.

[4]Guide to Qualitative Evaluation is adapted from the chart: *Guide to Teacher Evaluation.*Author unknown.

Chapter 5: Teacher Longevity

[5]Meshberg, Ron (2009, March). Reach The Children. *Connecticut Magazine, vol.72,no.3.* p35.

DiVito, Danny; Shamberg, Michael; & Sher, Stacey (Producers). LaGravenese, Richard (Director). (2007). *Freedom Writers* [Motion Picture].Paramount Pictures.

Friend, Brenda (Producer). Haines, Randa (Director). (2006). *The Ron Clark Story* [Television Movie]. TNT.

Larson, Glen A. (Creator). (1976-1983). *Quincy, M.E.* [Television Series]. NBC.

Chapter 6: Teacher on Teacher

Stein, Jess (Editor in Chief). (1979). *The Random House College Dictionary, Revised Edition.* New York, NY: Random House Inc.

[6]Ripley, Amanda (2008, December 8). Can She Save Our Schools. *Time, vol. 172, no. 23,* 36-44.

Chapter 7: Celebrity Musings

[7]Sharples, Tiffany (2008, June 30). Steve Carell will now take your questions. *Time, vol. 171, no. 26,* 6.

Quindlen, Anna (2005, November 28). The Wages of Teaching. *Newsweek,* 100.

[8]Archibald, Timothy (2008, August 4). John Madden will now take your questions. *Time, vol. 172, no. 5,* 6.

Chapter 8: The Business of Education

Herndon, James (1971). *How To Survive in Your Native Land.* New York, NY: Simon and Schuster. p. 109-110.

A Nation at Risk: The Imperative for Educational Reform. A Report to the Nation and the Secretary of Education, United States Department of Education by The National Commission on Excellence in Education. (1983, April).

Chapter 9: How Shit Happens

[9]Adapted from *In the beginning was the plan.* via www. Author unknown.

Chapter 10: The Others

Simon, David (Creator & Producer). (2002-2008). *The Wire* [Television Drama Series]. United States: HBO.

[10]Guthrie, Arlo. (1967). *Alice's Restaurant Massacree.* [Recorded by Arlo Guthrie]. On album: *Alice's Restaurant.* Reprise Records.

Frankfurt, Harry G. (2005). *On Bullshit.* Princeton, NJ: Princeton University Press. p 33, 61, 3.

[11]*If you tell the truth. . .* from "Zen Sarcasm." via www. Author unknown.

Williams, John. (1980). *The Imperial March.* [Film Score] *The Empire Strikes Back.* George Lucas (Producer). Irvin Kershner (Director).

Chapter 11: The Joys and Perils of Broad Certification

Grazer, Brian (Producer). Reitman, Ivan (Director). (1990). *Kindergarten Cop* [Motion Picture]. United States: Universal City Studios.

Fulghum, Robert (1989). *All I Really Need to Know I Learned in Kindergarten.* New York, NY: Villard Books, a division of Random House, Inc.

Chapter 12: No Hope of Parole

Herndon, James (1971). op.cit. p. 99-102.

[12]Hollas, Betty. (2005). *Differentiating Instruction in a Whole-Group Setting.* Peterborough, NH: Crystal Springs Books. p. 49.

[13]Kluger, Jeffrey. (2008). *Simplexity: Why Simple Things Become Complex (and How Complex Things Can be Made Simple).* USA: Hyperion

Friedman, Thomas L. (2008). *Hot, Flat, and Crowded.* New York, NY: Farrar, Straus and Giroux.

WSOBP = World Series of Beer Pong.

Forget Committees. Author unknown.

Williams, Bernard (Producer). Oz, Frank (Director). (1988). *Dirty Rotten Scoundrels* [Motion Picture]. United States: Orion Pictures Corporation.

[14]*Federal Arithmetic and Reading Test.* via www. author unknown. Appeared on blog: *The Kentucky Democrat* (2004, December 30). Attributed to "a cousin."

Chapter 13: Pretend Education

Friedman, Thomas. op.cit.

Chapter 16: Blind-sided

[15]Automated Answering Machine is adapted from *School Answering Machine.* via-email. Attributed to the teachers of Pacific Palisades High School in California. author unknown.

Chapter 18: NCLB

[16]Adapted from *NCLB Football Version.* via www. author unknown.

[17]Remsen, Kenneth (2004). *No Cow Left Behind.* School Administrator, vol. 61, part 2, pages 48-49. The American Association of School Administrators.

[18]Taylor, John (2002). *Absolutely the Best Dentists.* Retired Superintendent of Schools Lancaster County School District, Lancaster, South Carolina.

Chapter 19: Conflict Resolution

[19] *People Over 40 Should Be Dead.* via www. Author unknown. Adaptation.

Chapter 20: Let's Get Physical

[20] *Importance of Play.* Author unknown.

Caplan, Frank & Theresa. (1973). *The Power of Play.* New York, NY: Doubleday.

Chapter 23: Duties

Stein, Jess. op.cit.

Guthrie, Arlo. op.cit.

Chapter 26: Tools for Living

Zaentz, Saul (Producer). Forman, Milos (Director). (1984). *Amadeus* [Motion Picture]. United States: Republic Pictures Corporation.

Ginott, Haim. (1995). *Teacher and child: A book for parents and teachers.* New York, NY: Collier.

Spencer, Nina. (2006). *Getting Passion Out Of Your Profession: How to keep loving your living…come what may.* Sherbrooke, Quebec, Canada: Transcontinental Metrolitho Book Group.

The First Tee, World Golf Village, St. Augustine, FL. www. thefirsttee.org.

Albom, Mitch. (1997). *Tuesdays With Morrie.* New York, NY: Broadway Books.

Breinigsville, PA USA
05 April 2010
235451BV00006B/1/P